BLOODY SOUTHERNERS

BLOODY SOUTHERNERS

CLOUGH AND TAYLOR'S BRIGHTON & HOVE ODYSSEY

SPENCER VIGNES

\Bb\
Biteback Publishing

First published in Great Britain in 2018 by
Biteback Publishing Ltd
Westminster Tower
3 Albert Embankment
London SE1 7SP
Copyright © Spencer Vignes 2018

Spencer Vignes has asserted his right under the Copyright, Designs and Patents Act 1988 to be identified as the author of this work.

All rights reserved. No part of this publication may be reproduced, stored in a retrieval system or transmitted, in any form or by any means, without the publisher's prior permission in writing.

This book is sold subject to the condition that it shall not, by way of trade or otherwise, be lent, resold, hired out or otherwise circulated without the publisher's prior consent in any form of binding or cover other than that in which it is published and without a similar condition, including this condition, being imposed on the subsequent purchaser.

Every reasonable effort has been made to trace copyright holders of material reproduced in this book, but if any have been inadvertently overlooked the publisher would be glad to hear from them.

ISBN 978-1-78590-436-3

10 9 8 7 6 5 4 3 2 1

A CIP catalogue record for this book is available from the British Library.

Set in Adobe Caslon Pro

Printed and bound in Great Britain by
CPI Group (UK) Ltd, Croydon CR0 4YY

In memory of Roy Chuter, Paul Lewis and Steve Piper – three fine football men of Southwick, St Athan and Worthing respectively, gone too soon.

'These are the times that try men's souls.'
THOMAS PAINE, THE AMERICAN CRISIS

CONTENTS

Introduction   xi

1   The White Hart   1
2   A Change Is Gonna Come   7
3   In the Beginning   21
4   'Who's Mike Bamber?'   39
5   Dark Days   59
6   The Perfect Storm   85
7   Son of the Desert   109
8   Sir Norman's Waterloo   129
9   When Two Become One   151
10   Utopia   179
11   Promises, Promises   199
12   The Turning Point   221
13   Rise and Fall   243
14   An Unlikely Legacy   261

And in the End   273
Acknowledgements   287
About the Author   289
Bibliography   291
Index   295

INTRODUCTION

There is, as I write, only one club among the ninety-two members of England's four elite football leagues that carries the name of two places in its title. Born out of a gathering held at the Seven Stars Hotel in Ship Street, Brighton, on 24 June 1901, Brighton & Hove Albion are regarded now as the kind of forward-thinking, dynamic animal that most soccer managers would jump at the chance of helming. Home is an aesthetically pleasing stadium packed with around 30,000 supporters every other week. Awards have been won for the club's pioneering work in the local community. The training compound is among the best in Britain. They will never be Manchester United or Liverpool, but, equally, 'Albion', as supporters tend to call them, are light years away from the cash-strapped Burys and Newport Countys of the English and Welsh professional game.

It wasn't always like this. For seventy-two years, Albion skulked around in what might kindly be described as the game's shadows, rarely doing anything of excitement to trouble the headline writers. Comedy relief was quite literally provided by Norman Wisdom, who, between 1964 and 1970, served on 'a committee that talked about things', as the late comedian once described the club's board to me. Training took place among the dog mess on Hove Park. If Brighton was a town that looked, according to the playwright Keith Waterhouse, like 'it is helping police with their enquiries', then Albion could equally have been described as a football club of the tired, end-of-the-pier variety.

And then Brian Clough walked in.

Just imagine Alex Ferguson quitting Manchester United during the high-water mark of his reign at Old Trafford to take over at Rochdale. Or José Mourinho walking out on Chelsea in the wake of the 2015 Premier League title triumph and joining Southend United. Scenarios like that don't tend to happen in life, let alone football, going against the grain when it comes to the upward career trajectories of anyone with a drop of ambition in their veins.

Except that, in November 1973, one did.

At that time Brian Clough was managerial gold dust, having led Derby County from the old Second Division to the 1971/72 Football League title. The following season, County reached the semi-finals of the European Cup, controversially exiting the competition to Juventus amid rumours of bribery and corruption concerning the referee appointed for the tie's first leg. Clough's maverick ways, success at club level and made-for-television soundbites meant he was the perpetual people's choice as next boss of the England national team. And yet the man who would later declare himself (maybe with a hint of tongue in cheek, maybe not) to be 'in the top one' of managers chose to join a club six places from the bottom of English football's Third Division.

As a journalist I had recalled Clough's improbable spell at Brighton & Hove Albion across a combination of newspapers,

INTRODUCTION

magazines and the club's official match-day programme, where for many years I have served as a feature writer. I met many of the players who were there, getting to know some as friends, and would never tire of hearing their stories about Clough, whose death in 2004 has done little to diminish his status as one of English football's iconic figures. Some of those stories showed him in a positive light, others not so, as you might expect of a true original who revelled in dividing opinion. But they were never dull. That in itself leaves me scratching my head as to why it took so long to think of this remarkable sporting odyssey as a book. Sometimes the best ideas are staring you in the face the whole time.

Is the world ready for another book about Brian Clough? That's a question I asked myself several times before committing pen to paper, or rather hand to laptop. The answer always remained the same, and here's why. Every nook of Clough's career both as a player and manager has been thoroughly dissected on celluloid and in book form, with one exception – nobody has ever focused solely on his time at Brighton & Hove Albion. In many ways, that's the most intriguing part. What motivates a man at the top of his game to take a job which appears so monstrously beneath him? It made little sense back in 1973, even allowing for Clough's trademark eccentricities. It makes more sense to me now that I've researched and written this book. Even so, no matter how I probed Clough's thought processes for logic, the whole affair has the word 'surreal' written through it like a stick of Brighton Rock.

What's more, as good as the majority of books, films and documentaries about Old Big Head have been, I've found myself becoming increasingly riled at the degree of artistic licence taken with elements of the Brian Clough story. The footnote traditionally occupied by Brighton & Hove Albion tells of a club low on resources and going nowhere. That simply isn't true. After seventy-two years on skid row, Albion had an ambitious new chairman in place who was prepared to spend money. Lots of it. In fact, Mike Bamber, for that was his name, would part with more cash in transfer fees during Clough's nine months in charge than any other chairman outside the First Division (the equivalent of today's Premier League), not to mention several inside it.

It has also become de rigueur to talk up Clough's admittedly remarkable achievements at Nottingham Forest by playing down the stature of the East Midlands club that he inherited in January 1975, six months after his departure from Brighton and following an ill-fated 44-day spell as manager of Leeds United. In 1967, Forest had come within touching distance of winning the Football League and FA Cup double. That would have been their third FA Cup triumph, the second having arrived as recently as 1959. Forest may have been in the doldrums when Clough took over, but such a CV doesn't square with my understanding of what constitutes a small provincial football club. That, however, is what they have become in the creative rush to laud him.

This is the story of what happened when Brian Clough, together with his assistant, partner, shadow – call Peter Taylor whatever you will – went to manage a genuinely small provincial football club. In 1973, Albion had never finished higher than twelfth in the old Second Division or progressed beyond the fifth round of the FA Cup. But something was beginning to stir on the south coast of England. Clough would later argue that the task of achieving success at Brighton was 'like asking Lester Piggott to win the Derby on a Skegness donkey' – a quote which leads me to surmise that he either didn't comprehend or didn't wish to acknowledge the club's untapped potential. Indeed, 'What would have happened had Brian Clough stuck around?' is a question that has long fascinated Albion supporters of a certain age, especially in light of what transpired at Nottingham Forest.

Brighton & Hove Albion was far from Brian Clough and Peter Taylor's finest hour. It bore witness to the first major fracture in their relationship, a trial separation in a union that ultimately dissolved into acrimony, bitterness and regret despite yielding silverware aplenty. However, neither was their stint beside the seaside the complete washout it is often portrayed as. Quite the contrary. In fact, it would, in the long run, prove to be the making of a football club.

Spencer Vignes
Cardiff, Wales
September 2018

1

THE WHITE HART

Catalyst, rebel, man of the people, one-off, thinker, strong-willed, passionate, compassionate, revolutionary, independent of mind, academic underachiever, self-taught, visionary, quick-witted, complex, opinionated, difficult, controversial.

Almost certainly, Brian Clough would have got along famously with the idiosyncratic character who was Thomas Paine.

Before leaving England and emigrating to Philadelphia, where his writing championing a republican form of government under a written constitution played a pivotal role in rallying support for American independence, Paine spent six years from 1768 living in the town of Lewes, Sussex. Nestling beneath the protective arm of the rolling South Downs hills, Lewes already had form when it came to non-conformism. It was here, during the mid-sixteenth century, that seventeen Protestant martyrs were burned to death for their faith during the Marian persecutions of Queen Mary's reign, or 'Bloody Mary' to her detractors. Every year on 5 November, in union with Guy Fawkes Night marking the uncovering of the 1605 Gunpowder Plot, local people continue to salute the martyrs amid raucous scenes. How else can one describe the enthusiastic torching of multiple effigies, including that of Pope Paul V, whose tenure coincided with the Plot?

Paine lodged over a tobacco shop, married his landlord's daughter and became a member of the local debating society based at the White Hart Hotel in the High Street. There he honed the theories that formed the basis of his revolutionary politics. All of which gives the White Hart a pretty strong claim to be the cradle of American independence, as declared on a modest blue plaque now fixed to the front of the building.

As for the hotel's other brush with fame? Well, you won't find details about that on any plaque. It exists only in the memory of the people who were there, or at least those of them still alive. On Friday 2 November 1973, Brian Clough and Peter Taylor came to the White Hart to meet Brighton & Hove Albion's players for the first time. And, to a man, it wasn't an encounter any of them were likely to forget in a hurry.

The rumours had abounded all week – not that any of the players seriously believed them at first. Why would the self-proclaimed (albeit with good reason) best manager in the business be poised to join a Third Division football club? And a struggling Third Division club at that. Yet, with every passing day what had initially been dismissed among the squad as newspaper talk began to take on more substance. Then on the Thursday came confirmation: Brian Clough was Albion's new manager, Peter Taylor his assistant.

The news was greeted by the players with a fusion of laughter, incredulity and genuine excitement as they gathered for training on Friday morning ahead of the following day's home game against York City. There was also a message from the club's chairman, Mike Bamber, awaiting them. After training, they were to return home, pack an overnight bag and make their way in smart attire to the White Hart for dinner and an introductory meeting with Clough and Taylor.

Come 4 p.m., eighteen members of Albion's squad – a mix of seasoned professionals and younger players, plus a couple of youth team rookies – had gathered at the White Hart along with brothers Joe and Glen Wilson, both former Albion players who'd gone on to share a variety of roles within the club including trainer, kit man, scout and caretaker manager. All were escorted through to a dining room, where dinner was served. By 5 p.m., the food had long since disappeared, and still there was no sign of Clough or Taylor. Was this a deliberate ploy of theirs aimed at raising the suspense levels another couple of notches? Nobody knew.

The waiting continued. Striker Barry Bridges and left midfielder Peter O'Sullivan were half wishing Clough for one wouldn't turn up at all. 'I'd only ever seen him on television before and he'd always be doing his "Young man" thing,' recalls O'Sullivan, once on Manchester United's books as a teenager and regarded as Albion's chief playmaker. 'You know, "Young man, you should be doing this" and "Young man, you should be doing that." I knew if he came in and said "Young man" even once then I'd be in trouble because I wouldn't be able to keep a straight face. Barry was the same. That was nervous laughter, I can tell you. You don't want to laugh but you can't help it because of the situation you find yourself in.'

Like many hotels, the White Hart piped music through speakers into its communal areas supposedly for the benefit of guests – easy-going tracks such as Harry Secombe's 'If I Ruled the World', which by some uncanny coincidence happened to be playing when, at long last, the door to the dining room opened and in walked Brian Clough, closely followed by Peter Taylor.

The good news for O'Sullivan was that the words 'Young man' didn't so much as pass Clough's lips. The bad news came in the form of his collar-length hair, a real no-no in the manager's eyes, even circa 1973, when it was all the rage. Fortunately, Clough's attention was drawn first to utility player John Templeman, whose flowing locks far outshone O'Sullivan's.

'He went straight to John and said, "I understand you're called Shirley Temple because of your long blond hair,"' remembers defender Steve Piper, whose twentieth birthday it was that day. 'He had a right go at him. I'm sitting there thinking, "That's not nice but at least while he's on at John he can't find fault in me." But the hair was always going to be a thing with Clough.'

'Yeah, he was quite sarcastic about it, put it that way,' concurs Templeman, wincing at the memory.

What happened next came out of left field and caught everyone present off guard. 'He [Clough] has shaken a few hands and said a few things to people,' says Lammie Robertson, Albion's resident Scotsman able to play up front or in midfield. 'Suddenly he goes, "What do you want to drink?" And everyone's looking at each other. One by one we start saying, "I'll have an orange and lemonade," "I'll have an orange and lemonade," and so on. And he goes, "I mean a drink!" So, we had to write down what we wanted to drink. I still had a soft drink, but I think a couple of the lads said, "I'll have a pint" because that's what he wanted to hear.'

'That was like, "What the fuck do we do?", because it was a Friday night,' adds O'Sullivan. 'We drank back then, of course we did, but you're not supposed to be drinking the night before a game. I definitely had a beer along with one or two of the other guys, but most didn't. I thought it would be rude not to. Brian certainly had a beer and Peter had something stupid like a Campari and soda. And then, like he'd done with John, he copped hold of me and told me to get my hair cut.'

Even the introduction of alcohol couldn't dispel the uneasy atmosphere that now hung across the room, much as a sea mist carpets the Sussex coastline on a late spring morning. Many of those present, including Joe and Glen Wilson, were nervous about their futures now that a new management team was in place. Clough and Taylor were bound to want to make changes that could well extend to the backroom staff. The players knew it. Clough knew that they knew it. So, having addressed the unruly haircuts and attempted quite literally to inject some spirit into proceedings, his attention switched to the team in general.

'My first impression was that he was a complete headcase,' says Brian Powney, whose remarkable agility as a goalkeeper more than compensated for his slight stature, at least compared to the vast majority of other players in his position. 'The things he was saying, and the way he was saying them, all delivered in that accent of his. He said, "If you're lucky enough to be here next year, we will be going places." What a thing to say to a team that's going to go out and play for him tomorrow – "If you're here next year." That's not exactly going to inspire, is it? And because he didn't turn up until God knows when, that's what we had to go to sleep on. Thanks for that – thanks a lot. Just incredible.'

'Right from the very first, that's what he was like,' says Lammie Robertson. 'You never knew what was going to happen next, what he was going to say, what he was going to do. He was an oddity from the start. And you know what? I think he loved being like that.'

2

A CHANGE IS GONNA COME

'It was a hot afternoon, last day of June, and the sun was a demon.'

Bobby Goldsboro was right, at least from a Sussex point of view. The sun was indeed a demon on the last day of June 1973, just as his song 'Summer (The First Time)' – the tale of a seventeen-year-old boy's sexual awakening at the hands of an older woman – began attracting the attention of disc jockeys on the eastern shores of the Atlantic Ocean. In fact, the sun was a demon in the skies over Sussex throughout most of June and July – good news for the thousands of day trippers and holidaymakers to the coast but agony as far as Frankie Howard, groundsman for over a decade at Albion's antiquated yet homely Goldstone Ground, was concerned. A former left-winger with 219 appearances for the club to his name, Howard was the kind of man who spent more time tending his precious football pitch than his own garden. Sunshine was a good thing, up to a point. Now he, or rather his pride and joy, craved rain.

The last day of June 1973 fell on a Saturday. A day of rest for the majority, but not Frankie. Albion's squad, having returned from their summer breaks for pre-season training, required the pitch for a workout on the Monday. Howard had expressed reservations, given the parched conditions, only to bow to manager Pat Saward's wishes. The pitch wanted watering and that meant being there over the weekend to operate the sprinklers. Anything to help Saward – a man Howard respected and yet feared for. In May 1972, Albion had been promoted to the second tier of English football's pyramid system for only the second time in the club's history. The celebrations were short-lived. Thirteen consecutive defeats spanning November 1972 and January 1973 meant Saward's men were doomed to relegation long before the final ball of the season was kicked. Howard knew that a decent start to the 1973/74 campaign was imperative or the manager would be out of a job. That's the way it goes in a results-driven business when you're not getting results. Some said Saward was lucky not to have been fired already.

The pitch needed water. The team desperately needed a lift. The club needed a manager who would provide that lift, be it Saward or a fresh face. Just as well, perhaps, that things were on a surer foot in the boardroom. In December 1972, Albion had made the somewhat unusual move of appointing two men – Mike Bamber and Len Stringer – to work as joint chairmen. Stringer, a local funeral director, would soon relinquish his position, leaving Bamber in sole charge. Partial to cigars, jazz and foreign holidays (hence his 'Miami Mike' nickname among some of the players), Bamber was a firm yet likeable businessman who, in the words of one former Albion director who worked alongside him, 'seemed incapable of passing a pie without putting a finger in it'. He was a farmer. He was a property developer. He ran a restaurant that doubled as a nightclub. And he'd also formed a genuine attachment to the football club on the doorstep of his Hove mansion, the one that had underperformed so spectacularly throughout most of its existence.

For well over a century, right up until Crawley Town were promoted into the Football League in 2010, Brighton & Hove Albion stood alone as the only professional club in Sussex. The catchment area in terms of people who might want to watch a game of football was huge by English standards, the county's borders encompassing 932,335 acres inhabited by a population of over 1.2 million people according to the 1971 census. The nearest Football League clubs to the north and west were Crystal Palace (forty-six miles) and Portsmouth (fifty miles) respectively. As for the south and east? Well, there weren't any – at least not until you hit the French coast.

Mike Bamber wasn't alone in noticing that on the rare occasions when Albion threatened to wake from its seemingly eternal slumber, so the people of Sussex had responded in impressive numbers. On 30 April 1958, more than 31,000 of them converged on the Goldstone to watch their local team gain promotion from the old Division Three (South) with a 6–0 win over Watford. Fourteen years later, more still were present to witness the 1–1 draw against Rochdale that confirmed the club's return to English football's second tier – 34,766 souls shoehorning themselves into a rickety old football ground completely at odds with its genteel surroundings in well-heeled, reserved Hove.

Others had acknowledged Albion's potential but failed to do anything about it. So long as he was chairman, however, Bamber decided things would be different. Besides himself (few if any football chairmen, then as well as now, are bereft of an ego), Bamber recognised that the most important person at a football club was the manager. A better manager meant attracting better players. Better players meant a better standard of football. A better standard of football meant larger attendances. Larger attendances would not only sustain the whole operation financially but also open up the possibility of moving to a better ground. That, as Albion geared up for the 1973/74 season, was Bamber's business model.

Was Pat Saward the man to spearhead Albion's revolution? Len Stringer hadn't thought so, disagreeing with the manager on virtually everything from team selection to the strength of the half-time tea. Bamber also remained unconvinced. He liked Saward, as stylish a dresser as he'd been an inside-forward during the 1950s for Aston Villa, and recognised the fine job he had done in guiding Albion to promotion in 1972. But the 1972/73 season had been shambolic. With Stringer poised to step down as co-chairman, Bamber chose to see how results panned out during the opening weeks of the 1973/74 campaign before deciding whether Saward was his man.

'Pat was a very smart, articulate guy with a great presence, almost like a bit of a film star,' says goalkeeper Brian Powney, Albion's longest-serving player at the time, having joined the club's ground staff as a fifteen-year-old in 1960. 'He'd taken over from Freddie Goodwin, the previous manager, during the summer of 1970, and I soon realised he was a manager I wanted to play for – a very good coach who always joined in training. But when we got promoted [in 1972] he didn't have any money to spend and we went straight down again. We struggled. I suppose he could well have got the sack then, but I for one was glad he was still there at the start of the [1973/74] season.'

'The team that got promoted in 1972 was made of up twelve or thirteen guys who were the core of the side,' says Ian Goodwin, a Goliath of a centre-back initially signed on loan from Coventry City by Saward during the 1970/71 season. 'Then, having gone up, Pat decides [defender] Norman Gall isn't going to be good enough, and that somebody needs to come into midfield because Barry Bridges is getting to the end of his career, and so on. One of the first games we played that season we lost 6–2 at Blackpool. I got booked twice and wasn't sent off – nobody noticed – but that's beside the point. Instead of standing by us, giving us the chance to dig ourselves out of the hole we'd created, he starts making changes – too many changes. We deserved an opportunity as a team for maybe half a dozen games or more, but we didn't get it. Those changes, in my opinion, cost us our team spirit.'

'I first broke into the side as a youngster during that disastrous season because he [Pat] made those wholesale changes to the team,' says Steve Piper, signed on a semi-professional basis as an eighteen-year-old after impressing at centre-back for the local amateur club Rottingdean Victoria. 'Maybe that was his downfall, making so many changes, but if he thought the players that he had weren't good enough – and if he didn't have any money to buy new ones – what else was he supposed to do other than throw in some youngsters? There was myself, [winger] Tony Towner and [striker] Pat Hilton who were brought in and the three of us were just teenagers. But in terms of being a coach Pat was second to none and a really nice man.'

Lammie Robertson was an exception to the rule. Pat Saward had managed to crowbar some cash from Albion's coffers to buy the combative Scot who'd cut his teeth playing in defence, midfield and up front for Bury and Halifax Town. 'We [Halifax] had played Brighton a couple of times and got beat at home in one game,' says Robertson, signed by Albion in December 1972 for £17,000 plus a player swap; striker Willie Irvine went in the opposite direction to Halifax. 'Pat told me afterwards that he liked my attitude. We'd got beat but I'd banged a wall in frustration and he remembered that. They [Albion] were struggling against relegation from the old Second Division and the philosophy was "We're going to buy a lot of players and spend our way out of trouble." But it never happened. I think it may only have been me who they actually paid money for. That was it. So we didn't get out of it and got relegated. That pissed me off. It seemed as though a lot of the players were kind of giving up on it as well before we were actually down.'

That said, Robertson could see the club had potential. 'It was a bit like going back to Burnley again where I'd started my career in English football but hadn't cracked the first team. The ground was one of those places that could hold 25,000 or more, which Bury and Halifax weren't. Even when we struggled against relegation the crowds hadn't been too bad. There were some good players there as well like Sully [Peter O'Sullivan]. Great left foot, and a funny guy as well. We were playing up at Hull on a Friday night towards the end of that [1972/73] season and this official-looking guy came in the dressing room. I'd just got back in the team from an injury. Sully collared the guy and asked him if there were any changes. I wasn't in the programme as I'd been injured. It was just "Robertson, number 10", so the guy asked, "What's his name?" And Sully goes, "Fyfe." Now I don't know if you remember but Fyfe Robertson used to be this old fella on the television who'd do the news and current-affairs programmes. And that's what was announced by this guy over the tannoy before the game: "Changes, number 10 for Brighton, Fyfe Robertson!" That was Sully for you. A good lad, and a good player.'

With the exception of Mick Brown and Ronnie Howell, a defender and a midfielder signed over the summer months on free transfers from Crystal Palace and Swindon Town respectively, the Albion team that took to the field for the opening games of the 1973/74 season in the Football League's Third Division (now League One) read exactly the same as the side that had been relegated a few months previously. Very little new blood, in other words, bought with zero pennies.

In his programme notes for the first home match of the season, a League Cup tie against Charlton Athletic on Wednesday 29 August, Saward was open about his own shortcomings as well as those of the team's over the previous season. 'It is factual, but unbelievable, that this time last year we were marching like gladiators to our first match in Division Two versus Bristol City, and the rest of the story is too painful to relate,' he wrote in prose every bit as slick as his dress sense. 'The relapse which followed our triumphant victory was inexplicable. Tenacity and determination were not lacking but I would be less than honest if I were to deny that these earlier performances were a disaster. I have made mistakes but at the time I firmly believed they were the only decisions. It is a manager's unenviable task to envisage the future, not only of his club but all the other league clubs as well, and naturally the human element of wrong decisions is bound to happen from time to time. The important thing is to learn from these results and I have. Each season is a walk into the unknown but with our dedication and knowledge of last season I am quite confident that we shall be playing positive football this season which will be thoroughly enjoyable.'

To Frankie Howard's chagrin, the sun continued to beat down on his prized turf as August made way for September. Even worse, his fears regarding Saward's future were also coming to pass. In the league, a 1–1 draw away to Rochdale on the opening day of the season was followed by a first home defeat at the hands of Bournemouth. Two away games within the space of three days yielded a 1–0 win at Plymouth Argyle and a point in a 1–1 draw against Southport, only for the team to stutter again at home, losing to Charlton Athletic and Oldham Athletic, both by 2–1.

By the time September was out, Watford had also taken maximum points at the Goldstone under the old two-points-for-a-win system, abolished at the end of the 1980/81 season in favour of three for a victory. That left Saward's men sitting twenty-first in a league table consisting of twenty-four clubs. Consecutive away games at the start of October brought relief in the shape of a 1–0 win versus Oldham followed by misery at Blackburn Rovers, Albion surrendering a 1–0 half-time lead to lose 3–1.

Then came Halifax Town at home: another defeat, this time by 1–0, making it five reverses out of five in the league at the Goldstone and six out of six in all competitions. At which point the levee containing any last drops of supporter goodwill towards Saward for his previous achievements finally broke.

If there was one thing football club chairmen hated more than losing back in the 1970s, it was falling attendances. In the days prior to mass advance season ticket sales and television deals ending in multiple zeros, clubs depended largely on whatever cash came through the turnstiles on match days for income. Having averaged a fairly respectable attendance figure of 14,188 over the course of the 1972/73 season, despite the dire results, Albion's gates dropped alarmingly during the opening weeks of the 1973/74 campaign as defeat followed defeat. When only 6,228 bothered to turn up for the Halifax game on Saturday 13 October, Bamber's patience finally ran out. Win or lose the following Saturday at home to fellow strugglers Shrewsbury

Town, he decided that a board meeting should take place immediately afterwards with just one item on the agenda: the sacking of Pat Saward as manager.

In the intervening days between the Halifax and Shrewsbury matches, Saward carried the air of a dead man walking about him. Rather than acting as a rallying call, his column for the Wednesday edition of the local *Evening Argus* newspaper – headlined 'I'm Staying to Pull the Club Back' – read more like a suicide note. 'A chance remark by a tradesman to my wife this week put Albion's dilemma in a nutshell,' Saward wrote.

> He is a supporter and said quite simply 'We don't feel part of the club anymore.' This man was one of the 30,000 who joined in praising the promotion side the night of the Rochdale match. Now, as he freely admitted, he is anti-everything at the Goldstone although he continues to watch matches. Once, and not very long ago, he enjoyed watching the Albion. He even went so far as saying that the time we went up he could have got down and kissed my feet. Now he wants to kick my backside and there must be many more like him. 'I have the feeling now that everything has disintegrated and all that wonderful spirit has gone down the drain,' he says. This is it exactly. We have lost that feeling of togetherness at the club. Unfortunately I feel we are going the other way and attracting failure.

If Saward had any inkling that Bamber was about to fire him, and wanted somehow to change his chairman's mind, then as pleas in mitigation go there have been better.

As if in sympathy with Saward's plight, the weather well and truly broke across Sussex towards the end of that third week in October. On the Friday, gale-force winds and mountainous waves caused a 75-ton barge to break loose and smash into Brighton's Palace Pier, sending amusement kiosks, walkways and a helter-skelter tumbling into the sea. The following day, a paltry crowd of 5,308, Albion's lowest home attendance of any description since 1963, paid to see Ronnie Howell and Ken Beamish score the goals that beat Shrewsbury 2–0. Saward wasn't even there to witness it, the reason for his absence being a supposed scouting mission for players. Afterwards, as arranged, the club's board convened to agree on the manager's sacking. The only surprise, other than Albion managing to win a home game, was that news of his dismissal took until Tuesday 23 October to break, Saward himself being informed on the Monday.

'This is a decision by the board who bore in mind that the most important thing is the club,' said Bamber in justification. 'I have just seen Pat Saward. He is very upset and very sick. I would also feel very sick, but we have had six home defeats and are down to crowds of 5,000 wonderful people. No club can live on such gates. The running of the team is the manager's responsibility. I feel sorry for managers in a way, but if they want to be managers it is up to them. Naturally, some of the players are upset at him going, but I have just had a meeting with the players and morale is high.'

Bamber denied that the club had already lined up a successor, confirming the job would be advertised 'to get a really top manager'. Money would also be available to buy players. 'It is not easy to get them and we have been after a half-dozen this year without success,' he added, conveniently sidestepping questions over where that money might come from and why, if funds existed, so little had been made available to Saward for team strengthening.

'I still cannot believe it has happened, but I will say nothing to knock the club,' the now ex-manager told a small huddle of journalists waiting outside the Goldstone. 'The reason I have been sacked is that they say I can no longer motivate the players. What I need now is a holiday to get away from it all.'

'Pat took his sacking really badly,' recalls Brian Powney. 'In fact, I don't think he ever really got over it. Years later I was in London staying in a hotel on business. I came down in the morning and was having a cup of tea in the lounge with my work colleague before getting a taxi, and I heard this voice that I knew. And it was Pat Saward. He was being interviewed for a job. He was as chuffed to see me as I was to see him, but he didn't get that job. It wasn't for a league side. It was a non-league side. That upset me a bit. He seemed to fade away, which was a tremendous shame because he was better than that.'

'We [the players] didn't get consulted about Pat's dismissal,' adds Lammie Robertson. 'Maybe one or two of the senior players did, I don't know, but I certainly wasn't asked. I'd been places where the directors or the chairman had meetings with you, sometimes one on one, to ask what you thought about things. And you know in the back of your mind what's happening, that they're thinking of maybe changing the manager. But nothing was discussed with me or anyone else as far as I'm aware. He just went.'

If there was a clue as to what lay ahead regarding the possible identity of Albion's next manager, then it was Bamber's fondness for mixing with celebrities. Property development may have been his forte, but there was always something of a frustrated entertainer lurking within Albion's chairman, who, in the years immediately after the Second World War, had drummed semi-professionally with several jazz bands around the London area. His part-restaurant, part-nightclub in the village of

Ringmer, twelve miles north-east of Brighton, attracted many of Britain's top acts of the time, including the likes of Bruce Forsyth, Des O'Connor and Les Dawson. It being a relatively small venue with a limited capacity, Bamber would often reach into his own pocket to meet the large fees commanded by such celebrities. The Ringmer Restaurant, as it was called (later to become the 2001 Discotheque), wasn't quite a vanity project, but it wasn't far short.

'The one thing I always found about Mike was he was a bit star-struck,' says Brian Powney. 'He liked being seen with celebrities, very much. And it would cost him money sometimes to have these people with him. Quite often if they were appearing at Ringmer then he'd get them down to watch a game. One time we were in the dressing room before kick-off and Mike comes in with the guy from Peters and Lee, who were a very successful act at the time. And he [Lennie Peters] was of course blind. So he's sitting there and everybody's looking at each other going, "What's going on here?" We're more politically correct now, but back then it seemed a bit bizarre. You're about to play a football match and you're all thinking, "How's he going to see the game?" I remember [singer] Frankie Vaughan coming in once and he was like an excited schoolkid because it used to go in tandem: footballers liked showbiz people and showbiz people often wanted to be footballers. It used to criss-cross all the time. I met many, many celebrities while I was Brighton.'

Did Bamber really intend to advertise for a new manager, or was there somebody he had in mind all along to replace Saward? Only the chairman himself together with one other man could ever have answered that question. At the beginning of October came confirmation that Albion director Harry Bloom had been appointed as the club's vice-chairman, in effect stepping up to plug the gap created by Len Stringer's departure. It was Bloom who would act as Bamber's confidant over the weeks, months and years ahead, fulfilling various important roles including that of intermediary between the ambitious chairman and his managers whenever team matters and boardroom politics threatened to overlap. Bloom would also play a pivotal role in the negotiations to land Albion's next manager, helping guide Bamber through the minefield of having to deal with one of the quickest wits, not to mention brains, in the game.

Call it journalistic intuition, but *Evening Argus* sports writer John Vinicombe, who covered Albion throughout the 1970s right up until his retirement in 1994, had a hunch about who Bamber might try to persuade to take the manager's job. It seemed almost too ridiculous to contemplate, let alone write, but that hunch needed to be aired in print despite the risk of public – not to mention professional – ridicule. 'Could the club afford Brian you-know-who?' he speculated on Thursday 25 October, one seemingly throwaway yet carefully calculated line aimed at drawing debate on what he already suspected.

More than a few people laughed at Vinicombe when that story hit the streets. Not that he cared. Within forty-eight hours, the *Evening Argus* man would have the scoop of his career.

3

IN THE BEGINNING

Long before the European Cups, league titles and other assorted silverware won by Brian Clough the manager, there was Brian Clough the player.

In the 1950s, two types of centre-forward ruled the British game. The first was the tall, strapping, bull-in-a-china-shop variety; men such as Bobby Smith of Tottenham Hotspur (and, later in his career, Brighton & Hove Albion), Bristol City's John Atyeo and Nat Lofthouse of Bolton Wanderers who would run through brick walls to put the ball and, if necessary, the goalkeeper into the back of the net. The second kind relied more on subtlety and mobility, strikers who read the game in order to be in the right place at the right time to pass rather than bulldoze the ball into the goal. Clough – along with players such as Manchester United's Tommy Taylor and Charlie Fleming of Sunderland – belonged in the latter category.

The record books vary slightly according to the source, but are startlingly impressive no matter what you choose to believe. In 222 appearances for Middlesbrough spanning 1955 to 1961, Clough scored either 204 or 207 goals in 222 appearances (Clough himself plumped for the former in his second autobiography). Following his transfer from Middlesbrough to Sunderland he went on to net an undisputed sixty-three goals in seventy-four games for the Wearsiders before being forced into premature retirement aged twenty-nine, the result of medial and cruciate ligament damage to his right knee sustained in a collision with Bury goalkeeper Chris Harker at Roker Park on Boxing Day 1962. Many a club suffered at the hands, or rather boot, of the prolific Clough whose outstanding form, albeit in the Second Division, was barely recognised at international level. 'Two bloody caps' was Clough's own take on the derisory number of England appearances that came his way. However, it's fair to say some clubs suffered more than others.

In April 1958, courtesy of crushing Watford 6–0 at the Goldstone Ground, Brighton & Hove Albion were promoted to the English Second Division for the first time in the club's history. Their reward was a trip to Middlesbrough's Ayresome Park ground on the opening day of the 1958/59 season, Saturday 23 August, to face a team stuck in something of a trough having been relegated from the First Division in 1954. Nevertheless, with the prolific Clough up front, Middlesbrough always posed a threat in front of goal. So it proved that day as Albion, with understudy Dave Hollins deputising for first-choice goalkeeper Eric Gill, were thrashed 9–0.

And Brian Clough scored five of them.

'I kicked off nine times and I think I touched the ball more than anybody on our side,' says former Albion striker John Shepherd of a result which, at the time of writing, remains Albion's record defeat. 'Cloughie got all those goals, I got five or six kicks to my legs, and I don't think I even had a shot at goal. It was one of those games where you weren't in it at all. Afterwards it was a bit like, "Flipping heck, what's this all about?

What have we let ourselves in for?" Everything went right for them and nothing went right for us but when someone single-handedly scores five goals against you, then you know he can't be bad.'

Four months later, Middlesbrough travelled to Sussex for the return fixture. The match proved to be an absolute cracker, Clough scoring a hat-trick as the visitors won 6–4, taking his season's tally against the Second Division newcomers to eight. The following campaign he bagged another two when the sides met again at Ayresome Park, Middlesbrough triumphing 4–1, before Albion finally managed to exact some revenge with a 3–2 win at the Goldstone on St George's Day 1960. No prizes for guessing who scored one of Middlesbrough's consolation goals.

'People remember him as a manager and of course his struggle with the demon ale during the last few years of his life, but they forget what a talented centre-forward he was – and he really was talented,' says Adrian Thorne, himself no slouch in front of goal, scoring forty-four times in eighty-four appearances for Albion between 1958 and 1961. 'He took us to the cleaners in those matches. I suppose having recently played in the Third Division we were used to competing against centre-forwards who would miss as many chances in front of goal as they took. He didn't seem to miss, or at least miss the target. If it didn't go in, then the goalkeeper usually had to make a save. I didn't know him as a man, but what a tremendous player.'

As prolific a striker as he was, Clough was far from the most popular player in Middlesbrough's dressing room. Despite failing his eleven-plus exams at Marton Grove School and being ranked fifth-choice centre-forward at Ayresome Park after joining the club on turning seventeen, the former ICI messenger boy – born at 11 Valley Road, Middlesbrough, on 21 March

1935 – wasn't short in the confidence stakes. Clough's self-belief came laced with a cocky arrogance, the kind that took older players to task for their failings on the field and younger ones for simply being in the wrong place at the wrong time, as former Middlesbrough left-back Mick McNeil experienced in his very first encounter with the club's star striker.

'We [McNeil and goalkeeper Bob Appleby] used to go along in the evenings after work and train under the stand, in the sweat box, the "soot box" we called it because it was full of dust,' McNeil recalled in *Nobody Ever Says Thank You*, Jonathan Wilson's 2011 biography of Clough. 'One evening Cloughie was there, playing table tennis with some first team player. We were just young lads doing our training. We were doing step-ups. The box had a wooden base and it moved when you tried to do these things as quickly as you could. So the floor was bouncing. I heard this voice: "Hey, Buster!" The first words Cloughie ever spoke to me. "Hey, Buster, do you mind? We're trying to play table tennis." Bobby and I said under our breaths, "And we're trying to train", but we sat on the seat and watched him finish his game, then we carried on.'

Clough's directness extended, albeit with some justification, to certain members of Middlesbrough's team, whose defensive naivety seemed to go way beyond the occasional lapse. In his second autobiography, *Walking on Water*, Clough asserted that 'it doesn't take a master mathematician to produce the theory that a team with a centre-forward as good as I was, scoring as many goals as I did, should have been promoted.' And yet still Middlesbrough languished in the Second Division. Why? Because matches were, so he believed, being fixed.

'I was suspicious,' Clough continued. 'I'd kept an eye on our defenders and to my mind something had to be wrong.

Not even incompetence or crap players could explain the way Middlesbrough were letting in goals.' Clough's misgivings were understandable. Despite beating Brighton & Hove Albion 9–0 and 6–4 over the course of that 1958/59 season, Middlesbrough somehow conspired to finish below the Sussex club in the final league table (Albion coming twelfth, one place above Middlesbrough). Two of the players Clough most suspected of dirty dealing, Ken Thomson and Brian Phillips, were both later named in an investigation by the *Sunday People* as being involved in widespread match-fixing within the English game, receiving prison sentences and life bans from the sport.

Whether there was anything fishy going on at Middlesbrough circa 1958/59 has never been firmly established, but against such a backdrop Clough can almost be forgiven for cutting something of a brooding presence within the dressing room. 'The injustice of it all at Middlesbrough, the good work I did that was so blatantly undone by others in the team, produced more than anger and resentment,' he admitted of a period which had a profound effect on his managerial ethos of later years, namely that good teams are built from the back. 'There's no point in having the best and most prolific attack in the league if you can't keep the ball out of the net at your end. The Middlesbrough episode taught me a fundamental footballing fact of life – defenders need to be as good at their jobs as any forward.'

Clough's arrogance, aloofness and outspoken nature created individual enemies within the Middlesbrough squad, especially during the 1959/60 season, when manager Bob Dennison elected to make him captain (prompting a players' revolt, Dennison holding firm against a round robin asking for Clough be stripped of the mantle). However, on a team level, Clough continued to be tolerated for the simple reason that he was very good at his job. 'He [Clough] used to say, "I'm not wasting energy running out to the wings or chasing back,"' former Middlesbrough winger Billy Day would recall. 'That's what you lot get paid for. He'd say, "My job is in the penalty area scoring goals and that's what I get paid for." And you wouldn't argue because he was the one who got you your win bonus.'

In Clough's defence, his levels of competiveness far outstripped those of many of his teammates content simply to plod along week after week in the Second Division, something likely to have further fuelled the 'us' and 'him' environment which almost inevitably arose at Ayresome Park. In the same way that Roy Keane, himself a graduate of Brian Clough's managerial style at Nottingham Forest, railed against anyone whose appetite for the game (and in particular winning) failed to match his own, Clough strived to try harder all the time in order to improve and be successful. Otherwise what was the point?

That's a question Middlesbrough goalkeeper Peter Taylor had been contemplating after losing his first-team place in 1960, some five years after signing from Coventry City. Taylor was Clough's one true friend on the playing staff at Middlesbrough, someone who immediately identified his talents as a striker. However, whereas Taylor openly championed Clough as potentially the greatest goal-scorer in England, he himself was already eyeing a different career path within football, having grown wise to his own limitations as a keeper. While at Coventry, Taylor had served under Harry Storer, a member of the new breed of post-war managers who lived, breathed and slept the game rather than treating it as a pre-dinner inconvenience. Storer loved nothing more than embarking on scouting missions, which often yielded unsung yet capable players who cost little or nothing. That type of coaching position, Taylor decided, was where his future lay.

In 1961, Taylor left Middlesbrough for Port Vale before transferring again in May 1962, this time to non-league Burton Albion. Seven months later, he became their manager, embarking down the road – so Taylor hoped – to becoming another Harry Storer. Clough, bereft of his closest ally at Middlesbrough, departed Ayresome Park soon afterwards for Sunderland, where he continued terrifying defenders until that fateful afternoon in December 1962 when, in the process of chasing a slightly overhit through ball on a heavy pitch, his right knee made contact with Chris Harker's shoulder. Hitting the ground hard, Clough blacked out briefly before attempting to climb to his feet. Unable to stand, he was carried from the field and taken from Roker Park to Sunderland General Hospital, his career all but over.

It was almost two years before Clough bowed to the inevitable. The first attempted comeback, late in 1963, came to nothing, causing news of his supposed retirement to make headlines in the local *Football Echo*. By August 1964, Clough was training again, graduating to the reserves and then the first team where he made three appearances in the First Division, scoring one goal against Leeds United. Alas, it was to be a false dawn. Shorn of his speed and limping through matches, Clough's playing career had come to an end, leaving him feeling vulnerable, angry and uncertain about his future.

'I went berserk for a time,' Clough would confess of the period around his retirement. He drank alcohol, heavily. He lashed out at his teammates, including Len Ashurst, the full-back who had delivered the overhit pass in the build-up to the injury, appearing to blame him for the incident. He castigated the coaching staff, directors and seemingly anyone unfortunate enough to cross his path. Eventually George Hardwick, who had recently replaced Alan Brown as Sunderland's manager, decided enough was enough. Rather than have him moping around Roker Park, Hardwick asked his ailing striker to start working with the youth team players every afternoon. Brian Clough the manager had arrived.

'Thanks to George Hardwick's generosity – and it was generous because neither he nor I knew whether I could coach – I was given a head start on others my age,' Clough remarked of his lucky break, albeit amid unfortunate circumstances. 'I was able to take the first tentative steps on the road to a managerial career five years ahead of schedule.' Although he would never fully recover mentally from the blow of having to retire so early from playing, Clough soon realised that he was indeed cut out for management. Still young and skilful enough to impress on the training field, his verbal dexterity also proved inspirational, especially when it came to convincing teenagers that they were better players than they perhaps were. He sat a Football Association coaching exam, guided Sunderland into the semi-finals of the FA Youth Cup and as a consequence became Sunderland's official youth team manager. There was something else as well, a confession he almost apologetically acknowledged in *Walking on Water*: 'The truth was that I'd developed an instant liking for being in charge.'

For all his achievements during those few months spent coaching the kids, by the summer of 1965 Clough was out of work. When Hardwick was controversially sacked despite comfortably keeping Sunderland in the First Division, Clough found himself exposed to hostile fire from the directors, who hadn't forgiven him for his volatile behaviour while injured.

Sure enough, his marching orders followed a few days after Hardwick's dismissal. It left a sour taste in the mouth, especially as the club pocketed virtually all of the £40,000 insurance pay-out on his knee injury; Clough received just £1,500 plus the proceeds from a testimonial arranged by Hardwick attended by 31,000 appreciative Sunderland fans. His mistrust of directors and dislike of football politics, a seam that would run throughout Clough's managerial career, was duly cast.

Out of work and already marked down within certain boardrooms as a card-carrying member of the awkward squad, Clough's prospects appeared slim. That is until Hartlepools United, perennial strugglers towards the foot of the old Fourth Division, came calling. Clough was initially third choice for the managerial vacancy which arose in October 1965, but with the former Sunderland great turned football scribe Len Shackleton fighting his corner he got an interview. Offered the job by chairman Ernie Ord (a man who in Clough's words 'turned out to be an absolute shit'), Clough realised almost immediately that he needed a wingman alongside him who knew the avenues and alleyways of the game, particularly in the lower divisions. There had been little contact between himself and Peter Taylor since their days together at Middlesbrough, but he knew instinctively who that wingman should be.

When the pair met at a hotel in York to talk about potentially joining forces, Taylor was shocked by his old friend's appearance. 'His face reflected a dreadful year,' the former goalkeeper admitted. 'It was an overweight and careworn Brian Clough I was looking at. He had a young family to support and Hartlepool was the only hope.' Clough told him he'd been offered the Hartlepools job and had accepted, provided Taylor went as his assistant (a white lie – Clough had already informed

Ord he would accept the position). Taylor, recognising it as an opportunity to coach in the Football League, agreed to take a pay cut on his Burton Albion salary and move north. Ord knew nothing of this arrangement; Clough neatly sidestepping any potential flashpoint by designating Taylor as trainer rather than assistant, bucket and sponge perched at his feet in the dugout during matches. Hartlepools may have been in a mess – 'with defenders who couldn't defend, strikers who couldn't score, apart from a lad called Ernie Phythian who bagged a few, and the only thing the midfield could create was confusion among themselves,' according to Clough – but at least the pair of them, arguably the first proper managerial partnership in the English game, had a foot on the bottom rung of the Football League ladder.

* * *

'I don't know what's going on at this club. You're better than anybody here.' Those, according to Brian Clough, were the first words Peter Taylor ever said to him, spoken after a 1955/56 pre-season Probables *v.* Possibles trial match at Middlesbrough while Clough was still fuming over the injustice of being Bob Dennison's fifth-choice centre-forward. Besides being exactly what Clough needed to hear, it also told him that Taylor was a shrewd judge of players. It didn't matter that their personalities were poles apart, the gambling-loving, outwardly dour middle-of-the-road goalkeeper versus the financially astute, brash, prolific goal-scorer. When it came to football, or more specifically talking about football, the pair had chemistry in spades. Whether it be travelling to and from training, sat in train compartments bound for away matches or relaxing together in their respective family homes (Taylor was already married with young children, whereas Clough at that stage still lived at Valley Road with his parents and siblings), they would nearly always be discussing football – 'an incompatible couple fatally attracted to each other by a single passion', as Taylor put it. And, as neither had many other friends, an awful lot of football was discussed.

At Hartlepools United (as the club was known until 1968, when the 's' was dropped), the two men finally got the opportunity to put into practice what they had for so long preached. At least to an extent. Bereft of adequate training facilities and living out of tumbledown surroundings in the shape of the Victoria Ground (now more commonly known as Victoria Park), improvisation often became the norm. Whenever possible, Clough and Taylor arranged for team workouts to take place on the beach at nearby Seaton Carew, often tipping off the media for a good photo opportunity. To help save money, Clough secured a public service vehicles licence in case he was ever needed to drive the team coach (he wasn't). In terms of column inches, he was gold dust, even at that early stage of his managerial career. As Clough later boasted, 'Hartlepools suddenly found themselves getting more publicity, relatively, than some of the top clubs in the country.' He wasn't wrong.

The division of labour was clear right from the very start. Neither one of them bothered to formalise it. Their respective skills and personalities meant it happened naturally. Clough was the salesman, the man out front exuding self-confidence and delivering snappy one-liners. Taylor, less fond of the limelight, remained in the background, contacts book at the ready, itching to hit the road in search of untapped talent. Of course, there was more to Taylor than that. Behind the dour exterior lay a dry sense of humour – not everyone's cup of tea, admittedly, but it was there. Professionally, he offered Clough advice. Privately, he offered him companionship. Besides Barbara Clough, his wife, Taylor was perhaps the only person he really listened to, there to rein him in whenever he veered into the wrong or threatened to overstep the mark. Neither of them particularly liked taking training, preferring later in their careers when more money was available to employ other people to drill the players while they oversaw proceedings, but when it came to preparation and attention to detail they were spot on. Instructions to players were always kept simple: the game starts at 3 o'clock, not five past; get the ball down and play; no talking back to referees – it ruins your concentration and we can't afford the bookings; whatever you do first in a game – a tackle, pass, header – do it with total efficiency; cut off the supply to the left winger or you'll be sitting in the dugout alongside me; we've watched this lot, they're not as good as you, now go out and prove it.

Under Clough and Taylor's guidance, Hartlepools were spared the humiliation of having to apply for re-election to the Football League at the end of the 1965/66 season and went on to finish as high as eighth the following campaign. But the lack of training facilities and decrepit surroundings weren't the only flies in the managerial team's ointment. A draper who had made his fortune during the Second World War, Ernie Ord ran Hartlepools like a dictatorship. On selling the business, the football club became his all and the meddling promptly escalated. Ord would often ring Clough's office at 4.55 p.m. just to check that he and Taylor hadn't left early, hanging up immediately if anybody answered. It wasn't long before Clough began telling him where to go, something Ord simply wasn't used to and abhorred.

'Ord couldn't have been the big man if he'd tried,' Clough wrote in *Walking on Water*. 'As a bloke who was hardly tall enough to peer over the steering wheel of his Rolls-Royce, he was at something of a disadvantage. But like so many of his ilk, and so many in the game even now, he wanted to be seen as the man who ran the place and he wanted to be sure he took the credit.' If the decision within Sunderland's boardroom to relieve him of his youth team duties lit the match, then Clough's experiences at Hartlepools saw that match tossed onto the bonfire. 'I suppose it was Ord who made me wary of football club chairmen, right from the start,' he added.

In the event, Clough and Taylor would outlast Ord at the Victoria Ground. When the chairman declared that he wanted to sack Taylor because he cost too much, Clough refused to entertain the idea. Ord then told Clough that he'd sack him as well. Clough called his bluff and went nowhere – it was either the chairman or him. A board meeting was called and John Curry, who appreciated just what the Clough/Taylor axis brought to the club, rallied enough support for Ord's decision not to be ratified. With that, Curry was installed as chairman in Ord's place.

'Beating Ord was equal to winning the European Cup,' Taylor later insisted regarding the significance of Clough's stand on his behalf and the chain of events that followed. 'If we had lost, we'd have gone our separate ways, but once we'd survived, I knew we could take any job, face any challenge.'

Nevertheless, Taylor was already getting itchy feet. He wanted Clough and himself to move onto bigger things where there might be more money not only to buy players but also to boost their pay-packets, particularly his own. The more conservative Clough took some persuading, a combination of his sentimental attachment to the north-east (which Taylor, hailing from the East Midlands, didn't have) and a feeling that they had unfinished business at Hartlepools causing him to demur. Eventually, however, he came around to Taylor's way of thinking.

Once again it was Len Shackleton who would play fairy godfather, the former inside-forward turned journalist engineering a meeting between Clough and Derby County chairman Sam Longson, who had just sold his successful haulage business and had money to burn. Clough's sales pitch went something like this – he and Taylor had revived Hartlepools United on the pitch, left the club solvent, and now wanted to give the people of Derby a team they'd be proud of. Longson was seduced even though Clough, much as he had done on taking the Hartlepools job, failed to mention that he wanted to bring Taylor along as his assistant. Only once he'd been offered the job, and was negotiating from a position of strength, did Clough insist on his friend being there as well. Longson not only agreed, putting Clough on a wage of £5,000 per year compared to £2,500 for Taylor, but also promised to make £70,000 available for team strengthening.

'Taylor and I were in our element,' Clough reflected. 'We were never more excited or effective than when we were building teams from basics, getting rid of the dead wood and planting fresh new saplings.' The overhaul that followed during the second half of 1967 saw players, not to mention backroom staff, come and go from Derby at a remarkable rate as Taylor mined his extensive network of contacts to find the right blend. Even so, it took a while for the green shoots to appear, County finishing the 1967/68 season eighteenth in the Second Division shipping seventy-three goals from forty-two league games in the process. After which everything started to click. The following year they won the league by a country mile. Further team rebuilding ensured that County were soon challenging for the First Division title, an honour they achieved in 1971/72 finishing a single point above both Leeds United and Liverpool. The season after that Derby reached the last four of the European Cup, exiting 3–1 on aggregate to Juventus amid allegations that the referee for the first leg in Turin, Gerhard Schulenberg, had been fixed (the referee for the second leg, Francisco Marques Lobo, also revealed he'd been offered $5,000 plus a car if Juventus won, UEFA's subsequent investigation pinning the attempted bribe on the notorious Hungarian fixer Dezso Solti rather than the Italian club). Allegedly corrupt officials notwithstanding, County were doing just fine under Clough and Taylor on the field of play.

It was off it where the problems were starting to build with a vengeance.

For all County's success, far beyond anything the club had ever experienced in its entire history, an underlying tension lay just beneath the surface more or less from the day Clough and Taylor walked into the Baseball Ground. At its core was the gradual breakdown in the relationship between Clough and the man who had employed him, Sam Longson. Clough felt let down at the failure of the club's archaic administrative structure to capitalise on the hubbub of business and public relations activity generated not just by the club's success, but by him. Longson seethed at Clough's cavalier attitude towards signing new players, Colin Todd's arrival from Sunderland for a British record fee of £175,000 – a sum the manager agreed to pay without first checking with his chairman – being a particular bone of contention.

There were other things as well. Several of Derby's directors questioned the role of Peter Taylor and whether it was necessary to have him on the payroll, something that infuriated Clough. At the same time, Taylor felt betrayed on learning that Longson had quietly increased Clough's salary by £5,000, neither party bothering to inform the assistant manager. Clough's burgeoning media work, something which soared in parallel with County's success, meant Taylor was often left managing team affairs back in Derby while his old friend did the rounds on television. And yet that was all the thanks he got. While at Hartlepools the pair had agreed to divide any bonuses or external earnings equally between themselves, an arrangement Clough clearly reneged on. Taylor never forgot that, creating a sense of injustice which chipped away at him not just for the rest of his working relationship with Clough, but for the remainder of his life.

Clough's extra-curricular media activities would prove to be the straw that broke the camel's back at Derby. During the summer of 1973, London Weekend Television offered him the job of presenting their football coverage as a replacement for Jimmy Hill, who had left for the BBC. Clough opted for the best of both worlds, choosing to remain at Derby and work for LWT on a part-time basis. That meant leading a double life built around shuttling up and down the M1 motorway between the East Midlands and TV studios in London – not exactly an ideal scenario when you're supposed to be managing a top-flight football club.

As if that wasn't enough, one of Clough's newspaper commitments had also landed him in hot water. Over the course of several months spanning 1972 and 1973, his columns began to veer from the mildly controversial to outright attacks on anyone or anything that raised his hackles. In August 1973, Clough launched a blistering tirade from the pages of the *Sunday Express* on Leeds United and the Football Association. Leeds had been found guilty by the FA of 'persistent misconduct on the field' during a fiery game against Birmingham City and were handed a suspended £3,000 fine. Clough, whose dislike of Leeds and their manager Don Revie had grown over the years, felt the punishment was hugely inadequate. He wanted Revie fined and Leeds demoted to the Second Division. 'The Football Association should have instantly relegated Don Revie's team after branding them as one of the dirtiest clubs in Britain,' he wrote. 'As it is, the befuddled minds of the men who run the game have missed the most marvellous chance of cleaning up soccer in one swoop. By "fining" Leeds and Birmingham £3,000 they have allowed the "bad boys" to laugh at authority.'

The FA were not amused and charged Clough with bringing the game into disrepute. Longson was equally riled. Having tolerated Clough's excesses, becoming the subject of ridicule in boardrooms up and down the country for his perceived leniency, Longson grew adamant that Derby County as well as their manager would be in the firing line should a guilty verdict be returned. Clough for one was facing anything up to a three-year ban from football if the decision went against him.

Patience nearly exhausted, Longson issued Clough with an ultimatum ahead of the FA charge being heard. All television appearances were to be curtailed unless permission was granted in advance by the club's board. All newspaper articles were also to be vetted by the board before being published. Clough and Taylor weren't having it and threatened to resign. On 15 October 1973, their resignations were accepted following a board meeting. Having seen off Ernie Ord at Hartlepools,

Sam Longson – despite being left battered and bruised by his encounters with the pair, particularly Clough – had proved a tougher nut to crack.

Long after the dust had settled, Longson maintained that he had simply been calling Clough's bluff. Clough, in turn, regretted resigning. But the deed was done. He and Taylor were no longer in charge of Derby County. What's more, by resigning rather than being sacked, Clough departed without receiving so much as a penny, having agreed a five-year contract only the previous year. Born and raised in an area ravaged by the Great Depression of the 1930s, the fear associated with having no source of income cut to his very core, especially with a wife and three children to support. What's more, if the forthcoming FA charge brought further bad news, there could potentially be no source of income for years.

For all his bravado, the odds were beginning to stack against Brian Clough. He needed a job, and fast, before the FA could pass judgement on that piece in the *Sunday Express*. The only question, as he scoured the soccer map for any opportunity worthy of his talents, was where?

4

'WHO'S MIKE BAMBER?'

From his office chair at the Goldstone Ground, Mike Bamber surveyed the Derby County soap opera as it unfolded 200 miles away to the north and began hatching a plan.

The news that Clough and Taylor's resignations had been accepted by County's board came two days after Brighton & Hove Albion's 1–0 home defeat to Halifax Town, the result which convinced Bamber of the need to relieve manager Pat Saward of his duties. Bamber, himself something of a rags-to-riches story, recognised a kindred spirit in Clough, believing his restless spirit wouldn't allow him to sit still for long. The situation remained messy at Derby, where word had it that County's players wanted the pair reinstated. A so-called Protest Movement had also been formed by supporters who were busy organising marches and meetings campaigning for their return. For the time being, Bamber chose to observe from afar and see what panned out over the coming days. Once Albion's board had convened the following Saturday after the Shrewsbury Town game with the express intention of firing Saward, then the situation might have become clearer. Would Brian Clough really want to come to Brighton & Hove Albion? Given the right sales pitch and financial incentive, Bamber reckoned he just might. After all, if you don't ask, you don't get.

Although the picture did become slightly clearer at Derby in the days that followed, things remained turbulent around the Baseball Ground. The Protest Movement had gained momentum. The players did want Clough and Taylor reinstated. Longson, stung by the criticism coming his way, counter-attacked through the press insisting it was time people 'hear my side'. Yet one thing was also becoming patently obvious: despite all the noise, County's board were never going to take them back. In fact, they were busy moving on, wisely appointing Dave Mackay – a Clough/Taylor signing and Derby's on-field general during the club's ascendancy to the First Division – as manager, arguably the one man who the players would defer to, thus taking the sting out of any dressing-room rebellion. Bamber, sensing Longson wasn't for turning, decided to make his move.

'We had nothing else in the pipeline but quitting is made easier when you know alternative offers will not be in terribly short supply,' Clough reflected in 2002 of his immediate post-Derby career options. In reality this wasn't quite the case. Clough was out of control throughout much of 1973. For all his motivational talents as a manager, few chairmen were prepared to tolerate such a loose cannon on their premises, especially one with a ban from the game hanging over his head. Nottingham Forest, seeking a replacement for the Derby-bound Dave Mackay (who had become Forest's manager in 1972), made an enquiry, but nothing firmer than that, the lacklustre nature of their approach seemingly dissuading Clough from following it up.

That was it, the only prospective job offer on the table, and a half-baked one at that. Until Friday 26 October 1973, when, out of the blue, Mike Bamber got in touch not with Clough, but with Peter Taylor.

In *The Damned United*, the 2009 film based on David Peace's somewhat controversial part-fact/part-fiction novel about Clough's 44-day tenure as Leeds United manager spanning July to September 1974, there's a scene where Derby County's players gather at their former manager's house to discuss taking action in order to get Clough and Taylor reinstated. In the background, a telephone starts ringing. Barbara Clough answers, interrupting her husband with the news that Mike Bamber is on the line. 'Who's Mike Bamber?' asks a baffled Clough, portrayed by the actor Michael Sheen. Peter Taylor, appearing at his side in the form of Timothy Spall, puts him straight in six words: 'Chairman of Brighton and Hove Albion.'

The scene was fictional, a way of combining several different story strands in one go, yet Sheen's reaction on celluloid genuinely reflected that of Clough. He had never heard of Mike Bamber. In reality, it happened something like this. On Friday 26 October, Taylor received a phone call at his home from Bamber, who, over the course of a conversation lasting around twenty minutes, outlined his ambitious plans for Brighton & Hove Albion. Yes, he knew Albion were only a Third Division club. Yes, he knew Clough was facing an FA charge which could jeopardise his future in the game. Yes, he'd heard the boardroom talk about how Clough was impossible to work with. None of that, Bamber said, bothered him. He wanted Clough and Taylor to come and work on the Sussex coast and was prepared to pay handsomely for it, a sum of £15,000 (more than they'd been on at Derby) being mentioned to be split between the two of them.

'If Taylor was obsessed with anything beyond building football teams and winning matches, it was money,' Clough wryly observed in *Walking on Water* of the circumstances that led to them joining Albion. A touch harsh perhaps, but with some justification. Taylor loved building teams from scratch. He was certainly impressed by Bamber's vision and persuasive nature. None of that, however, would have mattered a jot had the salary on offer been paltry. Bamber was talking First Division wages, a sum well in excess of what many top-flight clubs might contemplate offering. Taylor was unquestionably a man out to better himself financially, and money would become a major issue between the two men further down the line in their relationship, but you can hardly blame him for being seduced by Bamber's proposition. In Taylor's opinion it had everything he thrived on right down to the perfect location, his love of English coastal resorts being something Clough often poked fun at.

Taylor called Clough straight away, told him who Mike Bamber was, and relayed details of the offer. Clough wasn't over-enthused but didn't kick the prospect into touch either. Taylor then rang Bamber back to arrange a meeting. Initially that was set to take place in the Midlands on the evening of Saturday 27 October following Albion's game at Hereford United. However, when Clough and Taylor were then invited to the London Weekend Television studios on the Saturday afternoon, the venue was switched to the Waldorf Hotel in Aldwych. Clough attended with Taylor, Albion being represented by Bamber together with club vice-chairman Harry Bloom.

John Vinicombe's exclusive in Saturday's *Evening Argus*, under the headline 'Talking To Clough', was right about pretty much everything except the venue for the talks, the late change of plan rendering the need for 'a secret rendezvous in the Midlands' redundant. This being the pre-digital age, Albion's players remained oblivious to Vinicombe's scoop, their minds focused on the match at Edgar Street, which Hereford won 3–0. Afterwards they boarded a train bound for London's Paddington Station before transferring across the capital by coach to catch another train from Victoria Station to Brighton. Only the sharpest eyes in the party noticed that, on arrival at Paddington, in the words of Brian Powney, 'Mike Bamber and one of the other directors just disappeared.' It wasn't until the following week, once the story grew legs, that 'we put two and two together about where they'd gone.'

That first meeting between the four men lasted around an hour and a half. Once introductions had been made, Bloom left the floor to Bamber, who once again pitched his vision of where Brighton & Hove Albion were going, this time more for the benefit of Clough's ears. By now the sum on the table, to be split between the pair, had risen from £15,000 to £20,000 per year. Money would be made available to strengthen the squad, an absolute necessity given Albion's perilous position towards the bottom of the Third Division. Clough could also continue with his extra-curricular newspaper and television work – anything, within reason, as far as Bamber was concerned, that might enhance Albion's public profile.

Clough was impressed, yet refused to commit. The meeting broke up amicably and over the course of the next two days talks between Bamber, Clough and Taylor continued in a series of telephone calls. 'They are both interested in coming to Brighton,' declared Albion's chairman in Monday's *Evening Argus*. 'It is a question of terms but I think there is a good chance of them coming. They are just what is needed here.' If it had been down to Taylor, contracts would have been signed there and then at the Waldorf Hotel. But still Clough hesitated. Albion being in the Third Division wasn't an issue – it was the club's geographical rather than league position that made him balk. He was, at heart, a dyed-in-the-wool north-easterner who had compromised enough to move his family as far south as Derby. Sussex was closer to France than Derbyshire, a county of Tory constituencies and picture-postcard villages compared to the Labour strongholds and industrial heartlands that had shaped him as a person. Derby County weren't going to take him back, he realised that, but surely there had to be a more viable option closer to home, irrespective of Mike Bamber's highly tempting offer?

On the flip side, the clock was ticking. That FA hearing, scheduled for Wednesday 14 November, loomed ever closer and Clough needed employment in case the verdict went against him. It was unlikely anything as financially attractive as Bamber's proposition would materialise before then. Bruised by his encounters with Ernie Ord and Sam Longson, there was also the somewhat peculiar prospect of working for a chairman he'd warmed to almost immediately, a man who seemed honest and straight-talking. And so, despite still having reservations, Clough decided to fall in with Taylor, the pair of them signing five-year contracts to manage Brighton & Hove Albion at the Midland Hotel in Derby on the evening of Wednesday 31 October.

At which point the football world went into complete shock.

The news broke late the following morning and made headlines all the way from Hove to Hobart. 'In a move that will surprise many, Brian Clough, the former manager of Derby County, is to take charge of Third Division Brighton & Hove

Albion with immediate effect,' declared the BBC's World Service in its Thursday bulletins. 'The publicity the club will get in future will undoubtedly be out of all proportion to their station in the league, and this is something Mr Bamber will be banking on,' wrote Norman Fox in *The Times*. Bamber himself told the growing posse of reporters at the Goldstone that it was 'the greatest thing ever to happen to Brighton' (as in the town in general). Excessive, definitely, yet perhaps understandable given he had just pulled off a sporting coup to rival any. 'Now we can really go places,' he continued. 'We've been playing recently to gates of only 5,000 but I feel certain Sussex people will now rally round us and I hope we see a crowd of 20,000 here on Saturday when we meet York City.'

'I would have been twenty-one at the time and had only just started working for [BBC] Radio Brighton,' recalls football reporter and commentator Peter Brackley. 'I got a tip in the office that Brighton were about to make a new appointment. Somebody said, "You'd better get down there quick because it's going to be a big signing." I don't even think I was aware beforehand that it was going to be him [Clough], certainly not that I can remember. And suddenly there they [Clough and Taylor] both were, walking through the little tunnel that went behind the West Stand at the Goldstone. It was a big shock for everyone. I mean it was only eighteen months or so since he'd won the title with Derby. For whatever reason the TV people from the [BBC] *South Today* programme couldn't get there in time, so they said to me, "You'll have to do it." I said, "Do what?" And they said, "You'll have to do the interview." I said, "I'm on local radio, I can't do that!" So my first ever TV interview was with Clough. There I am with my hair down over my shoulders in a kipper tie and a ridiculous jacket because I've dressed for radio, not TV. I actually said to him, "Are you going to be controversial, Mr Clough?" And he just looked at me and said, "I prefer to call it a touch of honesty, young man."'

Clough may have had reservations in private about taking the job, but they certainly weren't evident that Thursday afternoon at the Goldstone during what proved to be a whistle-stop question-and-answer session. In fact, he carried the air of a man on a mission, despite being unable to resist poking a jab in the direction of his former employers. 'I am anxious to get started and I understand there is quite a bit of work to be done,' he said. 'Peter Taylor and I meet the players tomorrow afternoon and, let me say this, Brighton's chairman and his directors did a better job of selling Brighton to me than I did trying to sell Derby County.' Asked how long it might be before he and Taylor were guiding Albion into the First Division, Clough was remarkably restrained in his reply for a man prone to boasting. 'We are now in the bottom six of the Third Division. It will take a lot of hard work to get them into the Second. Before anyone starts talking about the First, let's get into the Second. I think I would settle for staying in the Third for a few months.'

Not one journalist appears to have questioned Bamber as to whether Brighton & Hove Albion could afford to engage the services of two, let alone one, of the English game's highest earners. Basic arithmetic suggests the club was gambling on attracting attendances of over 20,000 for each home game in order to bankroll not only their new managerial duo but also the team strengthening that would be necessary. Print deadlines meant there was no mention of Clough and Taylor's appointment in the match programme for the York City match. However, in a statement published in the programme for the following home league game against Chesterfield on Saturday

17 November, Albion came as close as the club ever would to revealing how the Clough/Taylor revolution was going to be funded.

'Brighton & Hove Albion ... Brian Clough ... Peter Taylor,' the statement began.

> A great volume of publicity on television, radio and in the press began when negotiations were first reported, grew as Albion's hopes rose, and resulted in nationwide coverage as soon as the exciting deal was completed. Albion have received praise for their enterprise and initiative with our chairman Mr Mike Bamber, and vice-chairman Harry Bloom, skilfully and patiently conducting the negotiations. Mr Clough paid tribute to their ability when he met television and newspapermen after the decision had been made, and we know that everyone with the club at heart will wish him and Mr Taylor a very pleasant and successful stay with us. But there is no complacency, no sitting back and waiting for miracles to happen. We all know that much has to be done, and jobs are being tackled keenly and urgently. One thing is very important. We need your support now more than ever before. We shall rely far more upon gate revenue than in the past, for we have a forward-looking board of directors and manager, and big crowds for every match can help them carry out their plans. The support for the team is also vitally important, for we have to improve our league position, clear the first FA Cup hurdle, and with the fans roaring them on this becomes a little easier.

With barely any time to make a proper analysis of Albion's squad, Clough and Taylor chose to regard the York City match as little more than research. Taylor had made some calls to contacts of his at Third Division clubs while negotiations with Bamber and Bloom were in progress, just to get an idea of what they might be inheriting. Bamber also briefed the pair about some of Albion's key players, including Peter O'Sullivan, on the transfer list at his own request in a bid to escape the clutches of Division Three, and long-serving centre-back Norman Gall, who Clough was delighted to learn was a Geordie. While several Albion players came away from that first meeting with Clough and Taylor at the White Hart Hotel in Lewes feeling disappointment verging on anger, Gall would not be among them.

'He [Clough] goes, "Who's the Geordie?" in that unmistakable voice of his,' remembers Gall. 'I said, "Me." He said, "Right, you're the captain." I'm guessing it was because I was from the north-east and he felt he could trust me. And I had the same feeling about him, being a northerner. He was so tied to the north. It was where he'd grown up, where he'd played, where he'd managed, and as far as I was concerned it was great to have him there. Maybe he felt a little bit the same way about me, a familiar accent around the place, because I never lost it even though I'd been living down south for quite a while by then. So suddenly I'm captain, which I was really happy about. Eddie Spearritt [who had clocked up over 200 appearances in Albion's defence and midfield] didn't like it though. He'd been captain up until then. In fact he didn't talk to me after that. That was the beginning of the end for Eddie.'

Born in Wallsend near Newcastle in 1942, Gall was of the perfect time and place to appreciate just what a phenomenon Brian Clough the player had been. As a teenager, he along with many of his classmates at school had idolised the prolific centre-forward, Gall's enthusiasm even providing an early insight into the Jekyll and Hyde nature of Clough's personality that he would encounter much later while playing for Albion.

'Brian could be a funny man, and I mean funny as in strange,' says Gall. 'As a kid I used to collect autographs. He was playing at Middlesbrough then, and when I heard he had been selected for the England under-23 side to play at Newcastle, quite a lot of us lads went and stood outside the hotel they were staying at – the Grand Hotel, right by the station. We got all of the players as they came out. They signed their autographs, one by one, all except for Brian. We actually followed him, three or four of us, right the way through Newcastle while he was looking in the shops. And he just wouldn't sign. He sort of ignored us. When he came to Brighton – and I got on quite well with him actually to begin with – sometimes he'd have me walk around the pitch with him rather than train because my fitness was a bit of an issue by then. "Let's have a little walk round together," he'd say, and we'd chat about the old days, Northumberland and things like that. And one time I told him that story about the autographs. He said, "Yeah, I know, I was a really nasty man, wasn't I?" And I said, "Yes, you were!"'

* * *

In more recent times the fortunes of Brighton & Hove Albion and York City have veered in wildly contrasting directions, May 2017 witnessing the former winning promotion to the Premier League while the latter suffered the ignominy of relegation to the sixth tier of English football, otherwise known as National League North. Back in November 1973, it was York who were in the ascendancy, sitting fourth in the old Third Division (compared to nineteenth-placed Albion) having lost just one of their opening fourteen league fixtures. No mugs, in other words.

A little before 10 a.m. and with five hours to go until kick-off, Clough and Taylor arrived together at the Goldstone from their overnight stay in Lewes to be greeted by scores of cameramen and reporters. After sifting through a fraction of the many letters and telegrams piled on his office desk, the new manager, appearing uncharacteristically nervous, took to pacing the narrow corridors inside the bowels of the West Stand, eventually fetching up in the home dressing room. Taking offence at the tatty state of Albion's blue-and-white striped shirts laid out ready for the players to wear, Clough ordered a new strip to be delivered within thirty minutes. No supplier could possibly deliver a dozen good-quality shirts at such short notice, he was told. It took a brave man to say no to Brian Clough, but on this occasion the informant, their identity long forgotten, seems to have been listened to. The shirts stayed put.

By the time Albion's players took to the field shortly before 3 p.m., the Goldstone was buzzing yet nowhere near full, the official attendance of 16,017 falling short of the hoped-for 20,000 and considerably below the ground's then capacity of just under 35,000. Mind you, the hubbub made it feel a lot more than that. 'His greatness' proclaimed one of dozens of banners decorating the terraces. 'Brian C and Peter T, you're the ones the Albion are pleased to see' read another. Few heads among the scrum of cameramen now assembled at the mouth of the players' tunnel leading from the West Stand onto the pitch bothered to turn as the teams emerged. As far as the national media were concerned, they were of little importance. Today was all about one man. And, with all due respect to Albion's new assistant manager, that wasn't Peter Taylor.

Finally, Clough appeared, not out of the players' tunnel, ready to take up position in the home dugout, but high up in the West Stand, making instead for the directors' box. Cue mass adulation around the ground with the exception of a small pocket of York City supporters bearing witness. Renowned Welsh referee Clive Thomas blew his whistle to start the game and almost immediately Albion left-back George Ley sliced the ball straight into touch. According to Brian James of the *Sunday Times*, Ley 'seemed to shrink visibly' from that point on. He was far from alone. Out on the left flank, Peter O'Sullivan sensed almost immediately that the occasion was in danger of getting to some of his teammates.

'I was a left midfielder more than a left winger,' he recalls. 'At the start he [Clough] shouted to me, "Stay really wide on the line. Just stay on the line." And I'm thinking, "I'm staying on the line here. I'm not going to get much of the ball because I've got muppets inside of me that can't pass it." Anyhow, I did it, and I think he respected me from then as a player as I'd done what he asked. It's a bit like José Mourinho. If a player doesn't do as he says, he drags him off. Cloughie was similar to that with his man-management. You had to do what he said. If you didn't, then you were out, as simple as that. By out, I don't just mean out of the team – I mean out of the club.'

As the game progressed, so the majority of the nerves subsided. With O'Sullivan increasingly coming into play on the left, Lammie Robertson making a nuisance of himself upfield and Gall dominant at the back, Albion took control to such an extent that they were given a standing ovation at half-time. Yet clear-cut opportunities to score against a solid York defence were few and far between, Clough's new charges ultimately having to settle for a point in a 0–0 draw. Despite Albion's perilous position in the league and the lack of any goals, the supporters seemed largely satisfied, the occasion itself proving to be the main attraction. As one young woman commented on leaving the ground, having just witnessed her first match, 'I'm not interested in football. I only went to see Brian Clough. He's gorgeous.'

If there was a cloud on the horizon that afternoon, besides the slightly disappointing attendance, then it manifested itself when the time came for Albion's manager to carry out his post-match press duties. True, he and Taylor were new to the job, but Clough's lack of recent experience in the lower leagues shone through to the extent that he didn't appear to know or remember the names of his own players, not even the man he had just appointed as captain. 'They [Albion] played well enough to have won,' he told reporters gathered in the corridor outside his office. 'I would have liked to see them win but York aren't exactly the worst side in the Third Division, though I've not seen much of it. The number 10 for us [Robertson] got in good positions. There was a lot of effort on goal but I would rather have been the away side. York were lifted by coming here, the crowd and everything. Our lads were very nervous to begin with. They left some of their strength in the dressing room. I thought our number 5 [Gall] was superb, especially in the first half. His heading was as good as I've seen. He headed the ball remarkably well by Third Division standards.'

The fact that Albion's attendance for the game was several thousand down on what had been hoped for barely figured in the post-match analysis as seen through the eyes of both Bamber and Clough. Bamber chose to focus on the extra 10,000 punters who'd paid to come through the turnstiles compared to the previous home match against Southport, which had attracted a crowd of just 6,417. Instead of a mere £2,700 in gate money, Albion had benefitted from a £6,500 windfall – to the apparent delight of the chairman. In his *Sunday Mirror* column the following day, Clough's rather skewed financial logic had him bragging that 'I made more cash in one hour at Brighton than I did in four and a half years at Derby when we won the Second Division championship and league championship and reached the [semi-]finals of the European Cup.' He also claimed to be Britain's best-paid football boss, 'better off even than Don Revie and Bill Shankly' – insinuating that although the reported £25,000 salary for himself and Peter Taylor was awry, 'we are better off than most people think'.

After the rushed introductions of the previous week, the days immediately after the York City game saw all parties associated with one of the strangest managerial appointments in the history of British football slowly feeling each other out. Initially Clough and Taylor attended training sessions, although, to the immense frustration of the dressing room, this would soon cease to be the case. Bamber was also keen to see how his new employees would operate, the pair's very first training session in charge giving the chairman an opportunity to aim a gentle shot across the manager's bows. The session took place in heavy rain and yet Clough – dressed in tracksuit and football boots and claiming afterwards to be exhausted – emerged from it dry as a bone. When Bamber pointed out this inconsistency, an embarrassed Clough dithered before quickly admonishing teenage winger Tony Towner, leaning against a nearby wall, for not standing up straight in the presence of his manager and chairman.

However, with Albion continuing to dominate the headlines in the wake of Clough and Taylor's appointment, Bamber was in no mood to issue stern reprimands. A glance through the national sports pages of November 1973 shows Brighton & Hove Albion attracting as many column inches as the likes of Manchester United, Liverpool or Leeds United. Of course, Clough generated plenty of them himself through his own newspaper columns, yet by and large much of what he said in public tended to find its way into print anyhow. One quote in particular from his early days in charge appeared in just about every national title, and represents a fair assessment of the scenario that Clough and Taylor found themselves in:

'It's tougher here than at Hartlepools where they didn't expect anything. Now we have a reputation, but there are no fairies at the bottom of Brighton pier. There are only sixteen professionals here. Only one goalkeeper, one trainer, one secretary, one groundsman, in fact one of everything. That puts Peter and me in the majority, for they have two managers.'

Equally, when other people voiced an opinion about Clough or Brighton & Hove Albion, so their words also had a good chance of being reported. Two days after facing York City, the last tie out of the hat in the draw for the first round of the 1973/74 FA Cup competition paired Albion away against Isthmian League minnows Walton and Hersham, from Surrey's stockbroker belt. Finding himself besieged by calls from journalists wanting a reaction, Walton and Hersham club secretary Adrian Cooke duly stepped up to the mark. 'It will be a bit of a laugh, but not for Mr Clough,' Cooke told *The Times*. 'Remember, we beat Exeter in the [FA] Cup last year though to be honest we are not quite as strong this season. Even so we have been beaten only once at home in the league in the last two years and must have a very good chance of winning. I would expect a capacity crowd of 6,500 because, after all, Brian Clough is a great personality. It really is a very attractive draw.'

The tie, scheduled for the afternoon of Saturday 24 November at Walton and Hersham's compact Stompond Lane ground, came less than seven months after Derby County's exit from the European Cup semi-finals at the hands of Juventus. If one single fact encapsulates Clough's extraordinary transformation in circumstances over the course of 1973, then it lies there.

Somewhat worryingly for Bamber, not to mention Albion's supporters, many of the Clough-related headlines continued to revolve around rumours of his imminent return to Derby. Although County's chairman and board were keen to move on and had no intention of re-employing their former manager, sections of the club's fan base were still actively campaigning to bring both him and Taylor back to the East Midlands. Worse still from an Albion perspective, word had it that Clough wasn't exactly discouraging them. Whereas Taylor had moved quickly to put down roots in Sussex, buying a large seafront apartment in Kings Gardens, Hove, within two weeks of becoming assistant manager, Clough was still living at the family home near Derby, providing ample opportunity to meet with members of County's Protest Movement.

On 11 November, the *Sunday Times* ran an article suggesting Clough was poised to return to Derby, quoting Don Shaw, a leading light in the Protest Movement known for his work as a scriptwriter on television shows, including the police drama series *Z-Cars*. 'Clough even told me he is prepared to give up his TV work and serve under Sam Longson's chairmanship again,' Shaw was reported as saying. When confronted about the article by John Vinicombe, Clough's response verged on borderline contempt for what was going on in Derby. 'I have met this man, Shaw, on two occasions,' he stated. 'There are so many hangers-on that it is difficult to know who is who. They are all over the place, but I am Brighton's manager and I just want to get on with the job. There is much to be done.'

Was Clough telling the truth about staying or hedging his bets? Either way, Vinicombe was spot on in his assessment that 'somebody up in Derby is giving the matter a king-size stir.'

That king-size stir gained further momentum when, bizarrely, the wives of Derby's players appeared on the scene expressing support for the return of Clough and Taylor. The players themselves then decided to rebel against Dave Mackay over the club's refusal to reinstate the pair, signing a letter of protest outlining their intention not to report for duty until 1 p.m. on Saturday 24 November, the day of a home match against Leeds United. In response, Mackay called their bluff, saying he would field a team of reserve players if necessary. Cliff Lloyd of the Professional Footballers' Association also declared that they would be in breach of their contracts if the threat was carried out. With that, the rebellion was quelled; Clough's increasing ambivalence towards the idea of returning to the Baseball Ground hardly helping the Protest Movement's cause. Under Mackay, Derby would finish third in the top flight that season and win the Football League title again twelve months later, his part in County's 1970s purple patch so often overshadowed by the achievements of his predecessor.

'The players were thunderstruck, but they got carried away with the media and the public,' Peter Taylor told the TV presenter and author Tony Francis long after the rebellion had lost steam. 'They were loyal to us but I wasn't sure how much I wanted their loyalty in a situation like that. I told Brian we weren't ever going back, so we should stop misleading people. He knew it was a loser from the start. All sorts of businessmen were jumping on the bandwagon, trying to promote themselves.' In his 1980 autobiography *With Clough By Taylor*, that reluctance to return to Derby County was spelled out in even more emphatic terms when set against his determination to unearth new players for Brighton & Hove Albion: 'I was too busy travelling to take much interest. One night I was standing in the crowd at Chester, the next night I was more than 200 miles away watching Norwich reserves. My job is observation, decision, replacement.'

In the midst of all the continued strife at Derby came Clough's date with the Football Association's disciplinary committee, charged with 'bringing the game into disrepute' over his comments three months previously in the *Sunday Express* about Leeds United and the 'befuddled minds' of the FA itself. The hearing took place in London in front of five committee members. The worst-case scenario was a three-year ban from football. On the flip side, Clough could be cleared altogether. Some felt a lesser ban, should he be found guilty, was inevitable in order to curb his perceived excesses. Clough attended in person along with Taylor and, after fifty-five minutes of deliberations, the committee decided he was innocent. 'A triumph for common sense' was how Clough described the verdict to the waiting press.

What might have happened had the verdict gone the other way? A ban of anything longer than six to nine months would almost certainly have spelled the end of his relationship with Brighton & Hove Albion. In fact, just days after the hearing Clough suggested in one Sunday newspaper that any form of guilty verdict, even if it had only resulted in a fine, would have caused him to resign as manager. John Vinicombe doubted that he meant this. 'After all, Clough knew full well before accepting the job that he was due before the FA disciplinary committee and that a fine or suspension was a possibility following his forthright criticism of the way the ruling body handled the Leeds United affair,' he wrote in the *Evening Argus* on Monday 19 November. 'I cannot believe Clough started as Albion's manager with such a drastic course of action in mind. Perhaps yesterday's published remarks are a bit tongue in cheek to satisfy seekers of sensation and controversy.'

Brighton & Hove Albion, or more specifically Mike Bamber, had provided Clough with a safe haven while the threat of a ban hung over him. Free now to continue working, everyone associated with the club drew breath to see if Clough would repay that loyalty, or whether he'd jump ship for a more attractive destination at the earliest opportunity.

5

DARK DAYS

Hard as it might be to believe, having read the previous pages, there was more to the news circa November 1973 than just Brian Clough.

Take a stoked-up cauldron of cheap credit and the resulting bubble of consumer confidence. Throw in the almost inevitable banking crisis which follows, plus raging inflation and stratospheric wage deals, before inflaming the whole situation with an Arab–Israeli war leading to a quadrupling in the price of oil. Oh, yeah, and the miners' union wants a 40 per cent pay increase. What do you get? A country that grinds to a near standstill, that's what.

In hindsight, the whole situation escalated remarkably quickly. On Monday 12 November, Britain's newspapers carried stories about power cuts being likely in London and some other parts of the country, the result of industrial action reducing the amount of power available through the Central Electricity Generating Board (CEGB). The following day, as cold weather moved in from the north, a state of emergency was officially announced across the UK on the advice of the Privy Council 'in view of the present industrial disputes affecting the mines and electricity supply industries'. The state of emergency allowed for the use of troops, should it be necessary, and the setting up of local committees with powers to safeguard essential supplies. Ration coupons were made ready for distribution through local post offices. Barely twenty-four hours after London was put on standby, large areas of Sussex, including the towns of Crawley, Burgess Hill, Eastbourne, Haywards Heath, Shoreham and Horsham, were warned of likely cuts to their supplies on Wednesday between the hours of 4 p.m. and 7 p.m.

Come December, the situation had deteriorated to the point where a three-day week was declared necessary in order to conserve electricity amid the diminishing stocks of coal. As of 1 January 1974, commercial users of electricity were limited to three specific days of consumption per week. Essential services, for instance hospitals and supermarkets, were exempt from the restrictions but television companies had to cease broadcasting at 10.30 p.m. Even football was affected, the state of emergency and subsequent three-day week (which lasted until 7 March 1974) resulting in matches kicking off during the early afternoon due to a ban on the use of floodlights. By mid-December, however, changing kick-off times were last on Albion's list of concerns. That's because the club was experiencing a state of emergency of its very own.

To begin with, Albion's results under Brian Clough and Peter Taylor were commendable. The 0–0 stalemate against high-flying York City was followed seven days later by another draw away against Huddersfield Town, Albion fighting back from 2–0 down to share the spoils thanks to a Ken Beamish header and a powerful eightieth-minute shot from Barry Bridges. On Tuesday 13 November came the first win, Pat Hilton's second-half header from Lammie Robertson's free kick enough to see off Walsall in the West Midlands rain. Had Chesterfield goalkeeper Jim Brown not pulled off a wonder save in the last few minutes at the Goldstone Ground to deny Peter O'Sullivan on 17 November, then Clough and Taylor would have been celebrating a first home win. Instead, the match finished goalless in the days when a draw always counted for more under the two-points-for-a-win system.

Five points from a possible eight, all garnered against opposition who were noticeably raising their games against a club that had suddenly become newsworthy. Hardly earth-shattering, but a solid start nonetheless, especially as Clough and Taylor were still coming to terms with the raw material at their disposal in the dressing room. 'Many people will be looking for miracles from him but I think it will take a considerable time to readjust to the priorities of Third Division football,' Walsall manager Ronnie Allen commented after his side's defeat to Albion. In the event, it wasn't Third Division football that brought the curtain down on Clough and Taylor's honeymoon period at the Goldstone. It was the supposedly inferior fare of the semi-professional Isthmian League.

Comedian Eric Sykes, the local mayor and a couple of high-profile national radio disc jockeys were among the 6,500 people who squeezed into Stompond Lane on Saturday 24 November to see Walton and Hersham take on Albion in the first round of the FA Cup. Of course, Clough upstaged them all from beginning to end, choosing to watch the match from an exposed seat placed near the touchline like football's answer to King Canute observing the incoming tide. Not that his regal posturing achieved anything positive. Quite the opposite.

Somewhat piqued, the home side went at Albion straight from the kick-off, the ball being played back to future

Wimbledon and Sheffield United manager Dave Bassett, who smashed it high in the direction of Brian Powney in the visiting goal. Off charged Walton and Hersham centre-forward Russell Perkins, a school teacher by trade, in pursuit. The ball came down and bounced up high. Powney and Perkins jumped together, jostling for possession. Powney collapsed in a heap, leaving Perkins to convert into the unguarded net. However, Walton and Hersham's joy was short-lived as referee Gordon Kew, despite first appearing to award the goal, then disallowed it for a foul on Powney. At which point the home crowd, feeling robbed, turned their ire on Clough for much of what remained of the ninety minutes. In that respect, Walton and Hersham can't have felt a lot different to the hostilities of Turin in the previous season's European Cup semi-finals. Clough, to his credit, refused to bite. The game ended in a 0–0 draw but the overriding feeling was that Albion had dodged a bullet. In Powney's words, 'We should have got beaten there.'

'The preparation was crap,' admits Lammie Robertson. 'There seemed to be an assumption that we were going to murder them when we went up there. There was nothing much we did in the way of homework. It was like, "Go out and play." They [Clough and Taylor] must have had them looked at but if they did then none of that information got passed down the line to us.'

'It wasn't really a football match,' adds John Templeman. 'The ball was constantly in the air being aimed at several large guys up front, which wasn't pleasant. Cloughie said afterwards that we'd win the home game, but I sensed there were a few in our team who weren't up to it. Maybe it was their way of getting back at Clough and Taylor for the way they'd been treated when they first came in. Some of them didn't seem bothered.'

Four days later, on Wednesday 28 November, the two teams came together again for the replay at the Goldstone, the early kick-off time of 1.45 p.m. stripping the normally vocal North Stand of its youthful regulars who remained in school or at work. The nightmare began when Perkins stooped to head Walton and Hersham into the lead with twenty minutes on the clock. Despite winning no less than eighteen corners, Albion simply couldn't make their pressure tell. As more men were committed forward in search of an equaliser, gaps inevitably started to appear at the back. In the eighty-second minute, Clive Foskett, a 26-year-old joiner at the Natural History Museum in London, made it 2–0 to the part-timers. Two minutes later, he scored again. Then, with sixty seconds of normal time remaining, Foskett completed his hat-trick to make the final score Brighton & Hove Albion 0, Walton and Hersham 4. It was, so John Vinicombe declared, the worst FA Cup defeat in the club's history. Few were prepared to argue with him.

'I was left so much space at the back by Brighton and I had time to think about all three goals,' said Foskett afterwards, revelling in his fifteen minutes of fame. Indeed, it was Albion's defensive frailties rather than their inability to put the ball in the opposition's net that most concerned Clough. 'Walton put the goals in beautifully but we were very slack at the back,' he said. 'In terms of results I can't remember in my career getting beaten by four clear goals. The very fact they are amateurs didn't help, although I must give them every credit. They are very competent amateurs. It was much easier for Walton this time. The pressure was off them. We were stretched completely. They were better organised and had better technique. Naturally, I was terribly disappointed. I am certain my players are sick, poor lads. I'm paid to get results. They are paid to assist me.'

Reality had well and truly bitten. For the first time since Clough and Taylor's arrival, dissenting voices began to be heard. The main bugbear centred on their absences from the club between matches. Taylor, admittedly, was doing what he did best, slogging up and down the motorways and A-roads of England and Wales searching for potential new players. But what of Clough, whose eagerness to return to his family home near Derby after games meant he had yet to even set foot on Albion's team coach? By now training duties had been delegated to the ex-Notts County player John Sheridan, previously a coach at Derby during Clough and Taylor's reign at the Baseball Ground, with Joe and Glen Wilson continuing their backroom duties. Since Sheridan's arrival, the manager's presence had been sporadic to say the least, the lack of adequate preparation – as highlighted by Lammie Robertson ahead of the Walton and Hersham cup ties – beginning to manifest itself on the field and test the patience of the players.

'He [Clough] would come down on the Thursday, or Friday, or even the Saturday and then go back on either the Saturday night or the Sunday,' says Peter O'Sullivan. 'He'd have a jockey on his bonnet to get back to Derby. That was his place, where he was God.'

John Templeman concurs. 'John Sheridan would do all the training sessions during the week. He would also take the Friday session, by which time Cloughie and Taylor would sometimes have come back. They'd be standing around watching, not taking part. In fact, they put no effort into it whatsoever as far as I was concerned. You'd want their input about this and that, what tactics to play, how to improve as players, but it was rarely there. We were all quite shocked and disappointed in all honesty because we thought, "Here's a couple who have been highly successful in management," and of course he [Clough] had been a decent striker. I – we – were expecting a lot, lot more than they offered.'

Steve Piper, nevertheless, found there was one big advantage to Clough and Taylor's somewhat lackadaisical approach. 'In a way it was quite nice because you didn't have him [Clough] breathing down your neck every day. That's the way he worked. He and Taylor would turn up on a Thursday or Friday, we'd all go over to Hove Park to train, they would walk around the grounds with Peter Taylor's dog – Bess, I think it was called – while the coach did the training. They'd stroll around, looking on, saying hello to the locals, while we were out there in the dog crap with people walking across as you were trying to train!'

Very occasionally, the status quo would be broken, but even then Clough's unfamiliarity with his new surroundings – a situation he appeared to be doing little to remedy – had the potential to throw spanners in the works, sometimes with unintentionally hilarious results.

'You would get phone calls at home with a sudden change of plan,' says Ian Goodwin. 'We all got a call one Monday from Ray Crawford [Albion's youth team coach]. "Be at the [Sussex] University at 4 o'clock for training." I said, "Ray, it's dark at 4 o'clock!" He was like, "Just be there." So we get there. What are we going to do? Do we get changed? Do we go out and start? Cloughie rolls up at half-past four and it's completely dark. There are no floodlights at the university so we ain't going to train anyway. Cloughie goes, "It's dark", and buggers off. I turn to Ray and say, "What was all that about?" And he goes, "You can't talk to the man, Reggie," which was my nickname. "You just can't talk to the man."'

'He didn't know the area at all, coming from up north, so

instead of driving he'd get other people to take him wherever he wanted to go,' adds Tony Towner, Brighton born and raised, who had turned eighteen in the May of 1973. 'In those days we often used to train up at Sussex University. We'd get changed at the Goldstone, get in our cars and then drive from the ground to training. I'd only just passed my driving test and I bought myself a little light blue Ford Escort Popular for about £350. The day after, instead of getting the bus, I drove to the ground and got changed. As I was about to get in my car and head for training, I heard this voice – "Young man, wait there." And he wanted a lift in my car. So he got in, I went to pull away, and he says, "Don't go anywhere, young man." At which point Peter Taylor got in with the club secretary and Peter Taylor's dog. So now I'm sitting in my car, a first-time driver, and I've got Brian Clough in the front, Peter Taylor in the back, the secretary of Brighton & Hove Albion sat next to him, and a great big black Labrador called Bess somewhere in between the two of them. You can imagine the weight of this car, and it was only an 1,100 engine size. I was petrified. In fact, I was shaking so much I could barely hold onto the steering wheel! As we approached Sussex University, I went to turn left, took the kerb too sharp, and smacked against it. Peter Taylor came over the back seat, the dog came over the top of me, and Brian Clough hit his head against the windscreen. He turns round to me and says, "Hey, young man, how long have you been driving?" And I said, "About a week." It was the funniest thing I've ever witnessed in my life. He didn't ask for a lift back. In fact, he never got in my car again!'

As far as Mike Bamber was concerned, it was still early days. 'Brian cannot move until Christmas because his children don't break up from school until then,' was how he responded to one question from a reporter regarding the manager's apparent reluctance to relocate to Sussex. As for the Walton and Hersham replay result? That, reckoned the chairman, was more to do with the players than the management. But was Bamber fully aware of the extent of Clough's absences and the lack of preparation ahead of games? If he was, then he chose not to say so. 'I feel as sick this morning as Brian must feel,' Bamber told John Vinicombe. 'Agreed that Walton played well, I still think this was a disgraceful performance by our team, but Brian Clough and Peter Taylor are going to make this a great club and when the tide turns, as it will very soon, it will prove their greatest achievement in soccer so far.'

Clough also chose to turn the spotlight on his 'poor lads' rather than admit, at least in public, that his absences may have contributed to the state of flux at the club. 'When we came here I knew virtually nothing about the Third Division,' he told journalists the morning after the Walton and Hersham defeat. 'I assumed the club must have some good players having only recently been in the Second [Division], but when I had the chance of really assessing what we have, I was shocked. I was shocked not only at the standard here, but what appeared to be the norm in the Third Division. So far I cannot say that I have seen many players who can play, but the point I must hammer home is that I don't want my players frightened of picking up a newspaper and reading about who is coming here next. Now this story about [Newcastle United defender] Bobby Moncur – this was dreamed up in the north-east by somebody. We have no interest in this player whatsoever. How could we? I saw somewhere that the price is £100,000. There isn't that kind of money here for players. But when I look and see how much has been wasted here on players in the last couple of years, I just cannot believe it. Fees out of all proportion to their worth have been paid. No wonder the club has such an overdraft. But that is in the past, over and done with. What I must do now is to get the best out of the players here and they must stop worrying what is going to happen to them next, especially the younger ones. Those who aren't interested, they will go, of course, but we have got to keep our heads and get down to a lot of hard work, and that cannot be achieved without job satisfaction. The players are feeding into me. I am giving them everything I can, but they must respond and act like real professionals. Had we not come here the club would have been heading for the Fifth Division.'

'I think the expression "being hung out to dry" comes to mind,' says Robertson with a wry smile at the memory of Clough's post-Walton and Hersham rant.

Things would get a lot, lot worse before they got any better. On the first day of December, Third Division league leaders Bristol Rovers came to the Goldstone looking to cash in on Albion's FA Cup misery. In Bruce Bannister and Alan Warboys, the Bristolians possessed arguably the most lethal strike partnership outside the English top flight. The afternoon started badly for Rovers when referee Tommy Dawes, spotting a potential colour clash, asked the visitors to change from their usual red-and-white-striped away shirts. Problem was, they had no alternative kit. Albion came to the rescue, offering Rovers the use of some brand-new orange shirts that Clough had ordered. The generosity should have stopped there, but it didn't.

And so began what became known as the 'Bannister and Warboys Show'. In the fifth minute, Warboys squared the ball across Albion's goalmouth for Bannister to give Rovers the lead. Twelve minutes later, Gordon Fearnley ghosted into a king-sized hole in the home defence to head past Powney and make it 2–0. Although Peter O'Sullivan quickly pulled one back, two goals within the space of three minutes saw Bannister complete his hat-trick to make it 4–1, at which point Warboys got in on the act, heading firmly past Powney to make it 5–1 at half-time.

After the break, the pain merely intensified. In the fifty-fifth minute, Warboys rounded the advancing Powney to make it 6–1. Eight minutes later, with Albion's defence in complete disarray, the striker sprinted onto a long punt upfield to complete his hat-trick. Seven minutes later it became 8–1, Warboys scoring from a possibly off-side position, not that it mattered by then. By the time Ronnie Howell scored Albion's second with three minutes remaining, most of the home supporters had long since made for the exits. Small wonder Rovers manager Don Megson made a cheeky offer to buy the borrowed kit after the final whistle.

Cue another post-mortem – Albion's second in the space of three days. This time the language being used on all sides was harsher. 'It was the most humiliating ninety minutes of my career,' blasted Clough to waiting journalists. 'I was ashamed for the town and the club that eleven players could play like that. I feel sick. We were pathetic. This side hasn't got enough heart to fill a thimble.' To add to Albion's woes, the whole fiasco was filmed by ITV for broadcast on *The Big Match*, the football programme which aired from 1968 until 1992 on Sunday afternoons, with Clough scheduled to make an appearance in the studios talking about the game with presenter Brian Moore. This is how their conversation went once the match highlights, which included footage of Clough sat in Albion's dugout with his young sons Simon and Nigel for company, had finished:

Moore: What a devastating day there for Brighton. Let's go straight to their manager, Brian Clough. There was a lot of speculation, Brian, this morning as to whether you would turn up today.

Clough: Well obviously they were wrong and they don't know me.

Moore: Has it been a bit of a hangover for you?

Clough: It was a terrible night last night, you know. I've got my family down at Brighton trying to house-hunt, and being on the receiving end of eight goals is not very easy. You get up the next morning, the sun was shining, and here I am wanting to talk football, wanting to discuss Brighton and any other aspect of the game you would like.

Moore: I tell you the thing that occurred to me yesterday was that, talking to you in *World of Sport* last night and listening to your press conference at Brighton as well, that is the most astonishing attack I've ever heard a manager deliver about his players, and no doubt you felt it was justified. We really don't want to cover that ground again. I'm sure you don't. But the thing that interests me is how do you now get them to play for you again? You said they haven't got a thimble full of heart between them.

Clough: Well, in that particular ninety minutes they didn't have. Things went wrong right from the start of the match, and this got on top of them, plus our Cup exit last Wednesday, and they just caved in. They were raw. They couldn't cope with this type of pressure, and they caved in, and they've got to have more spirit and more heart to play professional football than they showed yesterday.

Moore: But after what you said, can you get it back into them?

Clough: I can get it back into them 'cause I can show it to them how they caved in and tell them why they caved in, and I can ask them to behave like men. And I'm certain that when they see the full picture they will start doing just that.

The pair continued by analysing three of the goals scored by Bristol Rovers, during which Clough admitted feeling 'sorry for the goalkeeper', Powney having frequently been left exposed by his defence, and referred to Norman Gall as 'that very honest man'. Switching his attention to Albion's supporters, Moore suggested, 'They must be saying now, "When is he going to do something and how is he going to do it?"' Clough replied: 'They will be asking "How many players am I going to sign and when am I going to sign them?" And I don't dictate these types of things. I can only buy players from managers who are willing to sell. We will get players eventually and we will sign some, but how and when, that's a different thing altogether. You know 8–2 is a hell of a shattering result but I think we've been there five, six, seven matches and that's the first league match we've actually lost. We've not won a lot, obviously, but it's the first one we've lost. You know, the stand hasn't caved in. Brighton hasn't disappeared into the sea. They're in perhaps a worse position now than they were last week, but that's all. We've improved their position, and nobody's going to panic Peter Taylor and I into doing anything we don't want to do. If we've got to sit through 8–2 defeats for the next six weeks before the type of player who we require comes on the market, then we'll do just that. No newspapers, television or anything will move us from this particular style.'

'I don't think I moved so far and so quickly and so many times as I did that day,' says Gall. 'I was running all over the place and seemed to be the only one that was playing in the defence. I was absolutely shattered physically by the end. I don't know how many points I got out of ten in the papers, but I never ran so much because nobody was performing. And a lot of players didn't play after that. I don't recall Eddie Spearritt making another appearance. George Ley played maybe one or two more games, and Pat Hilton, and that was that. I think by that time most of us were just frightened.'

'I remember the dressing room just being quiet afterwards,' says Lammie Robertson. 'He [Clough] left us to stew. At some point he did come in and told us, "There's going to be changes." There was one goal they [Rovers] scored from a free kick and it went through the wall. And I'd been in the wall. Cloughie was determined to find out who it went through. He asked everyone. 'Not me,' 'Not me,' 'Not me,' came the replies. But of course it had been on television. And it was Eddie [Spearritt]. He'd lifted his leg up and it went under. And he never played again.'

Despite being left exposed by the majority of his defenders and keeping the score down to single figures with some excellent saves, Powney also found himself on the receiving end of Clough's wrath. 'The southern end of the pitch was frozen that day, all the way up to the six-yard box,' Powney recalls. 'It often used to freeze over because it would be the last to get the sun. I said to Cloughie before the game, "Boss, that south end is frozen. Do you think it would be OK if I was to take a spare pair of boots out, rubbers, and when we have to kick up from that end I can put them on?" And he said, "Don't be fucking silly." I wanted to change my boots because you can't wear studs on ice. You can wear little pimply rubbers, and that's what I wanted to do. We played the first half kicking down towards the south end, and I changed them at half-time. It was still bloody lethal though, even though it had thawed out a little, so the rubbers weren't doing a lot of good either. Anyway, one of the goals came when Eddie Spearritt had given away a square pass and they were clean through. I came out. On ice you can't come out, stop, and stand still. As soon as you stop, your feet go. You have to commit. So I had to wait until this guy kicked the ball just ahead of him to go down at his feet, which I did. I knew if I stood still, I wouldn't have got anywhere. I timed it, and as I went down he pushed it wide and from a very acute angle scored a goal. After the game Cloughie said, "You shouldn't sell yourself," and I said, "Boss, you can't stand up in that six-yard box. It's frozen. I had to commit myself." He wasn't having it though and kept at me. I said, "With respect, I disagree with you." And I knew at that moment that my days were numbered, because you didn't disagree with Clough.'

Pity, then, BBC Radio Brighton's Peter Brackley, whose job it was to ask the occasional awkward question of Albion's manager. In the immediate aftermath of the Bristol Rovers debacle, Brackley found himself as much in the manager's firing line as any of the players. 'There wasn't a press room at the Goldstone in those days,' he recalls. 'Clough would just come out of his office and we'd queue up down the corridor to listen and ask questions. You can imagine what it was like. He'd say, "Number five is a donkey," and it would get passed back down the line to the other journalists – "Brian says number five is a donkey," and so on. I put my microphone up to him and he absolutely tore into me, he really did, in front of everybody. He was going to do this to me and that to me and shove it down my effing throat. I was quite frightened for a moment because he was really in a foul mood, as you can imagine after a result like that.'

But then something happened which was, in many ways,

typical Clough. 'Everybody sort of stood there, and then began filtering away,' adds Brackley. 'It got to the point where I'm on my own. I go as if to leave, and I hear, "Oi, come back, young man." I'm thinking, "Oh no, he's going to have another go at me now." He said, "Right, in here." And he took me into the boardroom and gave me an exclusive interview on what had just happened, which I was able to use on national radio. That again was Brian, playing hot and cold. I remember him saying, "You can put eleven ladies on the goal line and still not concede eight goals… but we did." He said, "You're going to send this up the line to London, aren't you?" And I'm like, "Yeah, I am." And they loved it. I remember Paul Weaver, who wrote for the *Sussex Express*, coming up with a good line. He said, "If you are going to see Clough, take a bottle in one hand and a gun in the other, because you never know how he's going to react." And that's actually a very good way of summing up how it was.'

Until virtually his dying day Clough denied that, as a manager, he set out to rule his players by fear in order to get them to perform, or to separate the ones he wanted to keep from those who needed to be jettisoned. 'Somebody once accused me of producing sides that were frightened all the time,' he said at a fans' forum held in Derby during October 2002. 'What a load of bull. What a load of bull! In life you cannot, irrespective of what job you do and what career you're pursuing, do it to the best of your ability if you're frightened. Now if you think about it, if I was sending a side out at five to three on a Saturday like that, frightened, arms tense, nerves jangling, what kind of preparation was that? That was absolutely rubbish.' There was even a suggestion that some kind of act was involved. 'Sometimes I just pretend to be angry so the word will go round that Big Head's in a bad mood and you'd better stay well clear,'

Clough confided to the *Nottingham Evening Post* journalist Duncan Hamilton. 'No one ever really gets the hang of me. I don't want them to. I want them guessing instead.'

Clough – together with Taylor, himself no shrinking violet – might not have deliberately set out to rule Albion's dressing room by fear, but that's exactly the effect they had on many of the players, particularly during those first few weeks in charge at the Goldstone. The fear became so extreme that several players 'froze' in matches such as the Walton and Hersham FA Cup replay and the 8–2 defeat to Bristol Rovers, terrified not just at the prospect of being verbally assaulted in the dressing room after games but also about their future at the club, or rather the perceived lack of one.

'I would say that they ruled by fear more than anything,' suggests John Templeman. 'Some players react positively to that whereas others need an arm put round their shoulders. They weren't that sort of management team. It was just the heavy-handed approach, using threats – "If you don't do it, you're out" – and unfortunately a lot of the players who'd been there for years weren't used to that style of management. I always believe you play as a team and you win or lose as a team. Individuals might have a good or a bad day but when you've lost 8–2, to come in and blame it on a small number of players who were good servants to Brighton and played their all, week in, week out, I don't think that's right. I think that [the Bristol Rovers result] made Cloughie's mind up that he was going to have to do some wholesale changes at the club and it was going to need a big rebuilding exercise.'

'It was fear, and it was Taylor who was at the centre of it,' adds Norman Gall. 'He was a right bully. He threatened people that they would never, ever play again if they didn't do this or they didn't do that. He was like that all the time and it just got on your nerves. After about ten games, a lot of people said, "Right, that's enough, I don't want to know anymore." There was never anybody saying, "Well done, well played." It was silence or a nasty voice from Taylor. He was a bully, just horrible. Straight away he said we weren't good enough because we'd just got relegated. "You won't be here. You lot won't be here much longer." That's what he'd say. There were some good players there, but you can't play with people like that.'

Some of those good players, however, have a slightly different recollection. 'A lot of the guys didn't like him,' says Peter O'Sullivan of Clough. 'I respected him. Like José Mourinho, or anyone who's good at that man-management side of things, he could make players think they were better than they are. He'd tell you that you were a good player. I'm not saying he did that with every player, but he did say that to me, and because it was him and he'd won the league, done this, done that, you respected him. People say he frightened players. When someone tells you that you're a good player, you don't fear him, do you? It was black or white with him because if he didn't reckon you were a good player he'd just ding you out. There was no second chance, not unless he rated you or you were a little bit younger and maybe needed to learn.'

'I thought it was fear, but I wasn't scared of him,' says Steve Piper. 'He built me up. It was like, "Don't let me down. You go out there, do your thing, but don't let me down because if you do you're in big trouble. I will have you and make life miserable for you." Being youngsters, we had no fear anyway, having just broken into the side, so maybe that had something to do with it. We had no reputations. It was different, though, for the others, the older ones.'

Recollections may vary, but there is one thing Albion's players are agreed on all these years later – your age at the time of the 1973/74 season had much to do with the way Clough and Taylor regarded you. 'They had no time for the older players, to be honest,' adds Steve Piper, whose twentieth birthday, it should be remembered, had fallen on the squad's first meeting with the pair at the White Hart Hotel in Lewes. 'Maybe he [Clough] thought that the older players should be the ones bringing the football club up... and they weren't. He thought the older ones knew too much, or wouldn't follow his ways, although he did like Norman Gall. He thought he was an honest professional. And he was, to be fair. Obviously I never heard what he said in private but he never took to the likes of Eddie Spearritt, George Ley, Brian Powney and Barry Bridges. He could manipulate the younger players though, people like myself, Tony Towner and Sully [Peter O'Sullivan], who was a couple of years older than me.'

'He tried to manage by fear, but that's where I was perhaps different,' says Powney. 'With all due respect, I wasn't frightened of him. I'd had a long career anyway and I knew it was coming to an end because of cartilage and ligament damage in my right knee that I'd been struggling with for years. The fact was I just couldn't play for him. I just didn't like his ways, his arrogance, his ignorance. I'll tell you who I see a lot of him in – José Mourinho. I look at Mourinho sometimes and I think, "That's fucking Brian Clough all over again." I'd love it to have worked out differently. I'd been on holiday in Majorca the year before with my wife and son and some friends, staying in a place called Cala Millor. One of our friends said, "John McGovern [who played under Clough at Hartlepools United, Derby County and Nottingham Forest] is here." So one night

I saw him in the lounge and I went up and introduced myself and we got chatting. I said, "What about Brian Clough?" and I got the impression he would have run over Beachy Head for him. He thought Clough was the dog's bollocks. When Pat Saward went, I was upset, but I thought, "Well, they've got somebody big to do the job, the right man." And it was so disappointing when it just didn't happen that way. I was really looking forward to seeing this Messiah, because that's what he was built up to be.'

Only in his second autobiography, *Walking on Water*, did Clough deign to admit that fear had played a part in one of the 1,400-plus fixtures he had overseen as a manager, namely the Bristol Rovers match. Even then he attempted to deflect blame away from himself and onto Albion's players. 'The score line of a home game against Bristol Rovers is etched in my mind as deeply as the two European Cup finals I was to win years later,' he wrote. 'I tried to avoid instilling fear rather than imposing it but that day at Brighton when we conceded eight goals, I knew they were frightened because they were all inferior players who had never known success and never encountered anybody like me. If I told them to cut their wrists I believe every single one of them would have done it right there in the dressing room and that was before the match! They were rigid, virtually frozen to the spot by fear and out on the pitch there was so much apprehension that they couldn't lift their legs, let alone raise a gallop.'

In the days immediately after the Bristol Rovers defeat, the first of Clough and Taylor's new signings, centre-back Ken Goodeve and goalkeeper Peter Grummitt, arrived at the club. Although Goodeve, twenty-three at the time and bought from Luton Town for £20,000, would make only six appearances for

Albion before being sold to Watford in June 1974, Grummitt proved to be a far more successful acquisition. Initially signed on a month's loan, the former Nottingham Forest and Sheffield Wednesday keeper repaid his eventual £7,000 fee several times over by making 158 appearances before being forced into retirement through injury in 1977.

'I knew Peter Taylor and Brian Clough very well,' said Grummitt when interviewed in 2015 for Albion's official match-day programme. 'I'd known Peter for years through cricket. We used to play on a Thursday for a team called Nottingham Taxis. None of us had anything to do with taxis, but I think it was originally set up by taxi people and others had been brought in over the years. It was good fun. I was at Sheffield [Wednesday] and another person had been brought in and taken over my place in the first team, and I decided I wanted to be away. Peter rang me up and asked if I wanted to come down there. The fact Brighton were in the Third Division didn't bother me at all. I knew what sort of managers they both were and I knew straight away that I wanted to go. I met Brian Clough at a motorway service station, we had a chat, and I signed there and then.'

The first Powney knew of Grummitt's arrival was when he set eyes on him at training the day before Albion's away game at Tranmere Rovers on 8 December. Both of the new signings made their debuts at Prenton Park, but the story remained the same as the side collapsed in miserable fashion, going 2–0 down as early as the sixteenth minute before eventually succumbing 4–1. That made it sixteen goals conceded in just three matches.

Hell-bent on replacing many of the players they had inherited, by now Clough and Taylor's search for new talent was taking on added urgency. Besides Newcastle United's Bobby Moncur, newspaper speculation also linked Albion with a number of high-profile stars, including Liverpool defender Tommy Smith and even former England captain Bobby Moore. In reality, Taylor's sights were set on less distinguished names, players with potential or experience who for whatever reason were surplus to requirements at their clubs. Players such as midfielder Ronnie Welch and left-back Harry Wilson, both of Burnley.

'I was happy at Burnley, but if an offer comes in for you and they accept it then there's not much you can do,' says Wilson. 'I got pulled into the main stadium and Bob Lord [Burnley's chairman] was there. I was told to sit down and that there was an offer on the table they were willing to accept from Brighton. I thought, "Brighton, that's a long way away." And to be honest I didn't realise just how far away it was. And then they [Clough and Taylor] walked in the room. They must have been next door, waiting for Bob Lord to ask them through. It was a bit like being on *This Is Your Life*, just one massive surprise. I said something like, "Hello, Mr Clough", and I can't remember what either of them said back. You didn't say much when you were in his [Clough's] company. He spoke, you listened. He had everybody on eggshells. I do remember Peter Taylor standing behind him. That's the way it would be. If I was ever in the office in Brighton, getting a bollocking or something, Peter Taylor would be behind him, sometimes with a finger over his lip, his way of warning you not to speak. You did what you were told.'

Having just signed Wilson and Welch for a combined fee of £70,000, Clough and Taylor set off by car bound for the Football League's headquarters forty-five miles away at Lytham St Annes. Their mission? To get both players registered by 5 p.m. on the afternoon of Thursday 20 December in order for them to be eligible to make their debuts on the Saturday away against

Watford. They failed, by a matter of minutes. 'The fifty-miles-per-hour speed limit went by the board but the traffic was too heavy in Preston and we were a quarter of an hour too late,' Clough told journalists the following morning of a scenario that wouldn't have seemed out of place in the popular *Wacky Races* cartoon series of the time. 'What a barmy set up it all is but that's the rule and they can't play tomorrow.'

Wilson and Welch, nineteen and twenty years of age respectively, watched the Watford game unfold from seats in the stands at Vicarage Road, but only after they'd met Albion's players for the first time in the away dressing room prior to kick-off. Wilson had bought a new suit especially for the occasion, one that stood out for its garish nature. Lammie Robertson, who remembered both players as juniors from his time at Burnley, was handed the job of introducing them to the team. 'Harry was wearing this loud kind of checked suit, and Cloughie says, "Fucking hell, I don't want to ever see that suit again." And everybody started laughing. Harry had red hair and he was going red in the face as well. And then he [Cloughie] came out with a classic. He goes, "What the fuck are you all laughing at? They'll be in the team next week." He said that to all of us, to keep us on our toes.'

'He said I looked like a deck chair on Brighton beach,' is Wilson's recollection of Clough's unflattering piece of fashion advice. 'And I'd paid a good bit for that suit!'

Albion lost at Watford, this time by 1–0, sinking to twentieth in the Third Division, one spot above the relegation zone. Four days later, on Boxing Day, all four of Clough and Taylor's new signings played in the home game against Aldershot with Wilson making his debut in place of George Ley. Once again Albion were way off the pace, managing only one shot on target throughout the entire game on their way to another 1–0 defeat. Five consecutive reverses, just one victory from ten league and cup games since taking over, plus increasing dressing room unrest over managerial absences and the lack of preparation prior to games and tactics employed during them. It wasn't supposed to be like this. For once even Clough seemed speechless, departing the Goldstone straight after the Aldershot match without speaking to any of the waiting press.

Of equal concern from Mike Bamber's point of view were the home attendances. Having attracted 16,017 for the York City match, Albion's gates had since failed to come anywhere near the required 20,000-plus necessary to finance the whole operation under Clough and Taylor (14,148 versus Chesterfield, 9,657 for the Walton and Hersham replay, 10,762 versus Bristol Rovers and 14,769 versus Aldershot, the latter well below the figure traditionally expected on Boxing Day). Only the Walton and Hersham attendance had mitigating circumstances given that the match was played early on a Wednesday afternoon due to the state of emergency. Albion were, in effect, caught in a vicious circle. The big crowds the club could potentially attract were only likely to come if the team was winning or at least showing signs of improvement. Results suggested the team was actually regressing under Clough and Taylor, leading to a fall in attendances since the York City match. All Bamber could do was pray for an improvement on the field and a subsequent surge in public interest.

Paradoxically, the gates for Albion's away matches were anything but disappointing. Without exception, every club that entertained Clough and Taylor's side from November 1973 into the New Year saw a jump in attendance, often a considerable one (being the visiting club, Albion saw nothing of the money generated through the turnstiles at away league games). The reason for these increases was simple: the supporters of those clubs wanted to see Brian Clough and Peter Taylor, particularly the former, at close quarters – and hopefully on the receiving end of a beating. On top of that, a sizeable minority wanted to give the big fish now swimming around in a small pond some stick. Not that this seemed to bother the fish in question.

'Did you hear at Walton any of the crowd start to barrack my lads or start chanting?' Clough enquired of one journalist who dared ask what he thought of the abuse being directed towards him by opposition supporters. 'No, you didn't. They were too busy slating me. Great. I love it. If it happens at every away match, I shall be delighted. If the crowd upset my players, then their performance could suffer. They won't upset me, no matter what they say.' Broad shoulders, certainly, but then Clough always loved putting himself front and centre in any picture, even when the picture wasn't a particularly flattering one.

Still, given Albion had lost three and drawn two of Clough's five home games in charge, failing to score in four of them, there was a very real danger that the love exhibited by the Sussex public at the York City game would soon turn sour. Clough and Taylor needed a win, preferably at the Goldstone, to restore faith and turn the ailing ship around. It didn't matter if that win was ugly even by Third Division standards, the kind of forgettable encounter won by a shot trickling into the net off an unfortunate opponent's leg or a striker's backside. It just had to come. Fast.

6

THE PERFECT STORM

Edgar Street, Saturday 12 December 1970, Hereford United versus Brighton & Hove Albion, FA Cup second round, sixty-first minute. United, then a useful non-league outfit, win a corner. Ian Goodwin, twenty years old at the time, scans Albion's penalty area to see which opponent requires marking. Call it youthful naivety, but the man lumbering upfield towards him doesn't exactly strike fear into the strapping defender.

'I'm old-school,' says Goodwin. 'I don't do zonal marking. I've never seen a zone score a goal. My view is, "I'm going to pick you up," and on that occasion the guy I was man-marking was their centre-half. They get a corner and this old man hobbles up from the back into the penalty area. I look at him and think, "Is he taking the piss?" So I go to mark him. I'm twenty. This is going to be no problem. The next thing I know the ball is in the net, I'm in the net with it, and this old boy is leaning down over me going, "You alright, boyo? Can I help you up? Are you hurt?" And it's John Charles. I thought I'd been hit by a bloody bus. He just came in and took me, the ball and everything into the back of the net with him. I thought, "You prat, you'll get a right bollocking afterwards for this."

I didn't even know who he was at the time. I certainly did afterwards.'

Fast forward three years from his salutary lesson, courtesy of one of the game's all-time greats, in how not to judge a book by its cover. Goodwin's body, specifically his knees, are betraying him. The cartilage in both is shot to pieces. His career has become a merry-go-round of cortisone injections, playing, ice packs and repeat. The writing is on the wall, but Goodwin can't read what it says yet. However, Clough's arrival in November 1973, much like a sight test at the optician's, suddenly brings the words horribly into focus.

'I was getting treatment before one game, I'm pretty sure it was the Bristol Rovers one when we got beaten by eight, and this time it was a broken collarbone rather than anything to do with my legs,' says Goodwin. 'Mike Yaxley [initially a coach but who went on to become Albion's physiotherapist] was doing some ultrasound and Arthur Tabor, who was the official club doctor, was also there. Cloughie comes in and says, "You're training Monday." And Tabor says, "He's broken his collarbone. He can't train!" And there was hell to pay. They were really arguing. Tabor says, "Where did you get your medical degree from? Have you got one?" And he [Tabor] resigns, right there and then. I was like, "What have I done now?" From that point I seemed to become a marked man. Every week it would be "My office, Monday morning," which was ridiculous because he was never there on Mondays. He was always back in Derby.'

One particular summons had nothing to do with Goodwin's failing body. At that time, Clough's forthright opinions delivered in his trademark nasal whine made him an impressionist's wet dream, Mike Yarwood's endeavours in particular going down a storm with the British public, not to mention Clough himself. 'We'd been sitting around waiting for the son of a bitch to turn up, and we were bored,' says Goodwin. 'So I started to do a Cloughie impression. "Right, you, go and get me a tea. I want you to make a diagonal run towards the cake stand." That sort of thing. Anyway, he [Clough] comes in as I'm doing it. He goes, "Mike Yarwood is better than you. I want to see you in my office at 10 o'clock." I went, "OK, Brian." And he was never going to be there.'

One of the reasons Goodwin lost respect for Clough so soon after his arrival at the Goldstone Ground was that he had a pretty good idea what might actually be happening on those Monday mornings. 'In the early days he was still having meetings up there with the [Derby] players, trying to coax them into getting him reinstated,' says Goodwin. 'Players talk to other players. I knew players up at Derby, which isn't far from Coventry, where I'd been before joining Brighton. So word came through to me about what was going on. It was around that time that I started thinking, "There's got to be something better than this." The injuries were the main thing and I might have got away with it for another season or two, but throw it all together and I just wanted out. I'd been thinking about going to university. That was the plan: come back to Coventry and do a degree. I thought about teaching because you get six weeks' holiday every year in the summer! But then I discovered you needed money to go to university and to live. That's when my father-in-law came up with a job at Rolls-Royce. I became responsible for recruiting apprentices through to graduates. We'd take on about 140 people every year from single-skill lathe operators to graduates of the Royal Academy of Arts. After that came thirty years as a manager at Peugeot. It was completely different to what I'd been used to, but I enjoyed it and I'd like to think I was pretty good at it.'

It is often said that football operates according to its own rules. What would be deemed unacceptable behaviour in most walks of life is regarded as the norm in dressing rooms and on training fields. It's not until a player, accustomed to that kind of detached environment from an early age, steps out onto Civvy Street at the end of their career that the truth becomes apparent. Goodwin was wise enough to appreciate that conditions at the Goldstone under Brian Clough could be extreme, but it was only once he'd traded football for the car industry that the reality of it really hit home.

'You've got to look at what the guy achieved,' admits Goodwin. 'He won European Cups. He won the Football League title. The guy did well. Nobody can argue with his achievements. But what about the manner in which he achieved it all? I went on to become a manager myself in a different field. I look at his management style and think, "Who do you think you were? Hitler?" Nobody in industry could get away with managing like he did, except perhaps Donald Trump. I had no respect for this guy. I couldn't fathom out what he was trying to do. I couldn't understand the arrogance of the man. He did rule by fear. He bullied people, and I wouldn't get bullied. I know I'm not the sharpest tool in the box but I'm not stupid. In the end I spoke to Alan Leather [Albion's club secretary] and said, "Just cancel my contract, I'm out of here." And that's what happened. Out into the big wide world I went.'

Clough's attitude towards players who were carrying injuries continues to perplex many of those who were on Albion's payroll during the 1973/74 season. From the early days of his managerial career at Hartlepools United, right through until its dying embers with Nottingham Forest, stories of Clough's indifference bordering on scorn towards those with injuries are legion. As Goodwin says, 'He'd had a bad injury that had finished his career. You'd have thought he would have been sympathetic. Instead it was like you'd committed a sin. You were cattle.'

In *Nobody Ever Says Thank You*, author Jonathan Wilson recounts how Sunderland manager Alan Brown, in the wake of Clough's career-ending injury, prevented his players from going to see their stricken teammate until four days after the incident. Wilson speculates that Clough's latter aversion could well have been a case of him implementing one of Brown's strategies, keeping the injured out of sight and mind, thus minimising the risk of players fearing for their own safety on the football field. Or maybe it was something far closer to home – the sight of an injured player brought all the memories of Boxing Day 1962 and its aftermath flooding back.

Whatever the reason, Clough's antipathy towards injured players had the potential to offend potential allies and belittle people who deserved better. At Derby County and Nottingham Forest, Clough's behaviour was to an extent masked by the successes of his teams. At struggling Albion, it only threatened to make an already tricky situation even worse.

'We had a guy called Bert Parker, an absolute gentleman, who came on the scene properly when Pat Saward was there,' says Brian Powney. 'Bert was a local physiotherapist who, to begin with, we used to have to go and see quietly behind everyone's back. He had a shop, or rather a practice, at Palmeira Square in Hove. Archie Macaulay [Albion's manager from April 1963 until October 1968] had banned us from going there. We went because, to be honest, the club's medical facilities weren't that good then. A cold sponge and a heat lamp was about all we had. I'd been going to see him about my knee and he'd been first class. Later on, when Cloughie arrived, Bert went to introduce himself before one game. "Hello, Mr Clough, I'm Bert Parker, the club physiotherapist." Cloughie goes, "I'm not fucking interested" and walked out of the dressing room. Bert Parker left and we never saw him again. After all he'd done for us. Cloughie definitely had a thing about physiotherapists, that's for sure. And do you know why? Because of the injury that finished him in the game. He had no time for physiotherapists or anyone who could help on the medical side of things.'

Ken Beamish was another casualty of Clough's mental wall when it came to injuries. Despite carrying damage to an ankle, the striker was made to play in the home match versus Chesterfield on 17 November after receiving a painkilling injection. Barely able to walk from the kick-off, Beamish signalled to the bench that he was struggling. Nevertheless, Clough made him continue until the thirty-fifth minute, when common sense finally prevailed and he was withdrawn.

However, that episode pales into insignificance compared to an incident involving Steve Piper, which occurred eleven days later when Albion faced Walton and Hersham at the Goldstone in their ill-fated FA Cup first-round replay.

'I got injured after about twenty minutes of that game with a dead leg,' says Piper. 'I couldn't walk. After the game he [Clough] wanted to find people who he believed hadn't performed. He said to Glen Wilson, "Get Steve Piper in my office now. I don't believe he's injured." So Glen Wilson came into the dressing room and said, "Steve, he wants to see you. He doesn't think you're injured." And I couldn't walk. I literally couldn't walk and had a haematoma on my leg. So he went back to him and said, "Steve can't walk to come and see you. You're going to have to come and see him." And Clough goes, "I won't go and see him. Carry him in here." So Glen Wilson had to give me a piggyback into the manager's office to prove that I had this massive lump of bruising on my leg that was preventing me from walking. He carried me in on his back, sat me down on a chair and said, "Look, I told you, he can't walk!" And to be fair Clough did hold his hand up and say, "Sorry, I realise now. You can't walk, it's not your fault." But he was looking for scapegoats and I was one of the ones he was going to have a go at.'

As competent a journalist as he was, even John Vinicombe appears to have been hoodwinked by Clough and Taylor when it came to Albion's injury situation, or rather the peculiar lack of one. In a comment piece in the *Evening Argus*, Vinicombe wrote about the noticeable absence of players receiving treatment at the Goldstone, where 'masses of gleaming expensive equipment in one of the best injury care centres in the Football League remain unused week after week'. The reason, he concluded, was that

> Brian Clough and Peter Taylor don't believe in injuries and the message has got home to the players, so much so that they grin and beat the knocks. Right now there is not one player under treatment for a soccer injury out of the entire professional staff. It is an outstanding triumph of mind over matter.

The piece also quoted Taylor as saying,

> We have discouraged players from pampering themselves and in our experience we know this sort of thing happens. It is natural if it is allowed to go on unchecked. It is like getting hurt in a

match. The last thing is to show the other side that you are hurt. The aches and pains and bruises are still there but Brian and I just don't hear about them anymore.

Aches, pains and bruises are one thing. Serious injuries, the kind that can destroy a player's career, are something else altogether. Beamish dismissed the Chesterfield incident as nothing more than 'strange' and, within a couple of weeks, had overcome his ankle problem. Others, such as Ian Goodwin and Brian Powney, were not only being let down professionally but also having their long-term, post-career health potentially put in jeopardy. Attitudes within British football towards injuries were certainly different in the 1970s, when the bucket-and-sponge approach to knocks still prevailed (legendary Liverpool manager Bill Shankly famously referred to those on the injury list at Anfield as 'The Bastard Club'), but even accounting for the times, Clough and Taylor's attitude was startlingly callous.

There is of course a flip side to the coin. Clough and Taylor were accustomed to First Division standards both on and off the field. The lax environment at Third Division Albion would have appalled them both. Under Pat Saward, discipline had slumped to the point where the Goldstone became known in some quarters as 'the holiday camp'. Unpunctuality went unpunished. The free and easy air about the place meant the players, subconsciously perhaps, became too relaxed. In *With Clough By Taylor*, Taylor describes them as being 'casual, almost amateurish, joking about their plight instead of being concerned'. The pair's stance regarding injuries often beggared belief, but in other areas a wake-up call was undoubtedly necessary if Albion were going to avoid a second successive relegation.

In Clough and Taylor, the players got it with cathedral-sized bells on.

'Discipline is an overworked word in football today,' Clough once remarked while still in charge at Derby County. 'People say "How do you do it?" And you know I never really give it a thought because that side of the game comes rather easy to me. Of course, to do that you've got to be a little bit of a dictator, and yet you've got to have a little bit upstairs because you can tread on so many people's toes.'

* * *

Plymouth Argyle were a good team in 1973. Fortunately for Albion, several members of their side, including wingers Alan Welsh and Alan Rogers, were absent through a combination of injury and suspension when the Pilgrims ventured to the Goldstone on 29 December. Once again, the attendance fell way below the desired 20,000 figure, with just 11,181 passing through the turnstiles in the wake of Boxing Day's abject performance at home to Aldershot, the fifth home game without a win under Clough. Lose and there was every prospect of Albion dropping into the relegation zone. Expectations on the terraces were low, even against severely weakened opponents. If you can't beat Walton and Hersham at home, then you're unlikely to get much change out of a side boasting future Ipswich Town and England international Paul Mariner up front.

This time, more players seemed to want the ball. More players seemed to work harder. For the first match since Clough and Taylor's appointment, fans noticed a discernible difference in the way the team played. At long last, there appeared to be a plan. And it wasn't as if the visitors rolled over in the face of their selection problems. Plymouth played with a refreshing, attacking zest, yet Albion not only kept them in check but managed to create a few chances of their own.

It was from one of these, in the fifty-sixth minute, that Ken Beamish bundled the ball into the net from close range following a goalmouth scramble to give Albion a scrappy lead. In the final fifteen minutes, Argyle threw everything at the home side in a bid to at least take a point. Mariner, their twenty-year-old talisman, rattled Peter Grummitt's crossbar with a long-range shot before forcing the goalkeeper into a brave point-blank save. But Albion held out. At the sixth time of asking, Clough and Taylor had the home win they so desperately needed.

Injury-hit Plymouth were one thing; second-placed Bournemouth, at full strength and playing in front of their own crowd on New Year's Day 1974, were expected to be an altogether tougher proposition. This time Albion barely managed to get out of their own half of the field, let alone create any chances. However, in front of a bumper crowd of 17,091, the season's best at cramped Dean Court, the visitors put on the kind of rearguard action that made a mockery of their displays against Walton and Hersham and Bristol Rovers, albeit with a team featuring slightly different personnel.

'In eleven years of watching [Norman] Gall I do not recall him more masterful or dominating than he was at Bournemouth,' wrote John Vinicombe in his match report, which also speculated as to why Brian Clough hadn't been there to witness what ended in a 0–0 draw, Peter Taylor taking charge of the side instead. Was he away on holiday? Watching a potential signing? Spending time with the family over the New Year period back in Derbyshire? No one, so it seemed, knew for certain. Such was the quality of the performance, with Grummitt keeping a second consecutive clean sheet, that his absence didn't become more of an issue.

Walton and Hersham's sterling efforts in the first round of the FA Cup ensured that Gall and his teammates were without a game the following weekend as the third round of the competition got underway. Not that the additional break seemed to adversely affect the players. On Saturday 12 January, Albion travelled to south-east London to face a Charlton Athletic team lying seventh in the Third Division at the start of play. After a goalless first half, Ronnie Howell put the visitors ahead shortly after the restart with a scorching drive. In the fifty-seventh minute, Peter O'Sullivan centred for Howell to convert from close range and make it 2–0. When Charlton centre-back Bobby Goldthorpe then handled inside the home penalty area, Howell duly completed his hat-trick from the spot, all three goals arriving inside just seventeen minutes. Not to be outshone, O'Sullivan capped an outstanding individual display by hammering home a left-foot shot to make the final score Charlton Athletic 0 Brighton & Hove Albion 4.

Albion were unbeaten in three games and had opened up a four-point gap over the four clubs beneath them in the league table occupying the relegation places. You might expect Clough to be in a positive frame of mind and keen to talk about an outstanding away win.

You would be wrong.

'We just played well but there wasn't four goals in it,' the manager remarked brusquely as he hurried out of The Valley to catch a train, leaving the players behind to run the gauntlet of journalists desperate for a quote. Except that Clough had banned them all from speaking to the media.

'As soon as the game ended he said, "Right, whatever you

do, nobody talks to the press," who were waiting outside the dressing room door wanting a quote,' says O'Sullivan. 'Little Ronnie Howell, the crafty cockney, goes out and gives them an interview about his three goals. The following Saturday he wasn't playing. He [Clough] had dinged [dropped] him. I think that may have even been the last game he played for Brighton. You'll have to check the records. I went out and walked straight past them. It was, "Oh, Pete, a quick word?" and I was like, "Not a chance." If you didn't do what he said, you were fucked.'

Howell was dropped in the wake of the Charlton match but did return to play another eleven games for Albion. At which point Clough deemed the diminutive midfielder surplus to requirements and cast him adrift to non-league Tooting and Mitcham. It wasn't as if Howell had given a proper interview either. 'It's more than I dare do to talk. That is the orders we have all had from the boss. I'm sorry.' Those were his only words. But he had spoken. That in itself was enough for Clough, who, despite maintaining he paid no attention to what was written about him and his teams in the press, always seemed to have read everything.

'That's Brian for you,' remarked Mike Bamber on being informed of his manager's post-match gagging order over a drink in the Charlton boardroom. 'He laughs and smiles when we've gone down and you can't get a smile out of him when we've won. But what a result. I said when we engaged Brian that it would all come right in the end. Things are looking brighter. Every player gave his best. That's the main thing.'

Years later, Clough would tell the BBC reporter Pat Murphy that there was no better feeling in football than the journey home from an away game on the team coach after a handsome win. 'It's probably been a long haul, a few hundred miles, but me and the lads have done our jobs well,' he said. 'That feeling of team spirit is wonderful. It's a feeling that outsiders can't comprehend. It's shared by just those who were there for that game, either playing or sat in the dugout.' The trip back to Sussex from London after the Charlton match would have been the perfect opportunity for Clough to experience such a scenario as Albion's manager. However, despite having been in charge for two and a half months, he still hadn't even set foot on the team coach after an away match. If there wasn't a TV engagement in the diary or some other social function to attend, then all roads led to the Clough family home in Derbyshire. And, as the players couldn't help but notice, there seemed little sign of that changing anytime soon.

'I often wonder whether the chairman said, "Look, you haven't got to move down, just run the team from where you are," because we honestly hardly ever saw him from match to match,' says Brian Powney. 'We were told he would move down, that it was only a matter of time, but he never did. He was still turning up on Friday or even on a Saturday, an hour or so before kick-off, and the mood he was in would reflect his team talk. Sometimes he'd come in and go apeshit at everybody and break everyone's confidence. Other times he'd come in and talk to just one or two individuals. There was no pattern. It was left to John Sheridan to look after us during the week, the poor sod, and I think after a while he was starting to have enough of it all as well.'

When he was in town, Clough chose to use the Courtlands Hotel, located in a tree-lined avenue on the cusp of where Hove meets Brighton, as his base. Even when he wasn't around, the team orders prior to a home match, more often than not, would be to assemble there the previous evening for an overnight stay before walking to the Goldstone a couple of hours before kick-off.

'You'd all be walking along and he'd usually announce the team then,' says Lammie Robertson. 'I'd say, "Boss, where am I playing? Am I playing up front or am I playing midfield? You haven't said anything." And it would be like, "Oh, you're up front, son." And that would be as you're walking down the road! I could put up with that, even though it was odd, but others couldn't. He was a funny bugger, he really was.'

One of the others was left-back Harry Wilson, someone for whom preparation and fitness were everything. 'The days off used to drive me mad,' he recalls. 'We must have had three days off every week. I found that very strange and frustrating because I liked to train every day. Even if you wanted to do something he wouldn't let you train around the ground or even in the park, which was just over the road from the ground. It was the same later on when he was at Nottingham Forest. Sometimes he'd just take the players for walks along the River Trent, and that would be it. But I used to do a bit anyway because he couldn't watch you twenty-four hours a day, could he? I'd do lots of sit-ups at home, things like that. I kept myself fit alright.'

With the state of emergency and three-day week continuing to bite, football across the British Isles found itself having to think outside the box in order to balance the fixture schedule and the needs of supporters with the power restrictions that remained in force. Keen to try something new which might tap into the family market, and only too aware that attendances under Clough had yet to climb anywhere near the desired 20,000-mark, Mike Bamber announced that Albion's next home game against bottom-of-the-table Rochdale would be played on a Sunday.

The gamble worked but wasn't without incident – the kind that had little to do with the contentious decision to stage football on the Sabbath. The good news came in the size of the crowd, an attendance of 18,885 being the largest since Clough and Taylor's arrival. The bad news was that the club failed monumentally to consider the logistical pitfalls associated with making such a change. The poor public transport service available on a Sunday meant several of the regular turnstile operators had problems getting to the Goldstone, meaning some gates remained shut. That led to sizeable crushes building up around those turnstiles which did open an hour before kick-off at 1.30 p.m., a wholly inadequate timescale to admit everyone who wanted to see the match. In the event, only the self-control of the crowd prevented a serious incident taking place, although there were reports of several people fainting. Others, thankfully, took one look at the chaotic scenes unfolding in front of them and headed for home instead of joining the throng. Another of football's many there-by-the-grace-of-God moments on the long and sorry road leading to Hillsborough in 1989.

On the field, however, there were no such worries, as Albion maintained their mini-revival, Tony Towner finding the net from twenty-five yards out in the thirty-fifth minute to give the Dolphins (as was the club's nickname until late 1975, when it was supplanted in favour of Seagulls) a 1–0 lead. Four minutes before half-time, O'Sullivan crossed from the left flank towards Robertson, who wrong-footed the visiting defence by stepping over the ball, allowing the better-placed Ken Beamish to make it 2–0 from point-blank range. Although Leo Skeete pulled a goal back for Rochdale in the second half, the Lancastrians barely threatened otherwise, allowing Albion to see the game out relatively comfortably, climbing the table from twentieth to seventeenth in the process.

Four games, three wins, one draw and seven points from a possible eight under the old points system. A reason to be cheerful, surely? Alas, the discontent in the dressing room among all bar a small number of the younger players over Clough and to an extent Taylor's methods was continuing to mount. The manager's unexplained absence from the away match at Bournemouth on New Year's Day had been dismissed with little more than a shrug of the shoulders. When it happened again on the last Sunday of January, Cambridge United following Albion's example of going for a Sabbath kick-off, there could be no hiding place.

During the negotiations which took place regarding Albion's managerial vacancy, Clough had told Bamber that there were various long-standing engagements in his busy schedule that needed to be honoured. Whether Bamber realised that these engagements would prevent him from attending some matches is unclear, but the chairman, keen perhaps not to lay down too many obstacles, went with it. At some point after accepting the job, Clough informed Bamber that he would be going to New York City at the end of January to watch Muhammad Ali fight Joe Frazier at Madison Square Garden. This, so he said, was one of his long-standing engagements and would mean him missing the match at Cambridge United. With Taylor on hand to assume the reins, Albion's board gave its approval for Clough to go.

The Ali versus Frazier trip had been organised by the *Daily Mail*, Clough finding himself heading Stateside on board a charter flight accompanied by a large group of fight fans, some of whom, he later divulged, 'were said to include gentlemen from the criminal fraternity'. Ali won in twelve rounds by a unanimous decision and the following day, in a pre-arranged meeting, the 'Louisville Lip' – his face swollen from the previous evening – went face to face with arguably the biggest mouth in football.

'By the time we finished the chat and he said, "So long and thanks very much," the sweat was trickling down my back and I was shaking,' Clough later confessed in a rare show of humility. 'I was supposed to be famous, good at what I did, a bit of a public figure, recognised almost wherever I went back home in Britain. In the presence of Ali, I was nobody, and rightly so.'

Albion were lucky to come away from Cambridge with a point in a 1–1 draw, Mick Brown converting Lammie Robertson's cross from the left in injury time at the end of the game. In his match report, John Vinicombe went remarkably easy on Clough regarding his decision to put New York City over the day job, while also revealing that the manager was planning on heading to the West Indies to watch cricket. 'In no sense is Clough shelving his responsibilities,' he wrote.

> Judging from the way he looked when we last spoke the other day, a break will do him good. He is not showing signs of strain but his high-powered routine between Derby, where he still lives with his wife and family, commitments in London and at the Goldstone cannot go on forever.

Albion's supporters weren't nearly as sympathetic, as reflected by the vast majority of the many letters received by the *Evening Argus* over the following days. Wasn't Clough short-changing the club by spreading himself too thinly? And if he did have too much on his plate, then how come there was still time to gallivant around New York City mid-season with Albion still dangerously close to the relegation zone? Those were the common threads running through correspondence after correspondence, accusations that were hard to deny. Not that Clough was around to do so, having chosen to remain on American soil for most of the following week as well.

The next time Albion's players laid eyes on their manager was in the dressing room at Vale Park, home of Port Vale, six days after the match at Cambridge. They arrived at the ground not knowing who was in the team, whether Clough would even be there to mobilise them, and seemingly without a game plan. It took Vale just five minutes to get off the mark, Brian Horton (an Albion captain of the future) arrowing a powerful volley beyond Peter Grummitt, with Ray Williams adding a second before half-time. Although Ken Beamish got a goal back against the run of play after the break, Vale managed to run out 2–1 winners despite missing a penalty and having a man sent off with half an hour to go.

Clough had no doubt where the overall blame lay, and it certainly wasn't at his door. The following Thursday he launched an astonishing attack on Albion's players, many of whom were 'lacking moral courage'. On he went in increasingly brutal terms: 'We have now got the problem of facing a home match. At every club we have been connected with, this has never been a problem. Players have looked forward to performing in front of their own supporters. But I don't think our lot do, and the reason is that they don't accept responsibility. They duck out of it. They are exposed before their home crowd and they don't like this, but it is their job as professional entertainers.'

There was more to come. In some matches the team had 'simply died'. Certain players 'have not even attempted to learn their trade'. The second-half performance at home to Rochdale had been 'nothing short of criminal for the people who paid to see it'. As if that wasn't enough, Peter Taylor then weighed in with some punches of his own. 'The days of passing the buck at Brighton are over,' he said. 'It is going to be D-Day for these players and from now on supporters are going to see action.' There was, so Taylor declared, 'a gale going through this club and the players concerned are now about to feel the draught'.

Back came Clough: 'These players are selling the club, the crowd and themselves short. We have a crowd bonus system here and they take the money quick enough when the fans roll in, but never before have they been exposed for what they are lacking. Those who are not motivated will leave the club.' In jumped Taylor again: 'We are not discussing tactics. We are talking about application and moral courage, particularly moral courage. We have been here over three months and taken time to make this assessment. Our opinion is that we have a fantastic crowd which deserve more than they are getting at home.'

A perfect storm had descended on the Goldstone. One day, Clough seemed to care deeply about the club and its future; the next it was almost as if he couldn't wait to put distance between himself and its personnel. The majority of the squad were scared of their manager, disliked him, deeply resented his absences and rantings, or felt a combination of all the above. There was also a deep disappointment in the dressing room that the hunger to improve players which had been so evident under Clough and Taylor at Derby County seemed to have deserted them at Brighton & Hove Albion. Even some of the pair's new recruits found themselves becoming disillusioned.

'He used to call me the worst full-back he'd ever seen in his life, and he did it without a trace of humour,' says Harry

Wilson, who as a child growing up in County Durham had been taken regularly by his father to watch Clough play for Sunderland. 'I can take stick, but he just belittled me. And I didn't like that. We were at the Courtlands Hotel once and he accused me of being with my wife all night because I didn't have a particularly good game. "You must have been in your wife's bedroom all night doing things you shouldn't be doing." I was thinking, "Are you for real?" The worst full-back he'd ever seen – but I'd always prove him wrong. I never missed a game. Why did he used to say it? I have no idea. You could argue that he did it to get me going and play better, but this wasn't nice stuff. This was personal. But he did similar things to other players. He ruined Gary Megson at Nottingham Forest later on with similar comments, for whatever reason. And Gary's a superb fellow. But I wasn't going to let him beat me.'

Were Clough and Taylor aware of the sullen mood among the players, given their prolonged absences from the club? It's hard to know how they couldn't have been. 'In all honesty, John Sheridan, the guy who took all of the training in midweek, wasn't the most pleasant of people either,' says John Templeman. 'He [Sheridan] must have known by the atmosphere in the dressing room and on the training ground how the players felt about things. If he did go back and speak to the two of them about it, then they certainly didn't make any changes to show us they were prepared to do anything that would help.'

It was at this stage that the Professional Footballers' Association, the union which serves to protect, improve and negotiate the conditions, rights and status of professional players in England and Wales, came into the equation. Today nobody seems sure whether anyone in Albion's dressing room contacted the PFA directly for help, or if the union threatened to step in of its own accord having read Clough's explosive comments after the Port Vale game. The PFA chairman Derek Dougan, an occasional colleague of Clough's on ITV's football punditry panel, was certainly proactive in his stance. Albion's players should 'take their grievances to the Professional Footballers' Association,' he said. 'This sort of thing takes footballers back to the day when they were chattels. I'm bewildered to know what Brian Clough expects to achieve by this.' PFA secretary Cliff Lloyd also expressed his disappointment that the remarks had been made publicly rather than within the sanctuary of the dressing room. 'The main thing to be deplored is that the right of reply has been denied the players,' he added.

'There were a few people who wanted to get the PFA involved,' says Brian Powney. 'The trouble with Cloughie was that he was a nasty piece of work. He was the type who would tear up a contract and put you out of business. That kind of fear would have stopped people from talking about it openly or taking it any further. When I say Cloughie, I actually mean the two of them because they worked in tandem. They knew where one another stood in the relationship. But Taylor was a much bigger influence than people think. A lot of people reckon Taylor was Clough's assistant and did as he was told. But, to me, Taylor was often the senior partner in terms of ideas, suggestions, keeping a lid on Clough, hiding his alcoholism and those kinds of things.'

In his later years, it became increasingly difficult for Clough to mask the heavy toll that alcohol was taking on his life. For far too long he did his level best to hide the addiction, changing the subject whenever the issue was broached or denying outright that drink had ever affected his professional judgement. Yet, as his physical features became at first red and blotchy, then grey and gaunt, so he finally began to acknowledge that a problem existed, all the while seeming to shy away from the actual word 'alcoholic'.

'You never know exactly when the drink problem sets in,' he confessed in *Walking on Water*. 'Nobody can really put a finger on the precise moment.' Had it become an addiction during his time at Brighton & Hove Albion, as Brian Powney suggests, when Clough's physical appearance was still youthful enough to cover the truth? On that, opinion among the players is divided. Many of his adversaries in Albion's dressing room, perhaps not surprisingly, indicate that it had. 'He always had a drink on the go,' Ian Goodwin says flatly. 'He always smelled of drink,' adds Powney. Others remain less certain. 'We'd go to some of the hotels after games and have a little drink, a pint, or sometimes after a game he'd ask me to come into the room with him for a talk and he'd give me a glass of beer, but it was always very slow,' is Norman Gall's recollection. 'He'd have a glass of beer on the go, yes, but it's not as if he'd be knocking them back one after the other. You've got to remember that alcohol was an accepted part of the social side of football then. It wasn't like today where drinking is frowned on in the game.'

Whether Clough's poison was prevalent at Brighton & Hove Albion during 1973 and 1974 probably depends on your definition of an alcoholic. It's clear that alcohol was consumed on a fairly regular basis at times of the day when the average working man or woman wouldn't consider partaking. Peter Brackley, BBC Radio Brighton's all-seeing eye on Albion affairs, says he 'wasn't aware that the drink was becoming a big problem, although people did know that he [Clough] liked to drink'. On the modern-day assertion that alcohol and work don't mix, then it's reasonable to assume that it may have played some part in the issues that arose between Albion's manager and his players. Clough did admit after retiring from the game that 'drink was part of my working environment for most of my time in management except at Hartlepools – we couldn't afford a glass of milk there.' At Brighton, with Mike Bamber signing the cheques, even the milkman could afford to dine out on champagne.

Ultimately the PFA stayed out of events at the Goldstone, other than Dougan and Lloyd firing their warning shots across Clough's bows. The perfect storm, for the time being at least, lost power to become a mere depression. It would, however, return on a regular basis over the months to come, as manager, assistant manager, chairman and players continued lurching from one newspaper headline to another.

7

SON OF THE DESERT

'For your fullest enjoyment you must see this film from the very beginning.'

Not exactly the catchiest of straplines. But when you've got Paul Newman and Robert Redford's faces to sell a picture, words become almost superfluous. There they were, Hollywood hottest heartthrobs, plastered across Albion's match-day programme for the visit of Grimsby Town promoting the opening of *The Sting* at Brighton's ABC cinema. The film wasn't out yet, but the irony dripping from the full-page advert wasn't lost on those supporters who had heard the buzz from America, read the universally glowing reviews in Britain's newspapers, and knew the basic outline of the plot:

Two men set out on an elaborate plan, a long-con, to swindle enormous sums of money from a man with a formidable reputation. They do it so well that the mark has no idea he is being conned, until it is too late.

After the events of late January and early February 1974, not to mention much of what had gone before since Mike Bamber hired Clough and Taylor, perhaps some other form of editorial content or advertorial might have been more appropriate.

Bamber was on the whole a fair, generous man, but he could be firm and uncompromising. No way was he in the same league as mob boss Doyle Lonnegan, as played in *The Sting* by Robert Shaw, but the comparisons between fictional Chicago and real-life Brighton – home to more than its fair share of shady underworld characters over the years – were inevitable.

Maybe it was the prospect of intervention from the PFA. It could have dawned on him that Albion's form since Christmas had actually been pretty decent. Perhaps it was the unseasonably warm temperatures that brought day trippers to the coast for some unexpected rest and relaxation during traditionally grim February (despite his love of the sun, Clough was such a reluctant traveller that he rarely ventured abroad on non-football-related business other than visiting Cala Millor, his favourite resort, where Brian Powney had also encountered John McGovern). Or he might just have grown tired of being angry.

We will never know.

What is certain is that Clough seemed more focused on Brighton & Hove Albion following his post-Port Vale rant and the PFA's subsequent comments. He was present rather than absent, encouraging rather than critical, good-natured instead of gloomy. It wouldn't be long before Albion once again slipped from his radar, but for a couple of weeks that February it was almost as if Clough realised he had overstepped the mark. Without, of course, admitting it.

Albion's performance at home to Grimsby on 9 February was arguably their poorest since the lacklustre Goldstone Ground display against Aldershot on Boxing Day – Barry Bridges providing one of the game's few touches of class, clipping the ball beyond Town goalkeeper Harry Wainman to secure a 1–1 draw. You wouldn't have guessed it though, going by Clough's upbeat comments afterwards. 'More things were right for us today than for a long time,' he insisted. 'We kept going. We kept at it. We had a reluctance to be beaten and Grimsby were not exactly fairies. I was most pleased at the way we came back after losing the early goal.'

It was the same story seven days later, when Albion, missing captain Norman Gall through suspension, didn't so much as get out of jail but escape from Alcatraz at Halifax Town's expense. Two goals ahead and cruising thanks to a first-half brace from Terry Shanahan, the Yorkshiremen were incensed when defender Tony Rhodes was adjudged – wrongly, according to just about everybody inside the ground – to have fouled Lammie Robertson inside the penalty area in the sixty-fifth minute. Robertson looked as surprised as anyone at the awarding of a spot kick, but kept his composure to score after a lengthy delay brought on by a barrage of protests. To add insult to injury, Peter O'Sullivan then made light of the heavy Pennine rain to dance his way down the left flank and set up John Templeman at the far post, who netted to seal an unlikely 2–2 draw.

'If you are going to go places in this division then you have to get results at places like Halifax,' said a buoyant Clough, glossing over what had been, for all bar the briefest of spells, a dire display. Several players, Bridges and Robertson among them, were singled out for praise. Even goalkeeper Peter Grummitt, horribly at fault for the Halifax opener after misjudging a corner kick from David Ford, got off lightly. 'He missed it completely but he is entitled to a mistake now and again,' insisted Clough. 'In the last quarter of an hour he saved us.'

Having shown little interest up until then in wanting to improve the technical ability of Albion's players, Clough also began making an effort to impart his vast footballing knowledge, frequently employing humour, as opposed to ridicule, to get the message across. There were also some curious attempts at deconstructing players psychologically, climbing inside their minds to see what kind of stuff they were made of.

'We were having a meeting one day and he was having a bit of a go at Tony Towner,' remembers Peter O'Sullivan. 'Suddenly he says to him, "I want you to go in the other dressing room and shout, 'I'm in here' until I tell you to stop." So Tony goes in the other dressing room and he's shouting and shouting, then he finally comes back. And Cloughie goes, "Good. Do that in a game and you'll get more of the ball." We were laughing our heads off. There was Tony going, "I'M IN HERE, I'M IN HERE! HELLO? HELLO?" for ages. That was a simple way of getting a message across effectively, and it worked.'

'Football players play a lot of card games travelling to and from away matches on trains and coaches, and that was especially the case at Brighton, which seemed about as far away from Hull and places like that as you could get,' adds Lammie Robertson. 'I'd never known a manager join in, but he [Clough] started to. There was a game we used to play, I forget the exact name, which involved trying to get rid of all your bad cards by passing them to the guy next to you. Clough was next to me and he was passing me all good cards. It was like, "What are you going to say? Are you going to say anything? Are you going to do anything? How are you going to react?" He understood the game alright and knew exactly what he was doing. That was his way of testing me. You know, trying to find out what kind of guy I was.'

Not all of Clough's stabs at humour worked, an indication perhaps that too much water had already gone under the bridge when it came to some players. 'I was planning on getting married at the end of that season,' says John Templeman.

'One afternoon we were called into training to do a light session. We weren't going to be very long, so I decided to take my future wife along with me so she could sit in the car and wait, then we'd go into Brighton afterwards and go round the shops. Anyway, we trained, got back in the dressing room, had a shower, got dressed, and were then told to wait for Clough and Taylor because they wanted to have a chat with us. We waited, and waited, and eventually they came in and sat down virtually opposite where I was sitting. They were chatting away and then, all of a sudden, Clough said in that accent of his, "I've seen something this afternoon that I've never, ever seen in all the years I've been in football." We all looked around, thinking, "What's this all about?" Then he pointed at me and said, "You, young lad. If you ever bring your girlfriend or fiancé to training again and leave her sitting in the car, then I'll put a bomb underneath it." Which, coming from someone who used to take his young son, Nigel, to all the games, including the away ones, was a bit rich. To me, that wasn't at all pleasant or funny. Mind you, I didn't do it again.'

And then, much as a lighthouse beam illuminates all in its path for the briefest of moments before darting on, so Clough's attention turned elsewhere.

* * *

Once more, events on the national stage were moving at an incredible pace. On 1 February, the National Union of Mineworkers, looking to press home its wage demands, had presided over a strike ballot. Eighty-one per cent of their members voted to come out, the largest majority in favour of strike action in the union's history. Conservative Prime Minister Ted Heath knew only too well that the reputation of his government rested on managing the economy and making its policy of pay restraint work. Believing public sympathy would rest with the government following the NUM ballot, Heath called a general election for 28 February standing on the platform of 'Who governs Britain?' Win and the government would, in effect, have a mandate to stand firm against the miners.

On the evening of Thursday 7 February, having asked the Queen for permission to dissolve Parliament, Heath addressed the country on television. 'Do you want a strong government which has clear authority for the future to take decisions which will be needed?' he asked. 'Do you want Parliament and the elected government to continue to fight strenuously against inflation? Or do you want them to abandon the struggle against rising prices under pressure from one particularly powerful group of workers? This time of strife has got to stop. Only you can stop it. It's time for you to speak – with your vote. It's time for your voice to be heard – the voice of the moderate and reasonable people of Britain. The voice of the majority. It's time for you to say to the extremists, the militants, and the plain and simply misguided, "We've had enough." There's a lot to be done. For heaven's sake, let's get on with it.'

Right from the start, the Conservative Party's strategy of focusing its election campaign on industrial relations appeared unsustainable. With price rises seemingly out of control, inflation continuing to climb and the country at the mercy of a colossal balance of trade deficit, the all-too-obvious answer to 'Who governs Britain?' was 'Certainly not you!' However, opinion poll after opinion poll continued to have the Conservatives out in front, one indicating a lead as large as 9 per cent. The Labour Party, so it appeared, were heading for defeat.

One Labour stalwart who feared for his future was Phillip Whitehead, Member of Parliament for Derby North and a friend of Clough's from his time at Derby County. The longer the election campaign went on, the more it seemed as if Whitehead was on course to lose his seat. Then, out of the blue, Whitehead and his agent John Beadle were contacted by Clough, who offered to do whatever he could to help. 'How can you do that when you're manager at Brighton?' Beadle enquired. 'No problem,' was Clough's reply. 'I only go on Fridays and I'm back on Saturday night.'

Clough was no stranger to politics. Socialism had been as much a part of Middlesbrough as the blast furnaces that dominated the local skyline. Along with Peter Taylor, he had been to hear Harold Wilson, Labour's then shadow Chancellor, speak at a local working man's club in the town one Sunday afternoon during the late 1950s. 'I didn't have to drag him along,' recalled Taylor, who as a younger man held strong left-wing beliefs which seemed to fade as Clough's intensified. 'He was as fascinated as I was.' It jarred not with Clough that, later in life, he would live in a country mansion with a Mercedes in the drive. Those were the fruits of his hard work, justifiable according to the 'I want everyone to have a Mercedes' philosophy (as Clough biographer Tony Francis brilliantly put it). Over the years, rumours persisted about him standing for election, though they remained only that. Not until 1986, prior to the Derbyshire West by-election, did he actually join the Labour Party, seemingly stung into action by Conservative Party leader Margaret Thatcher, whose policies and leadership style he abhorred.

Clough threw himself into campaigning on Whitehead's behalf, canvassing from door to door as election day approached and delivering two well-received speeches at schools in the constituency. Almost inevitably, football threatened to hijack both events, although Clough tried as much as he could to ensure that Whitehead's cause took precedence. The 'When are you coming back to Derby?' question was met with a 'Let's get Phillip elected first, then we'll see what happens' answer. Against all odds, Whitehead won the seat by 1,200 votes, one of 301 to be taken by Labour against 297 for the Conservatives. Heath's gamble to call a snap election had backfired and allowed Harold Wilson into Downing Street, albeit at the head of a minority administration.

'He [Clough] had a considerable effect on the vote in an area of the country which was crucial to us,' recalled Whitehead. 'All the computers predicted failure, but we won by 1,200 votes. My greatest memory of him was on polling day, a bedraggled figure looming out of the sleet and drizzle with his loudhailer telling everyone, "I'm Brian Clough and I think you should come out and vote for the Labour Party. Get down to the polling station now." He went round the estate drawing people out of their houses like the Pied Piper.'

Whitehead's assessment as to whether Clough would have made a good Member of Parliament contains some interesting parallels with the way his career as a football manager panned out over twenty-eight years in the job. 'To be caught on the treadmill of our Parliament, which works longer hours than anywhere in the world and operates insanely by most people's standards, would, quite honestly, have driven Brian mad,' reckoned Whitehead. 'He is undoubtedly a political animal with a mesmerising style who cares about ordinary people. The trouble is he cannot suffer fools. Because he has been so successful himself, he expects others to be equally so. He would find the dolts and toadies one has to put up with in the House [of Commons] quite unbearable. Brian would have been marvellous on the big occasions but useless on the mundane ones. Sadly, they are the vast majority.'

For the big occasions, see Derby County, Clough's ambitious stab at taking on Leeds United, and Nottingham Forest. For the mundane, see Brighton & Hove Albion and a fixture list that included Halifax, Aldershot and York. As Clough himself said while attempting to justify his decision to fly to New York City for the Muhammad Ali versus Joe Frazier showdown, 'I am going to America for the big fight because I have missed the big time.'

While Clough was away banging his drum in support of Whitehead, Albion's squad went back to square one, left to fend for themselves on the treadmill that was Division Three. Taylor also continued to be a largely absent figure as he scoured the country looking for new recruits. Speculation that Bobby Moore was about to sign proved wide of the mark (the ex-England captain and Clough had been spotted together at the Metropole Hotel in Brighton, causing the story to snowball). Instead, the Blackpool pair of midfielder Billy McEwan and defender Paul Fuschillo arrived during the third week of February for a combined fee of £15,000, taking Clough and Taylor's spending on players to approximately £112,000. Neither would make a lasting impression at the Goldstone, appearing only twenty-eight and seventeen times respectively for the first XI before disappearing to pastures new, substantiating the growing feeling in the dressing room that there was something amiss with Albion's recruitment policy.

'I wasn't too impressed with some of the players they were bringing in, and I know I wasn't alone,' says Lammie Robertson. 'I think they were changing for changing's sake, bringing in players who weren't as good as the ones they were getting rid of when of course it should be vice versa. Peter Grummitt was a good goalkeeper and I liked the look of Harry Wilson, but some of the others just didn't seem up to it. Paul Fuschillo came from Blackpool and I thought, "He can't fucking play!" You can tell in training when you see a player's first touch and the way he goes about things.'

'Obviously we made anyone who came in welcome,' adds Steve Piper. 'However, there was a lot of chopping and changing going on with players coming and going, new faces here and there, and I didn't really think that helped, especially when it came to team bonding. You need a little bit of stability and of course Cloughie and Peter Taylor weren't always there to introduce the new players to us and explain what they wanted from them. It did feel like you were on a conveyor belt sometimes. Having said that, we did start to climb up the table.'

On Saturday 23 February, Albion defeated sixth-placed Blackburn Rovers 3–0 at the Goldstone in what John Vinicombe described as 'their best performance of the season so far'. At that stage they remained eighteenth in the league table, too close for comfort to the relegation zone but within touching distance of a close-knit pack of clubs just above them. The day before the general election, Fuschillo and McEwan made their debuts as Wrexham came to Hove for another midweek match with an afternoon kick-off due to the floodlight ban, this one a 3.30 p.m. start. Only 7,510 people were there to see it, significantly down on the 12,120 that had attended the Blackburn game due to so many fans being either at work or school. A goal down after twelve minutes, Albion battled back to win 2–1 with Ronnie Howell on target from the penalty spot and Peter O'Sullivan finding the net from long range, rising to fifteenth place in the process. Despite some questionable recruitment and the rapid turnover in players, they were indeed starting to climb the table.

'I think the football was as good as any since we came here,' said Clough, making a whistle-stop return to Sussex for the Wrexham match amid his campaigning on behalf of Phillip Whitehead. There was also praise for Fuschillo and McEwan, thrust into first-team action after spending most of the 1973/74 season playing in Blackpool's reserve team. 'The two new signings played well considering they've come straight out of the Central League. They were pacing it well towards the end. It is a big lift from what they have been used to just recently.'

Four days later, with Whitehead safely returned to the Houses of Parliament, Albion made it three wins on the bounce courtesy of a 1–0 away win at Aldershot in front of almost 10,000 people, more than ever appeared safe within the confines of their modest council-owned Recreation Ground. It proved to be a fiery affair with both Fuschillo and Aldershot's Ron Walton sent off by referee Alf Grey for violent play during the second half – this in an era when red cards were harder to come by than a day without some kind of industrial action. According to those who witnessed the full-blooded encounter, it could easily have been more than two.

'I thought we were superb in the first half,' declared Clough afterwards. 'All the lads played well, particularly Steve Piper and the two strikers again. The best ones hunt in pairs. That is what is starting to happen with us. Barry Bridges is doing more work for us now than he has done in the past ten years of his professional life. The other week he got two [versus Blackburn]. This time it was [Ken] Beamish. As I said, the best ones hunt in pairs.'

Beamish was on target again the following Sunday as Albion, sticking with their Sabbath experiment despite the near-calamitous scenes for the visit of Rochdale the previous month, won 2–1 against a Hereford side every bit as uncompromising as Aldershot had proved to be. They left it late in front of 17,061 spectators, Steve Piper scoring the first goal of his professional career with two minutes of normal time remaining to lift 'Brian Clough's Brighton', as the national media had grown accustomed to calling them, up to tenth.

In the space of ten weeks, Albion had risen ten places on the back of a twelve-match sequence yielding seven wins, four draws and just one defeat. Was promotion really out of the question? With twelve league games of the 1973/74 season remaining, Albion lay eight points adrift of Oldham Athletic, occupiers of the third and final promotion place. Going by their current form, it wasn't impossible. Clough, however, was having none of it – at least not publicly. 'You say people are talking about the mathematical possibility of us going up?' he asked one journalist following the Hereford win. 'Are they now? We couldn't get promotion if we had Einstein on our side, and he was pretty good at figures.'

Cue general laughter from the press pack. But then another reporter came in with a question that had nothing to do with promotion, Hereford, Steve Piper, the general election, Bobby Moore or going back to Derby County. It was a question no one saw coming, the sort that sends a ripple through a room, and to this day nobody seems able to recall who did the asking. But the wording went something like this:

'Is it true that you have had an offer to run the Iranian national side for £400 a week, tax free?'

Rather than bat the question away, Clough replied succinctly, yet with enough detail to suggest that the subject not only carried weight, but had at some stage been discussed with other parties. 'I was both delighted and flattered,' he said. 'Of course I'm not going. I'm staying with Brighton.'

Less than forty-eight hours later, however, Clough was on a plane bound for Tehran. Once again, the storm clouds were gathering.

The journalist's information had been solid. At some stage while back in Derbyshire campaigning for Phillip Whitehead, Clough had been contacted by one of the Shah's representatives about becoming manager of the Iran national team. It was an intriguing proposal, not to mention an extremely lucrative one by 1974 standards, the initial offer being more than double his £200-a-week salary at Brighton & Hove Albion. Clough got in touch with George Brown, the former Labour Foreign Secretary who lived in nearby Belper, to ask for advice. In his first autobiography published in 1994, Clough recalled Brown saying, 'If you've gone through the right channels they'll treat you like a God. They'll make you a bloody king. Your kids will go to the American school, you'll have cars at your disposal, and you'll be able to pick exactly where you want to live. And as for the salary, they'll virtually invite you to write your own cheque.'

Armed with this information, Clough told the Iranians he was interested. Arrangements were made for him to fly out first class on Tuesday 12 March accompanied by the journalist Vince Wilson, ghostwriter of his regular column in the *Sunday Mirror*, and Billy Wainwright, manager of the Midland Hotel in Derby, whom Clough regarded as one of his closest friends. Once there, he held talks with a gentleman introduced as the Master of the Horse, one of three right-hand men to the Shah who Clough assumed took responsibility for sporting affairs.

The job offer was for two years, starting as soon as his five-year contract with Albion had been prematurely terminated. Whether Peter Taylor's name was mentioned during the negotiations is unclear, but given Clough's circuitous methods in bringing him on board at Hartlepools United and Derby County, there is every indication they'd have remained a pair. As Taylor later said, 'We would have stuck together.'

Back at the Goldstone, an inwardly seething Mike Bamber was trying his best to exude an air of business-as-usual amid the growing furore. The problem was that on this occasion the media knew more than he did. On the Wednesday, having tried to find out what he could from various sources, including the Iranian Embassy in London, Bamber put on a brave face to give his version of events. 'There's been a misunderstanding,' he insisted. 'Neither Peter nor Brian are taking any job in Persia. On Sunday, Brian said to me that he would like to go over there to give them some advice. I did not realise at the time he was going this week. I thought he was going at the end of the season. I did not know he went yesterday.' Bamber had been made to look like a mug, and he didn't like it.

Clough always maintained he was serious about taking the Iran job, and that only the considerations of his family and the fact that 'the life was not for me' prevented him from doing so. What he never admitted was that for the first time, Albion's chairman – with the support of the entire board – stood firm, holding both he and Taylor to their five-year contracts. On the Friday, Clough returned to the UK, and the following morning met Taylor, Bamber and five of Albion's directors in Burton-on-Trent ahead of the team's match at Shrewsbury Town. Outwardly, the mood was jovial, even if there was a touch of the errant schoolboy being summoned to the headmaster's office about Clough. 'I've sold the drilling rights on the Brighton pitch and I've still got my interview suit on,' he joked to the waiting media, Taylor adding, 'Can I smell camels?' Once behind closed doors though, Bamber left his manager in no doubt as to how he felt about the whole matter, or 'stunt' as he later described it. The days of Clough using Brighton & Hove Albion as little more than a staging post were, he insisted, now over. Bamber didn't expect him to be at the Goldstone every day, but from now on there had to be more commitment plus a heck of a lot more honesty. And if he wanted to go to the West Indies to watch England play cricket, then that was up to him, but the board certainly wouldn't be sanctioning it.

A line had been drawn in the Sussex rather than the Persian sands. That afternoon, Albion's four-game winning streak came to an end, Shrewsbury edging yet another bad-tempered affair 1–0. On the Monday, Bamber, Clough, Taylor, several of Albion's directors, the media and even some fans gathered at the Goldstone for what was supposed to be a press conference but which ended up resembling more of a shareholder meeting. If Bamber intended it as a way of calling Clough to account for his straying – not just to Iran but in general – then he might have done better to think again.

'The idea of running a national side appeals to me immensely,' Clough admitted to the assembled throng. 'How many national managers are there in the world? Four, five, six? You tell me. If the chairman had given me his blessing, I would have gone to Persia, but I'm staying to do a job here at Brighton. The ultimate ambition in management is to take charge of a national side, but we are very conscious of the fact that we have signed long contracts. We have a job to do here and the chairman wants us to do that job.'

It was an honest answer and, when written down, the words seem earnest enough and relatively upbeat. But the manager's body language told a different story. Dressed in a tracksuit, a sullen-looking Clough spent much of the time either looking at the floor, fiddling with a pen, or both. At one point a journalist asked him if he was happy. 'Am I happy right now? Well, let's say I'm looking forward to the cricket season,' was his deadpan reply. It was a remarkable comment from a man on an excellent salary whose team had risen from the depths of the Third Division to stage an outside bid for promotion. When it appeared in print, as it inevitably did, Clough's frank confession provoked fury among many Albion supporters, yet little more than a shrug of the shoulders in the dressing room. 'We were doing OK on the pitch in spite of him, not because of him, so I don't think we cared what he did or said by then anyway,' is one anonymous player's recollection of how he felt on reading his manager's words.

Instead, it was again left to Bamber to try to put a positive spin on proceedings. 'Brian is very happy to stay here,' he quickly interjected. 'The more successful they are, the more offers we shall get for them. Brian and Peter had to be interested in the offer they received. It was fabulous. I would have been very interested if it had come to me, but they are not leaving Albion. Taking everything into consideration, we have all decided that they will stay.'

For once, the best quip of the day came not from Clough but a member of the press corps, just as the gathering was breaking up. Asked why he thought Clough hadn't taken the Iranian job, the journalist's off-the-cuff reply – 'There isn't room for two Shahs in Persia!' – had everyone within earshot in stitches.

Having fended for themselves during Clough's various

absences and Taylor's scouting missions, Albion's players emerged from the Shrewsbury game battered, bruised and in need of some actual hands-on management. Top of the casualty list was Peter Grummitt, stretchered from Town's Gay Meadow pitch with a broken pelvis. The goalkeeper remained in the Royal Salop Infirmary for most of the following week, scans thankfully revealing the injury not to be career-threatening. He would, however, miss the remainder of the season. That left Albion with only one fit goalkeeper, the man cast out into the wilderness following the Bristol Rovers debacle after more than a decade's sterling service between the posts: Brian Powney.

'It had happened before in my career, going to play in the stiffs [reserves], but it had never really bothered me,' says Powney. 'Yes, your ego gets damaged when you're dropped, but I was always fairly resilient and believed that I'd get my place back. I knew Cloughie didn't fancy me, but I just kept at it. I was always a good trainer. In fact, it used to make my day, going training. I'd do all the work with the squad, then go and do stuff on my own, then sometimes go back in the afternoon with the kids just to get balls hit at me. I had the cartilage and ligament damage in my right knee that I'd had for years, but all that training meant I was still pretty sharp. When Peter got his fracture, he [Clough] had to bring me back in. And I was ready.'

'I always remember one reserve team game that I played in around that period when I was out of favour. We were playing somewhere like Peterborough or Wycombe – north of London but south of Derby, put it that way. The game was in a park because whoever it was we were playing didn't want us using their ground. That meant we had to change in this recreation hall. I'm thinking, "Christ, from Villa Park to this!" So I've gone out there, I'm standing in my goalmouth, I look around, and who do I see walking through the trees? Brian Clough. He wanders round the pitch, then fucks off. Now there were a lot of young kids in that side. They would have thought, "Cor, the boss has come to see me. Come on, motivate me!" But he just disappeared without saying as much as a word. Weird.'

Peter Grummitt wasn't the only player who failed to last the entire ninety minutes at Shrewsbury. Steve Piper had entered into a running feud with Town's Alan Durban, once a part of Derby County's midfield during Clough's tenure at the Baseball Ground. Things came to the boil when Piper, in full view of the referee, booted Durban and got sent off. Realising he could ill afford to be without the promising young defender, Clough went overboard in his attempts to get Piper – arguably his favourite player out of the entire Albion squad – off the hook and back into the side without having to serve any suspension.

'I kicked him [Durban] up the arse off the ball and was quite rightly sent off,' recalls Piper. 'Clough was no problem about it at all, but it was what happened afterwards that really sticks in my mind. I was due to have a hearing at Lancaster Gate [former home of the Football Association's headquarters] and Brian came with me. He not only picked me up and took me there in a chauffeur-driven car from Brighton, but he also got Alan Durban to come down from Shrewsbury to say it had all been an accident. Alan goes, "It was my fault entirely. Steve turned because I provoked him, but there was no malice in it at all." All rubbish of course, because I had wanted to punch him. But between them they made up this story and I ended up getting off. That shows you what he could be like with me and some of the other youngsters. He would go the extra mile for you.'

With Piper restored to the side and Powney back in favour

after a sixteen-game absence, Albion went out to face Port Vale at the Goldstone on Wednesday 20 March, the lengthening daylight allowing for a slightly later kick-off at 5 p.m. This time both Clough and Taylor were present in the dugout, proof perhaps that Bamber's private dressing-down had struck a chord after all. Somewhat embarrassingly, given the events of the previous few days, Albion's programme editor – working to a premature print deadline due to the three-day week – chose to include a letter of thanks from the deputy principal of Glenrothes and Buckhaven Technical College in Scotland, Clough having delivered a lecture there entitled 'Management in Football' on 25 February. 'His ability to entertain, interest and inform at one and the same time was made crystal clear,' wrote A. S. McGlynn. 'Reaction to the lecture has been most favourable from all angles. Mr Clough succeeded in winning over his entire audience and the contingent of press representatives present. It is no exaggeration to say that he has created many new friends and admirers in Scotland.' Bamber wasn't aware that his manager had even been in Scotland on 25 February. However, as the lecture had taken place three weeks prior to the post-Iranian Burton-on-Trent showdown, he chose to look the other way.

Port Vale, like Albion, were one of twelve clubs separated by just four points in the league table, all harbouring ambitions of catching the Third Division's front-runners. With the finishing straight in sight and plenty of ground still to make up, even a single defeat at this stage of the season was likely to scupper any hopes of promotion. Albion's players seemed to sense this more than Port Vale's and started as though they meant business, goals from Barry Bridges and Billy McEwan giving them a 2–0 lead inside the opening twenty-five minutes. But from then on they were found guilty of cruising, Port Vale coming back into the game after the break when Powney, his vision impaired by the low-lying sun, misjudged Bobby Gough's corner, allowing David Harris to score with a header.

Albion were, in effect, down to ten men for the entire second half, Clough's decision to play Ken Beamish – running a high temperature and clearly in discomfort – almost backfiring amid scenes reminiscent of November's home game against Chesterfield when the striker had been made to start despite having an ankle injury. This time Beamish remained on the pitch rather than being substituted. 'A three-quarters fit Beamish is better than no Beamish at all,' is how Clough justified his decision afterwards. Somehow Albion got away with it and held out for a 2–1 win, rising to ninth in the process, their highest position of the season so far.

Brighton's date with destiny was rapidly approaching. In less than three weeks' time the eyes of Europe, let alone England, would be on the Sussex town. Unfortunately, all the razzmatazz had zero to do with Brighton & Hove Albion. And even Old Big Head would find himself being upstaged… by four relatively unknown Swedes.

8

SIR NORMAN'S WATERLOO

In 1955, the European Broadcasting Union, an alliance of public service media organisations from across the continent, decided it would be a good idea to hold an annual song competition as a means of promoting the burgeoning television industry, while at the same time helping to unify countries still reeling from the effects of World War Two.

Thus, the Eurovision Song Contest was born.

In 1972, Vicky Leandros, representing Luxembourg despite the fact she was from Greece, won with a number called 'Après toi' ('After You'). Victory meant Luxembourg got to host the competition the following year, when they won again courtesy of Anne-Marie David and her performance of 'Tu te reconnaîtras' ('You'll Recognise Yourself'). Unable to absorb the considerable financial burden associated with staging it for a second year running, Luxembourg shook its head at the prospect of an encore. Sensing an opportunity, the BBC offered to take the competition to the UK. 'Mais oui!' said the European Broadcasting Union, meaning the BBC had to find a suitable venue pronto.

Step forward, Brighton.

The show would be held on Saturday 6 April 1974 at the Dome, an arts centre adjacent to the town's famous Pavilion, which had once been used as royal stables by the Prince Regent (later to become George IV). As March wore on, so those with a vested interest in the competition began working their magic. Banners welcoming Brighton's European guests started appearing on the side of buses and hanging from lamp-posts. Foreign flags flew from polls in Old Steine Gardens close to the Pavilion. Men with paint pots tended to any railing within sight of the Dome and the many hotels accommodating those attending the event. There was, people recall, a general feeling of a town emerging from the gloom. Spring had arrived, flowers were in bloom, the clocks were poised to go forward and – perhaps most importantly of all – the three-day week had finally been lifted. Television was able to broadcast again after 10.30 p.m., pubs returned to trading after dark and football went back to being played under floodlights. No more 1.45 p.m. kick-offs on Wednesdays, in other words.

Even the music showed signs of rising above the usual pap offered up by the Eurovision Song Contest, with British entry 'Long Live Love' by Olivia Newton-John installed as an early 5–1 favourite by the bookmakers. Relatively unfancied at 20–1, despite receiving plenty of airplay on BBC radio, was the Swedish entry from a band called Abba. The general consensus among those in the know was that 'Waterloo' verged a little too much towards rock as opposed to the standard Euro-folk/pop fare, and was likely to score relatively poorly as a result. 'We will probably get several votes from northern Europe and possibly also from England,' said Björn Ulvaeus, one quarter of Abba, before leaving Sweden for Brighton. 'It's harder with the

Italians, the Spaniards and the French. In those countries they want their ballads. But we are working with the intention of winning. That's the only way to do it.'

Winning was something that Brighton & Hove Albion had become accustomed to as winter gradually made way for spring. All too often in the football calendar a dark horse comes from nowhere to win promotion. With five victories from their past six matches, there was every reason to believe that it could be them. Albion had beaten Port Vale without playing particularly well, the mark of many a successful side over the years, but with much ground still to make up they couldn't afford many more below-par performances if a place in the top three was to be achieved.

On Saturday 23 March, Huddersfield Town came to Hove for Albion's first 3 p.m. home kick-off since Brian Clough's inaugural match in charge against York City. Town, like Albion and Port Vale, also occupied the chasing pack and couldn't afford to slip up either. With so much at stake, it could easily have been a cagey affair, but wasn't. After twenty-three minutes, Alan Gowling, Huddersfield's former Manchester United striker, struck a fierce shot past Brian Powney to put the visitors ahead. Unperturbed, Albion hit straight back with a goal from Billy McEwan, his second since joining from Blackpool. Shortly after half-time, Gowling restored Town's lead with a header. As the minutes ticked by, so Albion threw everything at Huddersfield in an attempt to salvage at least a point: McEwan fired just wide; Ronnie Howell's effort appeared goalbound but cannoned back off a post; Ken Beamish broke clean through only to see Town goalkeeper Terry Poole spread himself like an octopus to beat the striker's shot away. At 4.52 p.m., referee Ron Crabb's final whistle echoed out around the Goldstone

Ground, sealing a 2–1 defeat. A disappointing result watched by a disappointing crowd, only 12,564 customers paying to come through the turnstiles despite Albion's decent run of form and the return of 3 p.m. football on a Saturday.

Two days later, Albion's upward trajectory was well and truly stopped in its tracks, Wrexham's 1–0 win at the Racecourse Ground ending any lingering hopes of promotion. To make matters worse, Ronnie Howell was sent off for deliberately kicking an opponent, the third Albion player to receive a red card in six matches. This time, unlike the Steve Piper affair, there was no sign of Clough going the extra mile in order to get the suspension overturned.

Two defeats on the bounce meant the 1973/74 season was as good as over. The players knew it. The supporters knew it. Albion wouldn't be going up, but they wouldn't be going down either. From now on the campaign would be about pride and the players playing for their futures. Under Clough and Taylor, the squad had swelled in size from the eighteen members present that November evening at the White Hart Hotel in Lewes to twenty-five. Such was the rapid turnover rate that it was often hard to tell at any given time who was on the payroll, who wasn't, and who was poised to sign. Twenty-five was too many for a club trying to function on attendances that were good by Third Division standards, yet nowhere near high enough to underwrite the kind of spectacle put in place by Mike Bamber. With new players continuing to arrive on a regular basis, some kind of post-season clearout became inevitable. It was just a question of who would be staying and who would be going. In that type of environment, coasting through what remained of the season with one eye on a relaxing summer vacation wasn't an option.

One of the most recent arrivals was a Manchester-born forward by the name of Ian Mellor, signed from Norwich City for a club record fee of £40,000 – although in Mellor's case perhaps arrival is the wrong word. In March 1973, 'Spider' (he stood at 6 ft 1 in. and weighed just eleven stone) had been dropped by Manchester City following a 5–1 thrashing at the hands of Wolverhampton Wanderers. While in something of a post-match sulk, he agreed to be transferred to Norwich. To cut a long story short, the move didn't work out. In March 1974, Clough offered to take him from the bottom of the First Division to halfway up the Third. Mellor agreed to go for one reason: Albion's manager. Then came the twist. Despite there being almost two months of the season remaining, Clough informed his record signing that he didn't want to see him again until May, when the team was due to go on a bonding trip to Majorca. The manager, so it seemed, needed 'Spider' physically and mentally fresh for August, not March. 'It was so frustrating,' Mellor told me in 2005. 'I was gutted. I think I just went home to Manchester to kill time. Very strange.'

Although the majority of the players still had much to play for in terms of their futures, the two longest-serving members of Albion's squad sensed long beforehand that old father time was working against them. As early as August 1973, Brian Powney had decided that the 1973/74 season would be his last in professional football, such was the extent of the damage to his right knee. He'd already started a vending machine business as a side-line, which was doing very nicely, thank you. Come May, he would be out of his own volition. Likewise Norman Gall, or 'Sir Norman' as he was known among supporters in recognition of his dedication to the Albion cause stretching back to 1962. In 1967, Gall had suffered a serious injury to his right knee during a game against Torquay United. He underwent treatment and returned to the side to play regularly for many more seasons, but the pain never really went away. Come the 1973/74 campaign, it was getting worse. Despite being made captain by Clough and putting in some of the finest performances of his career, 'Sir Norman' decided to inform his manager that he would be retiring at the end of the season.

'With all the pressure that I was under with my fitness, it was actually an easy decision for me to make,' says Gall. 'I went to see Brian to tell him about it. He asked me to stay for another season and I said I couldn't. He said, "I can't understand why. But if that's what you want, that's what you want." The next time the team sheet went up, I wasn't captain anymore. Whether it was Brian who made that decision or Peter Taylor, I have no idea. I would have thought Taylor. As I've said, he was an awful man and I never got on with him at all. Brian never said a word, so I didn't say anything either. I just got on with it.'

On Saturday 30 March 1974, Albion went toe to toe with York again, this time at City's compact Bootham Crescent home. It was to be one of those games that achieves significance only with hindsight, the match itself proving to be something of a washout from an Albion perspective as the team slid to a third successive defeat, this time by 3–0. In the fifteenth minute, Gall pulled his right hamstring and had to leave the field. He knew immediately that the injury would in all likelihood rule him out for what remained of the season and, therefore, spell the end of his career. Sure enough, York City away was Norman Gall's 488th and final appearance in an Albion shirt.

'Because I was injured playing for the first team, I should have continued to be paid as if I was still playing,' adds Gall. 'I should have been on bonuses for things like winning and attendances, that kind of stuff. Instead I just received my basic salary. Over my last two months at the club not one additional bonus was given to me. I could have gone to Mr Bamber or any of the directors to say, "Look, there's been a mistake here," but I didn't. It was an awful, awful period and I realised it was time to get out quick. I did go back to the Goldstone to collect my gear and while I was there bumped into Mr Bamber. I asked him if I could hang on to my existing pass card, something which all the players had, so I could continue to go and see Albion play. And he said that I couldn't. Don't get me wrong: I regard myself as having been so lucky to play for Brighton & Hove Albion. But that last year at the Goldstone was disastrous. It spoiled my whole experience of playing twelve years of professional football and 488 games at the club. If it had happened with some of my previous managers at Brighton, like George Curtis, then I would have been very sad to leave, but at the time it didn't affect me at all because the atmosphere was so bad. I just had to get away from there. Twelve years and you end up being called a crap player all the time by Peter Taylor and being stripped of the captaincy for being honest. In fact, Brian didn't say a single word to me after I told him I was going to pack it in. That was it – finished. All because I had a bad knee.'

Brian Powney also has good reason to remember the York City game for the wrong reasons. Albion's goalkeeper broke a bone in his right hand plus two fingers while diving at an opponent's feet, injuries which under normal circumstances should have put an end to his season. However, with Peter Grummitt still recuperating from his broken pelvis, the club had no back-up option for the back-up goalkeeper.

The Monday after losing at York, Albion asked the Football League for permission to sign a goalkeeper on a month's loan to deputise for Powney, the transfer deadline having passed on 14 March. The request was turned down flat. That left Clough and Taylor with two options for the home match against Cambridge United on the Wednesday, and indeed for the foreseeable future: stick an outfield player in goal, or use a goalkeeper nursing a busted hand.

'By the time we got back to Brighton from York, my hand had swollen to quite a size,' recalls Powney. 'Glen Wilson met me at Brighton Station and took me to hospital where I had X-rays which showed the extent of what had happened. We were due to play again at home a couple of days later and all the lads were saying, "Who's going to be in goal?" My hand was still swollen out of all proportion, so it wasn't going to be me. Then I got the message: "Brian, the boss wants to see you in his office." All the lads were like, "You're going to be playing tomorrow!" So in I go and there's Clough with his big mate Taylor, and instantly I think, "Uh-oh!", because Cloughie couldn't handle certain situations on his own. There were some things he had to have Taylor's backing for. Anyway, I went in, sat down, and it was: "Would you like a drink, son?" They had a bottle of brandy on the table between them. I said, "No thanks, boss," but they said, "No, have a brandy, it'll do you good, it'll warm you up," because it was a cold day. Then Cloughie says, "Well, son, you're going to have to play tomorrow." I said, "I'm going to have to play? How am I supposed to catch a ball? I can't punch!" And they said, "You're going to have to play because we've got no alternative." I said, "Well, as far as I'm concerned, it's your responsibility. If I can't catch a ball and it goes in the back of the net, then it's got to be down to you." Then I said, "I wonder what the PFA would think of this?" And Taylor went berserk. "The fucking PFA! I've played with broken hands, I've played with this, I've played with that." You'd think he'd played with a broken neck the way he was going on. And that's what happened. I ended up playing in goal. And to this day I don't know how I did it.'

A half-decent side when playing at home, Cambridge United travelled to the Goldstone dogged by a wretched away record of two wins, two draws and fourteen defeats from eighteen league matches. Just as well, really, considering Albion were, in effect, fielding a goalkeeper with only one working hand. Powney's ten teammates did just about everything possible to prevent the ball getting through to him, even to the extent of conceding a needless 43rd-minute penalty which Bobby Ross converted to cancel out Barry Bridges's opening goal. However, from that point an attack-is-the-best-form-of-defence game plan came into play, Ronnie Welch restoring Albion's lead on the stroke of half-time. Billy McEwan and Ronnie Howell then added further goals after the break to secure a 4–1 win.

'We played some really good football out there and I only hope the crowd were entertained,' said Clough, who singled out the contributions of John Templeman, Mick Brown and his battered goalkeeper for special praise. 'When a player like Brian Powney doesn't hesitate about playing, that is a spirit you cannot buy.' Of course, Powney *had* initially hesitated, understandably so given the nature of his injuries. Still, at least Clough was praising rather than criticising him. Knowing full well that his professional playing career was entering its Indian summer, Powney chose to go along with the ruse.

Three days later, Powney was back beneath Albion's crossbar for the visit of mid-table Walsall, his right hand still heavily bandaged. Once again, Bridges opened the scoring, this time with a beautifully weighted effort after ten minutes. Four minutes after that the striker received his marching orders for the first time in an eighteen-year career spanning five clubs, dismissed by referee Peter Walters for a clumsy foul deemed to be malicious.

Throughout his managerial career, Clough wore the excellent disciplinary records of the sides he produced like a badge of honour. Officials were there to be respected, not abused. Dirty play was frowned on. Bookings were a waste of playing resources, pure and simple. For a brief period spanning March and early April 1974, during which Albion accumulated four red cards in the space of just nine matches, those high standards went out of the window. Clough thought he knew why.

'They just don't know how to tackle in the Third Division,' he lamented not only of his own players, but the entire league in general. 'I had six years at Derby and long enough in the First Division to realise the difference. Most of the lads I'm dealing with now aren't villains or anything of that sort. Much of it is over-enthusiasm. They want to do well which is understandable, but they lack the right technique. They will learn. Believe me, they will learn.'

Down to ten men and with Walsall having equalised prior to Bridges's dismissal, Albion made light of the numerical disadvantage (not to mention their goalkeeper's handicap) to score an unlikely second-half winner, Lammie Robertson timing his run to perfection to head home Peter O'Sullivan's 61st-minute corner. While Clough addressed the waiting press on the poor standards of Third Division tackling, Bridges stood outside the main players' tunnel at the Goldstone defending himself to anyone who would listen. 'I admit it was not a good tackle I made,' he confessed, 'but I couldn't believe my ears when the referee said "Off!" There's far worse than that goes unpunished.

A yellow [card], perhaps, but not "Off!" That's not what I'm about.'

And with that he disappeared from the ground to join the multi-million-strong global army watching the Eurovision Song Contest on television. Tonight, Brighton would be the light-entertainment capital of the continent. Not that Brian Clough was bothered. His focus, as per usual on a Saturday evening, was on the northbound carriageway of the M1 motorway and the turnoff for Derby.

* * *

If Lammie Robertson was the undisputed hero of the Goldstone that afternoon, then Olivia Newton-John had the honour of being Brighton's belle. The 25-year-old singer, already a major international recording star, was the one all the photographers wanted to capture as the various acts began converging on the town in the days leading up to the competition. There she was on the front cover of Saturday's *Evening Argus*, cradled horizontally in the arms of six members of the Sussex constabulary. There she was in the national newspapers, walking along the seafront in the sunshine flashing a smile as broad as the English Channel. There she was on television at the Dome, preparing to run through the first of several dress rehearsals. 'Long Live Love', so it seemed, was on course to win big for the United Kingdom and break Luxembourg's mini-run of Eurovision victories.

The UK appeared second out of the seventeen participating countries and Newton-John sang her song perfectly. But it wasn't enough. After Yugoslavia had gone seventh, the four members of Abba took to the stage, accompanied by two backing musicians and led by conductor Sven-Olof Walldorf, dressed as Napoleon for the occasion. 'If all the judges were men, which they're not, I'm sure this group would get a lot of votes,' declared BBC commentator David Vine in a very of-that-age nod to Agnetha Fältskog and Anni-Frid Lyngstad, the band's admittedly alluring female personnel. 'Waterloo' did indeed lean more towards rock than your typical Eurovision entry, yet that didn't stop those inside the auditorium and the viewing public from loving it. 'Sweden have never won, but they've surely got to be up among the reckoning with that one,' declared Vine as the Dome burst into rapturous applause at the song's close.

Despite receiving nil points from Belgium, Greece, Monaco, Italy and (somewhat bizarrely, given what a hotbed of all things Abba it would become) the UK, 'Waterloo' won at a canter. The omens had been good from the start. On arriving in Brighton the previous Tuesday, the band discovered to their amusement that they'd been booked to stay in the Napoleon suite at the elegant Grand Hotel. 'A complete coincidence, by all accounts, but a good sign and one that made us feel very welcome,' Björn Ulvaeus would recall. As the fourth-placed Newton-John informed stunned journalists that she'd never really liked 'Long Live Love' anyway and would far rather have sung a ballad, so Abba hit the town in full-on party mode, only retiring to bed once the sun had come up. Small wonder the four of them appeared a touch bleary-eyed as they posed for pictures in front of Brighton's West Pier later that morning.

The Eurovision Song Contest was good for Brighton. A combination of clement weather, a slick-looking TV show and a memorable winning entry all added up to what the *Evening Argus* described as 'a priceless publicity bonanza'. The terrorist threats made beforehand against three of the participating countries – Israel, Greece and Ireland – amounted to nothing, although that didn't stop hundreds of police and security people from flooding the town in the week leading up to the competition and on the day itself. Always a popular tourist destination among the English, local hotels also reported a significant increase in foreign tourists over the following months, a rise attributable to Brighton's Eurovision exposure. That overseas interest continues to this day.

As for Abba? Life, so the four of them have subsequently agreed, was never really the same after Brighton. The town (or city, as it's since become) became their launch pad to global stardom and, as a result, has always occupied a special place in the band's collective heart. As Benny Andersson, Abba's musical driving force, once said, 'Those were days that I will never forget and the Dome was the perfect venue for it.' Likewise, Brighton owes a debt of gratitude to Abba for the portal they opened up to a wider world. The place has certainly never forgotten them. 'Abba were brilliant,' is Norman Gall's unabashed opinion. 'And the girls! They were beautiful. I think it's lovely that it happened down here and what they went on to achieve. It helped put Brighton on the map, definitely.'

The feel-good factor surrounding the staging of the 1974 Eurovision Song Contest lasted a good deal longer than it took the riggers to break down the several thousand feet of cable running in all directions around the Dome. Clough, however, experienced little if anything of it, failing to resurface again until Good Friday, 12 April, when Southend United entertained Albion on the Essex coast. Once again Powney somehow remained resolute as two second-half goals from Ken Beamish secured a 2–0 win, their third in succession. 'We absorbed them in the first half and took them to the cleaners in the second half,' said Taylor of a performance which sent Albion back up to tenth in the table.

Easter could be a brutal time for a footballer back in the days when fixtures on consecutive days were a relatively common occurrence. Just twenty-four hours after walking out of the tunnel at Southend, Albion's players did likewise almost 200 miles away in Chesterfield. Against the former they had been by far the better side. This time Chesterfield more than matched them, edging a closely fought contest 1–0. From there it was straight back to Sussex to prepare for Easter Monday and Southend's return visit to the Goldstone. In a complete turnaround of fortunes from Good Friday, Albion lost 2–0, producing the kind of display you might expect from a team that had travelled the length and breadth of England by coach and train to play three matches in four days. A worthy excuse perhaps, but then all clubs had to put up with extreme fixture schedules in 1974.

Clough certainly wasn't about to make alibis for a performance that John Vinicombe described as 'typical end of season stuff' in the *Evening Argus*. 'It's getting pathetic again,' raged Albion's manager. 'All the old faults are coming out. Mind you, they have to come out. You can remedy faults. You have to, or they lie buried below the surface.' Unsurprisingly the consensus in the dressing room among the majority of the players was that Clough had again overstepped the mark. If anything, the team, fielding an unfit goalkeeper for the fifth game in succession and managed by two men who were rarely present at training sessions, felt they were exceeding expectations. To cap it all, April also saw John Sheridan, the man hired to take training in Clough and/or Taylor's absence, ask to be released from his contract for 'personal reasons'. No other details were given but the suspicion was that Sheridan had grown tired of being the meat in the sandwich between the managerial duo and Albion's players.

As the season limped towards its conclusion, so Clough's fluctuating moods continued to inspire and exasperate those around him in equal measure. There were days when he seemed in it for the long haul; comments such as his 'Believe me, they will learn' admonishment in the wake of Barry Bridges's red card at home to Walsall giving every indication that Albion's manager planned on sticking around and leading his squad to better things. 'I am here for a long time,' he declared to those who doubted his loyalty to the club. 'They will have to shoot me to get me out.' Then there were occasions, much like the post-Iran press conference at the Goldstone, when his sombre demeanour made it seem as if he simply didn't care.

Harry Wilson recalls one incident around this time when Clough's see-saw persona spilled over into something far nastier. 'I'd been staying at the Courtlands Hotel again with Geraldine, my wife. Clough was there as well, and he decided he wanted a drink. When you went into the Courtlands, if you turned left, there was this bar there. Clough walks in and says, "Waiter, I want this and I want that." And the waiter didn't get it for him straight away. He had other people who needed serving beforehand. Clough didn't half have a real go at him. He really belittled him. He sometimes did that in public because he liked to be seen as the most important person in a room, the main man. He used to belittle me all the time, calling me the worst full-back he'd ever seen in his life. That was bad enough, but to do it to a waiter who's going about his job the best he can was a rotten thing to do.'

Clough's aura meant very few people ever dared confront him

about such unreasonable behaviour. Comedian Les Dawson belonged in that somewhat exclusive club. It was Mike Bamber who gave his manager carte blanche to enter the dressing room at the Ringmer Restaurant one evening and introduce himself to Dawson, who was preparing to go on stage. 'Les, good to see you,' exclaimed Clough. 'How are you?' 'I'm bloody working,' came the curt reply. That was it. End of conversation. Clough rapidly withdrew and, to his credit, saw the error of his ways. 'My timing was wrong,' he later admitted. 'I should have waited until after he'd been on stage and done his work. The comedy routine is funny to those who watch it, but to those who do the performing, it's a job. Like the chairman who wanders into my dressing room or the hanger-on who ventures into my working day at the wrong time or in the wrong place, I was being told to piss off.'

Bamber got it wrong on that occasion, yet in the main Albion's chairman was getting most things right as he attempted to navigate the day-to-day running of the club through some pretty stormy seas. Only too aware by now that Clough could potentially bolt at a moment's notice, despite having four and a half years of a five-year contract still to run, Bamber did his best to ensure that the players occupied as stable and happy a working environment as possible given their manager's unpredictable behaviour. On the first Monday of every month he would treat them, their wives and the backroom staff to dinner at the Ringmer Restaurant. Social trips to local racecourses became regular occurrences. On one occasion the whole squad went by coach to London to watch boxing at the Royal Albert Hall, paid for out of the chairman's wallet. Bamber also sanctioned the post-season trip to Majorca, recognising its importance for team morale, especially with so many old faces expected to make way for new players. His decision to deny Norman Gall

LEFT 'He took us to the cleaners in those matches.' Brian Clough in his playing days with Middlesbrough, 1959.
© THE NORTHERN ECHO

BELOW The Goldstone Ground, home to Brighton & Hove Albion from 1902 until 1997.
© THE ARGUS/BRIGHTON AND HOVE STUFF

BOTTOM LEFT Comedian Norman Wisdom, an Albion board member from 1964 until 1970, entertains fans at a home game.
© THE ARGUS/BRIGHTON AND HOVE STUFF

BOTTOM RIGHT The White Hart Hotel, Lewes, where Clough and Taylor met Albion's squad for the first time. © SPENCER VIGNES

ABOVE Former Albion player turned groundsman Frankie Howard tends to his pride and joy.
© THE ARGUS/BRIGHTON AND HOVE STUFF

MIDDLE LEFT 'Who's the Geordie?' Norman Gall, Brian Clough's choice as Albion captain.
© THE ARGUS/BRIGHTON AND HOVE STUFF

MIDDLE RIGHT Peter O'Sullivan, Albion's talismanic presence throughout the '70s.
© THE ARGUS/BRIGHTON AND HOVE STUFF

BELOW LEFT Lammie Robertson, Albion's resident Scotsman.
© THE ARGUS/BRIGHTON AND HOVE STUFF

BELOW RIGHT Harry Bloom, Albion vice-chairman, confidant, negotiator, intermediary and all-round father figure.
© THE ARGUS/BRIGHTON AND HOVE STUFF

Front page of Brighton's *Evening Argus*,
1 November 1973. © THE ARGUS

Front page of Brighton's *Evening Argus*,
2 November 1973. © THE ARGUS

ABOVE 'It's tougher here than at Hartlepools where they didn't expect anything.' Brian Clough takes his place in Albion's dugout alongside Glen Wilson.
© THE ARGUS

LEFT 'He tried to manage by fear, but that's where I was perhaps different.' Long-serving Albion goalkeeper Brian Powney claims a cross.
© THE ARGUS/BRIGHTON AND HOVE STUFF

LEFT 'His loyalty to me and the club was absolutely staggering.' Steve Piper, Albion stalwart and local hero.
© THE ARGUS/BRIGHTON AND HOVE STUFF

BELOW Stompond Lane, November 1973. Brian Clough prepares to watch his players take on Walton and Hersham in the FA Cup, flanked by Albion defender Graham Howell (left) and coach John Sheridan (right). © THE ARGUS

BOTTOM LEFT 'You, son, are going to be my new Roy McFarland.' Andy Rollings gets ready for training.
© THE ARGUS/BRIGHTON AND HOVE STUFF

BOTTOM RIGHT Like father, like son. Albion's manager focuses on the job in hand, accompanied by a young Nigel Clough.
© THE ARGUS

LEFT Anything but dour. A smiling Peter Taylor ready to go it alone as Albion's new manager, July 1974.
© THE ARGUS/BRIGHTON AND HOVE STUFF

BELOW Peter Taylor welcomes striker Ricky Marlowe (right) and coach Gerry Clarke (left) to the club, July 1974.
© THE ARGUS/BRIGHTON AND HOVE STUFF

'Supporters must already be wondering whether my methods are right.' Peter Taylor watches Albion take on Southend United, December 1974. © THE ARGUS/BRIGHTON AND HOVE STUFF

BRIGHTON & HOVE ALBION

Back Row (Left to Right): Ken Gutteridge (Trainer), Graham Winstanley, Harry Wilson, Ken Tiler, Peter Grummitt, Derek Forster, Steve Piper, Jim Walker, Ian Mellor, Glen Wilson (Assistant Trainer).
Front Row (Left to Right): Ernie Machin, Fred Binney, Peter O'Sullivan, Neil Martin, Peter Taylor (Manager), Brian Daykin (Assistant Manager), Tony Towner, Phil Beal and Jerry Fell.

Albion's squad line up under Peter Taylor ahead of the 1975/76 season. © FOOTBALL MAGAZINE

ABOVE LEFT Peter O'Sullivan duels with fellow Welshman Mickey Thomas as Albion entertain Wrexham at the Goldstone, October 1975. © THE ARGUS/BRIGHTON AND HOVE STUFF

ABOVE RIGHT Albion chairman Mike Bamber with new signing Peter Ward. © THE ARGUS/BRIGHTON AND HOVE STUFF

LEFT Brian Horton, arguably Albion's greatest ever captain. © THE ARGUS/BRIGHTON AND HOVE STUFF

ABOVE 'He is the hottest property in English football.' Albion supporters let Peter Ward know what they think of him, April 1976.
© THE ARGUS/BRIGHTON AND HOVE STUFF

LEFT Peter Taylor's successor at the Goldstone, Alan Mullery, takes charge of training, August 1976.
© THE ARGUS/BRIGHTON AND HOVE STUFF

ABOVE Assembled by Clough and Taylor, inherited by Alan Mullery. Albion line up ahead of the 1976/77 season.
© THE ARGUS/BRIGHTON AND HOVE STUFF

LEFT Gary Williams beats Peter Shilton from long range to give Albion the league double over Nottingham Forest, March 1980…
© THE ARGUS

LEFT …and is immediately swamped beneath a pile of jubilant teammates.
© THE ARGUS

a pass card to watch Albion play at the Goldstone during what remained of the season remains a rare, unexplainable blot on his character. Besides Gall, every player that I spoke to during the research process for this book was quick to praise Bamber's vision and generosity. In the words of Ian Goodwin, 'He was a good businessman and he was a gentleman.'

Bamber's business sense told him Albion's crowds would have to improve significantly the following season in order to bankroll the business model he had put in place under Clough and Taylor. On Saturday 20 April, only 9,593 spectators attended the final home game of the season against Tranmere Rovers. There was, admittedly, nothing at stake for either club in terms of promotion or relegation. Even so, the figure came as a massive disappointment given Albion's newsworthiness under Clough and the fact that avoiding relegation – the number-one priority when he and Taylor arrived – had been achieved with something to spare.

All told, the average attendance at the Goldstone for the sixteen league matches spanning the visits of York and Tranmere was 12,363, well short of the desired 20,000 target. True, power disputes had played havoc with kick-off times for part of the season, but excuses don't pay the bills. The local interest was there; Bamber knew it. However, he was also beginning to realise that the big attendances would only be achieved once the public were convinced that management and players were singing from the same hymn sheet. So far, Clough and Taylor's reign had been played out in an almost constant state of flux, rumour and innuendo. There needed to be a little less conversation and a lot more action before those missing thousands were prepared to part with their hard-earned cash at the turnstiles.

One familiar face absent from the Goldstone for the

Tranmere game was Peter Brackley. 'I was getting married that day,' recalls BBC Radio Brighton's Albion correspondent. 'The day beforehand I got a message in the office saying that Brian wanted to see me. So down I went like a little schoolboy to the headmaster's office. He said, "Hey, I understand you're getting married tomorrow, young man. Well you shouldn't be. We're at home to Tranmere Rovers and you should be here." I'm looking at him thinking, "Is he joking?" And he wasn't. He meant it. In his eyes I shouldn't have been getting married on a match day.'

Even Brackley, accustomed by now to expecting the unexpected when it came to dealings with Clough, was completely sidestepped by what happened next.

'He suddenly said, "Carpets. Do you want some carpets?" Within the space of a few seconds he went from telling me off to trying to get me a deal with a local carpet company he knew to improve my new home. He was genuinely trying to help me out. That was Brian – you never knew how he was going to react, not just from one day to the next but sometimes within the blink of an eye. He would walk past you, you would say, "Hello, Brian," and he'd just carry on walking. If you saw him again the next day and you didn't speak to him, he'd say, "Not speaking to me this morning then, young man?" That was also his secret with the players, I'm sure it was. They didn't know what to expect. They'd come in at half-time having played brilliantly and either Brian or Peter would slag them off. If anything, I think Peter was probably more the bad cop. Between them, they'd keep everyone on their toes.'

With the exception of Steve Piper, Billy McEwan and Ronnie Howell (who scored from the penalty spot), every single member of the Albion team received a slagging off from Clough and/or Taylor for their performance against Tranmere.

The visitors wanted it more and were good money for their 3–1 victory against a side 'woefully short of ideas', according to John Vinicombe. 'Tranmere played as though it wasn't the end of the season for them,' said Clough. 'I didn't think we had any worthwhile chances and we never had it in midfield. Let me tell you – we are looking forward to the close season.'

In the days immediately after the lacklustre performance against Tranmere, Clough and Taylor stepped up their attempts to attract more new blood in anticipation of the impending mass summer clearout. While in the process of signing Ian Mellor from Norwich City, the pair had been alerted to the presence of two strapping central defenders plying their trade in the reserves at Carrow Road. Steve Govier, aged twenty-two, had been unable to hold down a first-team spot since City's promotion to the top flight of English football in 1972. Andy Rollings, three years his junior, was in a similar predicament. Both had joined as fifteen-year-olds and, with almost 300 appearances between them in the second XI, were to all intents and purposes going nowhere.

'I was in a snooker club when I got the call,' remembers Rollings. 'The lady who served teas and stuff behind the counter said, "Is Andy Rollings in here?" This, of course, was long before mobile phones. So I went over to take the phone and it was someone at Carrow Road saying I had to go down there as quickly as I could. When I arrived, Steve [Govier] was already there. I said, "What's happening?" and he goes, "Cloughie's in there. He wants to take Spider [Ian Mellor], me and you to Brighton." Anyway, I got called in, and there Clough was, sat behind [Norwich manager] John Bond's desk. He just waved this bit of paper at me and said, "Right, son, sign this. It'll be the best thing you've ever done." That was his opening line.'

At which point Peter Taylor appeared and asked Rollings to go for a walk with him around the Carrow Road pitch. For the next half an hour he told the raw defender all about their plans to turn Albion into the next Derby County. Unsure what to do and in need of guidance regarding his contractual position at Norwich, Rollings asked to speak to his manager. John Bond, it emerged, didn't want him to go, but with new players expected to arrive couldn't guarantee the teenager any first-team football either.

'The moment he said that, I made my mind up,' adds Rollings. 'Norwich were in the First Division then and Brighton the Third, but this meant going to play football for Brian Clough. Having someone like him as your manager persuaded me it was the right thing to do. When Peter and I got back from walking round the pitch, Clough said, "You, son, are going to be my new Roy McFarland," giving all this praise to a wet-behind-the-ears nineteen-year-old. That was amazing to hear because Roy McFarland had been the lynchpin of his defence at Derby and everyone knew what a great player he was. I said, "Mr Clough, I normally have a chat with my dad about things like this," because there were no agents or anyone like that back then to advise you. He went, "Son, you are nineteen. You're a man now. You make your own decisions." I didn't have a clue what was in the contract. I didn't have a clue what the terms were. I signed without even knowing what I was going to get paid. I look back now and think, "Whoa! What was I doing?" But it turned out to be the best move I ever made.'

Ian Mellor had cost £40,000 on his own. Now Steve Govier and Andy Rollings combined were about to set the club back another £25,000. That took Albion's spending on transfer fees under Clough and Taylor to approximately £175,000, a substantial sum for the vast majority of clubs in 1974, let alone one in the Third Division. The time was rapidly approaching when several players would need to be sold in order to balance the books. But first, there was one game of the 1973/74 season still left to play.

9

WHEN TWO BECOME ONE

Bristol Rovers had already won promotion from the Third Division by the time Brighton & Hove Albion came to the West Country for what, in the case of both clubs, would be the forty-sixth and final match of the 1973/74 season. A goalless draw away to Southend United the previous weekend had been enough to seal it – the ultimate irony for a side that went twenty-eight games unbeaten from the start of the campaign, scoring goals for fun in the process. However, the league title was still up for grabs. Oldham Athletic and York City, in second and third place respectively and also both promoted, had games in hand and could still pip Rovers to the divisional trophy. Bruce Bannister, Alan Warboys and their teammates had been at the summit for months, and felt they deserved the title. That in mind, there would be no easing off against Albion. Another 8–2 was probably out of the question but, given the events that had played out at the Goldstone Ground on 1 December 1973, you can see why Rovers' players and supporters fully expected to take maximum points from the visitors.

For the majority of the Albion side, playing at Eastville on 27

April 1974 was about dignity and self-respect. 'We knew there would be a big crowd round the old greyhound track that used to circle the pitch there, and we knew given what had happened at the Goldstone a few months before that they'd expect us to get smashed again,' says Lammie Robertson. 'The thing was we were determined not to get beat. It didn't matter where they were in the league. We were that determined.' Several of the players boarded the team coach knowing, or with at least a hunch, that it was likely to be their last appearance in an Albion shirt, given Clough and Taylor's desire to sign new blood and the unsustainable size of the current squad. Brian Powney, one of those dropped following the 8–2 debacle, was among them.

'I'd already made up my mind about my future, but I discovered before the game that I wasn't going to be kept on anyway,' says Powney. 'We'd heard that he [Clough] would be taking the team, or at least *a* team, to Majorca on a close-season jolly. I needed to know if I was going because I'd got divorced that year and had a son to look after. My mum used to have him while I was at football but I had to plan ahead and make childcare arrangements. So I said, "Boss, there's a rumour going round that the team's going to Majorca. Can you tell me whether I'll be going?" And he said, "No, son, you won't be going." I knew then that was it. But, as I said, I'd decided to go by then anyway.'

On the day of the Bristol Rovers match, Powney witnessed an encounter involving Brian Clough comparable to the one Harry Wilson had recently experienced at the Courtlands Hotel (as recalled in the previous chapter). The episode stirred emotions within Albion's long-serving goalkeeper similar to Norman Gall's 'time to get out quick' reaction following his career-curtailing match at York in March and the shoddy way he'd been treated by the club afterwards. 'We went down by coach and stopped at this hotel somewhere near Bristol for a pre-match meal,' says Powney. 'Clough met us there having come down from Derby or wherever he'd been. We went into the restaurant, sat down, and started to order. I'll always remember the woman maître d' coming over, and she said, "Oh, Mr Clough, how would your players like their steaks?" And he goes, "I'm not interested in your fucking steaks!" I mean, why be like that? There was no need for it at all. It was just nasty, but that's what he was. He could do it to anyone, not just his players. You can't go to work in an environment like that.'

According to *Evening Argus* reporter John Vinicombe, Rovers supporters were literally rubbing their hands together in anticipation of what was to come as the teams went through their pre-match warm-up routines, pointing at Powney and making him the subject of terrace chants featuring the number eight. Once the match began, it was all one-way traffic. Except, to everyone's surprise, it was the visitors doing the pressing. Robertson opened the scoring after eighteen minutes and, had some of his teammates not been found wanting in the shooting department, Albion could well have led by three or four goals at half-time. Rovers, realising what was at stake, duly woke up during the second period and equalised through a late Bruce Bannister penalty. And that's the way it stayed. A season which had begun with Albion taking a 1–0 lead away from home before having to settle for a 1–1 draw ended eight months later in a mirror image.

'My hand was still playing me up during that game,' adds Powney. 'It had only been three or four weeks since I'd broken it. I'd been playing all that time as well, so it hadn't had a chance to heal properly. We came under a lot of pressure. I'd punched two or three balls and every time I did it my hand was killing me. But I had a cracking game. I almost got down to the penalty as well. I got a hand to it but could only push it inside the post. I so nearly saved the bastard. And do you know what he [Clough] did after the game? He came up to me and said, "Well played, son," and smacked the side of my face. I thought, "You bastard." That still pisses me off, looking back.'

Today, rules stipulate that each season must culminate with the final round of English league fixtures kicking off on the same day and at the same time. In 1974, that wasn't the case. Although most clubs did complete their fixture programmes on the last scheduled Saturday of the season, there were always some with games in hand left to play, which could take anything up to two or three weeks to fulfil. Three defeats and a draw from their last four matches saw Albion plunge from a respectable tenth in the table to a disappointing eighteenth on the evening of the Bristol Rovers match. Once all the stragglers had come in, they then sank one further place to finish nineteenth overall.

Still, it could have been worse. John Vinicombe wrote that although 'it won't look very good in the final table, if Clough and Taylor hadn't arrived in the nick of time the last rites might have been performed weeks ago'. Clough had some trouble later in life remembering where Albion had come in the league. 'We spent an absolute fortune, got knocked out of the FA Cup by an amateur side and all we managed to do was finish fourth from bottom,' he grumbled in 1990. Just as well he was wrong, otherwise Albion would have been relegated – Rochdale, Southport, Shrewsbury and Cambridge all sinking into Division Four having taken 21, 28, 31 and 35 points respectively.

Albion's toll of 43 points meant they ended up sixth from bottom in a tightly contested league; only 9 points separating Grimsby Town in sixth position from Port Vale in twentieth.

For the record, Bristol Rovers missed out on the title by a single point to Oldham Athletic. Had Bannister and Warboys been in the zone on that final Saturday of the season, then the trophy would have gone to Eastville. Instead, Brian Powney, appearing in his 386th and last Albion game, earned redemption of sorts at the expense of the club that had done so much to bury his career five months previously.

The close season is, traditionally, the time of the year when football clubs become ghost towns. All the games have been played out. The employees – manager, assistant manager, coaches, players, office staff, physio, even the groundsman – take off for a well-earned break, leaving behind empty stadiums and facilities. For a few brief weeks, no one comes and no one goes, except perhaps an overworked club secretary and the postman. Then everyone returns and the circus swings into action all over again.

Not so the Goldstone Ground from late April through to early June 1974. No sooner had the team arrived back from Bristol than preparations were being made for the following Friday's testimonial match against an All Stars XI in honour of Joe Wilson, who, aged sixty-five, was finally retiring after thirty-eight years' service to the club as a player and in various backroom roles. Albion's players were told that after the game a list of names would be pinned on the notice board in the home dressing room. If your name was on it, then you were going to Majorca on the post-season bonding trip. If it wasn't, you weren't.

The Wednesday happened to be striker Pat Hilton's twentieth birthday. Several of Albion's younger players went out to celebrate and, inevitably, one pub led to another. Not so inevitable was what occurred after the pubs had shut. 'Micky Brown,

Pat Hilton, Terry Norton and myself were all heading home in a car,' recalls Steve Piper. 'We happened to have a football with us, and as we were driving past the Goldstone someone said, "Let's go and have a kick-around." So we kicked the ball over the wall, climbed over one by one, went out on the pitch and started playing football. But then things got a bit out of hand. I put my hand through some glass where [groundsman] Frankie Howard's hut was and cut myself. Pat Hilton fell off the gate by the hut, cracked his head, so there's blood coming out of him too. We were all absolutely legless. And then we heard the police sirens.'

The Goldstone was fairly unique compared to other English football grounds in that it had a long line of houses overlooking its lopsided eastern terrace boasting uninterrupted views of the pitch. On match days, the majority of front-facing windows (and, when the weather was kind, gardens) would be occupied by residents observing the action free of charge. It was one of those residents who, during the early hours of Thursday 2 May, called the police to report some kind of disturbance inside the darkened stadium.

Within minutes, PC Peter Sims, a dog handler with Sussex Police, was screeching to a halt outside the ground. In the gloom, he observed a shadowy figure sliding down a wall. 'You're nicked,' bellowed PC Sims, or words to that effect. The shadowy figure started begging for mercy, all the while insisting that he was in fact an Albion player. Sims was having none of it and, once back-up had arrived, the suspect was carted off to a local police station where his identity was revealed as none other than Steve Piper. 'He was pretty good about it really,' the long-retired PC Sims told me many years later. 'He knew he was in the shit.'

Piper was, indeed, in the shit – as were his three teammates, also caught red-handed. 'I was perhaps the worst culprit, to be honest,' he admits. 'I was pissed out of my head. After the police came with the dogs and arrested us I didn't want to go home. I was distraught and worried what my parents would think. It was on the local TV news the next day that there had been a break-in at the Goldstone and that Brighton football players were involved, although they didn't say who it was. It was on the front page of the *Evening Argus* as well. I just felt horrible.'

Ever since the game turned professional, football clubs have used bad behaviour as a convenient way of offloading unwanted players. As the much-travelled manager Harry Redknapp once admitted, 'If a great player and a crap player commit the same crime, the club finds a reason to keep the great player and uses the transgression as an excuse to sack the crap one. Sorry, but it's true.'

The Goldstone transgression gave Albion enough ammunition to axe three fringe players – Hilton, former youth team captain Norton and defender Brown – from its already bloated squad. All were given their marching orders within days of the incident taking place. Piper, however, was retained without so much as an official club reprimand.

'I was in the team and worth money,' says Piper. 'The rest were sort of bit players. They were sacked almost immediately. About three or four days later I met Clough at Gatwick Airport when we were going out to Majorca. That was the first time I'd seen or spoken to him since it had happened. He called me over and said, "Steve, you stupid kid, what were you doing something like that for? Don't ever let it happen again." He didn't fine me or anything. He must have liked me otherwise I'd have been out the door in a flash like the others.'

Steve Piper was heading for Majorca, which meant his name had been on the list posted at the Goldstone after Joe Wilson's testimonial match. But there were several players conspicuous by their absence. It wouldn't be long before the significance of that list became horribly apparent.

Ken Beamish learned he was being made surplus to requirements from an unlikely source. 'Normally a club will come to you and let you know where you stand in the scheme of things, but I didn't know what was happening or where I stood at Brighton,' he told me almost thirty-five years later, while reflecting on his time as an Albion player. 'I had a neighbour who lived next to me in the Saltdean part of town. He came up to me one afternoon and said, "Have you heard anything?" I said I hadn't, and he replied, "You're on the transfer list." And I was! He'd heard it on Radio Brighton. They never even told me. In circumstances like that it was easy to leave. Soon afterwards, [Blackburn manager] Gordon Lee was on the phone and I signed for them at London Euston Station on that big wide concourse there. I never spoke to anyone at Brighton between the end of the season and signing for Blackburn. That was the disappointing thing, because I'd enjoyed my time at Brighton and made some good friends there. It was a sad ending to a happy period in my life.'

John Templeman and Lammie Robertson didn't even have to wait until after Joe Wilson's testimonial to discover they were being chopped from Albion's payroll. 'The strange thing about it was I'd played most of the games from when they [Clough and Taylor] had joined right up until the end of the season,' says Templeman. 'I'd been struggling with a minor hamstring injury when they arrived, so I was basically doing no heavy training during the week, just light training the day before a game and then playing. We played away at Bristol Rovers and then had Joe's testimonial, which we were all looking forward to. I got a phone call during the early part of that week asking me to be at the ground to speak to Peter Taylor. When I got there, he told me Exeter City were interested in taking myself and Lammie in part-exchange for [Exeter striker] Fred Binney. I still had a year on my contract left at Brighton and didn't want to go. Taylor said, "If you don't go to Exeter City, then you won't get another league club." I thought that was a bit strong. Mike Bamber was sat at the other end of the table in the boardroom and he said, "Well, Peter's the manager. What he says goes." So he obviously wasn't going to offer any support for me. I said to them, "I've been here eight years, I didn't cost a penny, and I probably haven't been on the same wage level as some of the so-called big-name players that the club has signed. I've played a fair amount of games and I think you're being a bit unfair by threatening me with this." And Peter repeated, "Well, if you don't go to Exeter, then you'll never ever get another league club." I was planning to get married that summer. I decided I wasn't going to change his mind and would only be putting myself in a very vulnerable position by staying. So, reluctantly, I went.'

'They wanted Fred Binney, who had scored something like thirty-five goals at Exeter the previous season,' adds Lammie Robertson. 'John Newman, Exeter's manager, wanted me and John Templeman. I – we – could have said no, but in that situation what's the point? My philosophy was if you're not wanted, you go, but in doing so you make sure you make some money. So I made sure that I went on some decent money. To be honest, I was pissed off. I'd gone to Brighton when they were in the Second Division. Now I was back in the Fourth Division where I'd been with Halifax a few years before. I thought, "I don't like this." But John Newman wanted to build a team to get promotion and he sold Exeter to me. I'd loved Brighton, though. Leaving was hard, I can tell you.'

Right-back Graham Howell, not on the list, was released and ended up at Cambridge United. Ronnie Howell (no relation), memorably dropped after his hat-trick at Charlton in January for disobeying Clough's instructions and speaking to the press, departed for Tooting and Mitcham. Barry Bridges bade farewell to Sussex and moved to South Africa, where he played for the Highlands Park club in Johannesburg. Eddie Spearritt and George Ley, frozen out of the first XI after the Bristol Rovers mauling, were finally offloaded to Carlisle United and Gillingham respectively.

Albion's night of the long knives was a painful experience for many familiar faces around the Goldstone, the manner of their dismissals often rude and callous. According to Clough and Taylor, the decision over which players to retain and who to cut loose was made as early as February. To release several without so much as a thank you reflects badly not just on Clough and Taylor's legacies but also, to a lesser extent, that of Mike Bamber, the person who otherwise did so much to foster a happy environment within the club. None of them, so it seems, appeared to regard it as their responsibility. Or perhaps it was more a case, to paraphrase the late American writer and humorist Helen Rowland, of men never knowing how to say goodbye.

Out in Majorca, those players who had made the list remained oblivious to the extent of the bloodshed back home. There was a gut feeling among some that a few of the absentees might not be around when the squad returned home but, hey, that's what tends to happen at football clubs during the close season; players come, players go. Mobile phones and social media didn't exist. The players were, to all intents and purposes, cocooned in sunnier climes. But there were clues.

'Quite a few of the players who came on that trip we'd never met before,' says Steve Piper. 'That's when Ian Mellor turned up. Then there was Andy Rollings and Steve Govier. Fred Binney arrived a couple of days later when we were already over there. He brought a mate along with him as well, as you do! I think that may have been the first we heard about John Templeman and Lammie Robertson leaving the club. So we knew changes were afoot. To be honest, it was just great being out there relaxing and having a few beers in the sun. Cloughie, Peter Taylor, Mike Bamber and the directors stayed in one hotel and we were in another, so we didn't really see much of them. I really enjoyed it.'

Inevitably it was Cala Millor, the number-one foreign holiday destination for both Clough and Taylor, that played host to Albion's mutating squad during their Majorcan break. The resort, situated on the Spanish island's east coast, was where they had taken Derby County's players on several trips in the past and they would continue to frequent it while in charge of Nottingham Forest in the future. It was while staying there in 1972 that County's players heard they had won the Football League championship after Leeds United and Liverpool failed to win their respective games in hand over Wolverhampton Wanderers and Arsenal. 'Nobody ever wanted to miss out on a trip there, whether in the close season or in mid-season when we just fancied a break from the old routine,' Clough wrote in his first autobiography. 'We've enjoyed some of the finest times of our lives in Cala Millor.'

Small wonder when your accommodation is of the five-star variety, as was the case for Albion's managerial duo, chairman and directors in May 1974. The players, however, had to make do with three-star surroundings under the watchful eye of Joe Wilson's brother, Glen, handed the thankless task of what amounted to herding cats. At some stage among the merriment, two friendlies had been arranged against local amateur teams. Just minutes before the second match kicked off, Clough ordered in a round of drinks, one for each member of the squad. Tony Towner was handed a brandy, even though he'd never tasted brandy before. 'That was a bit of a shock,' he recalls. Yet once the action got underway, no matter how average the opposition was, the mood changed.

'You did get the feeling that once you stepped onto the field, it was like totally serious,' says Andy Rollings. 'We were playing on these dusty, bumpy pitches, lethal really when you're talking about professional athletes. The first match we won something like 6–0. I played in that, then for the second I was on the bench. They wanted to try out some different permutations. This particular pitch was cut into the side of a hill. You had one side in the shade where the dugouts were while the other was in the sunshine. I started to have a little warm-up, so I went round the other side to do it. I wasn't sunbathing, just trying to catch a few rays. About twenty minutes before half-time I came back and Glen Wilson said, "Get yourself stripped, you're going on." So on I went. We came in at half-time, I think it was 1–0 to us, and he [Clough] suddenly goes, "You, you're off" to me. He subbed the sub! He didn't say why, so I didn't ask. I got showered, we finished the game, came back to the hotel and started having a few beers. Glen was there, so I said, "What was that all about then, me getting subbed?" And he went, "That'll teach you to go and sunbathe over the other side of the ground, won't it?" Anyone else would have probably called me back round to the dugouts at the time and said, "You don't do that." But that was Cloughie's way of doing things.'

So began a crash-course among the new recruits in how to deal with Brian Clough. 'A lot of us were in the same boat on that trip because we'd only just joined,' adds Rollings. 'You're trying to find your feet, work out what's expected of you, how you address the manager, that kind of thing. We were up at their five-star hotel one night where there was a band playing. It was like a social night. There was a bar at one end with a dance floor, and as you walked through the room there were these little alcoves along the side. I was walking along, heading for the toilet, and Clough was in one of these alcoves with Taylor and a group of people. As I walked by, close enough to be in earshot, I hear, "Hey, son, when you walk past next time say, 'Hello, boss.'" He'd had a right few sherbets, as you can imagine. The band had been playing but everything went quiet at that moment, it was such a loud shout. I was absolutely dreading walking past on my way back. In the end I literally stopped right by the alcove and went, "Alright, boss?" And everybody went quiet again, even the band, just to see if I would say it.'

'We were there a week, drank some beer, got to know some of the new lads, played some football – I think one of the teams we played against may even have been a bunch of waiters – and then came back,' says Steve Piper. 'And I – we – never saw Clough again after we left to fly home.'

* * *

It has often been said that Brian Clough was the best manager England never had. When it comes to the best manager England has ever had, the shortlist also tends to stop at one name:

Sir Alf Ramsey. His eleven-year tenure speaks for itself; won sixty-one, drawn twenty-seven, lost seventeen – and that at a time when the well-worn phrase 'There are no easy games in international football' actually carried some weight. Ramsey's CV is even more remarkable considering his reign began with a 5–2 reverse against France followed by a 2–1 loss to Scotland. Under him, England won the World Cup in 1966. Their failure to progress beyond the quarter-finals four years later was only viewed as such when measured against his own high standards. 'I rate him, by some distance, the greatest manager England have ever had,' Jimmy Greaves once said. That's the same Jimmy Greaves who was famously overlooked by Ramsey for a place in the 1966 World Cup final team against West Germany. When the man widely regarded as your sworn enemy makes that kind of declaration, then you had to be good.

Rather than hold a grudge, Greaves had plenty of time for Ramsey, which is more than can be said for certain Football Association officials and members of the press. Ramsey could be cold, arrogant, aloof, rude – and that was when England won. So long as England kept winning, Ramsey remained relatively secure in his job. When their form deserted them, as it did during the qualification process for the 1974 World Cup finals, he became horribly exposed. On Wednesday 17 October 1973, England had thirty-five shots on goal at Wembley compared to two by Poland, yet it was the visitors who qualified at the expense of their hosts courtesy of a 1–1 draw. That evening, Polish goalkeeper Jan Tomaszewski, labelled 'a clown' by Clough in his capacity as an ITV pundit, pulled off a series of miraculous saves to deny Ramsey's increasingly desperate team. In doing so, he helped usher England's knight of the realm one step closer to the door marked exit.

It took six months for the axe to fall, after which Ramsey was replaced by Joe Mercer, the former Aston Villa and Manchester City manager. Mercer publicly declared that he wanted only 'to hold the reins for a few weeks', meaning the hunt was on for a new, long-term incumbent. Various names were mentioned in the press, including Jimmy Armfield of Bolton Wanderers, Bobby Robson at Ipswich Town and Burnley's Jimmy Adamson. 'It will be interesting to know if Brian Clough, one of Ramsey's severest critics in his time, now offers himself to the firing line,' speculated Geoffrey Green of *The Times*. Even if he had, the likelihood of Clough becoming England's manager at that point was low to non-existent. Not only did the FA consider him to be a loose cannon, but nineteenth place in the Third Division was hardly going to set pulses racing among those charged with appointing Ramsey's successor.

Ultimately, it boiled down to a logical choice. Under Don Revie, Leeds United had become one of the major powerhouses in English football. Promoted from the Second Division in 1964, the Yorkshire club finished second, second, fourth and fourth in their first four seasons back in the top flight, losing the 1965 FA Cup final to Liverpool. In 1968, they won the League Cup, becoming Football League champions for the first time twelve months later. Over the next four years they finished second in the league three times, won the FA Cup in 1972 and came runners-up in the same competition twice. Ramsey's sacking just happened to coincide with the Football League championship heading back to Elland Road at the end of April 1974. Their combative, win-at-all-costs mentality throughout much of that time made Leeds revered throughout Yorkshire's central belt, yet widely reviled elsewhere. However, under Revie there was no denying United's effectiveness. By the time they captured that second championship, Leeds were even starting to win a few friends outside Yorkshire with the quality of their football.

On 3 July 1974, it was finally confirmed that Revie would be leaving Leeds to take over as manager of the England national team. That left a vacancy to be filled at Elland Road – an extremely attractive one for any ambitious manager, given what Revie was leaving behind. The general consensus among United's players and supporters was that the job would go to one of their own. Johnny Giles had blossomed into arguably the finest central midfield player in the country and, at thirty-three, was at the right age to take the step up into management. Although Giles played down the speculation, he did admit Revie had offered him the position. However, that decision wasn't Revie's to make. Instead, Leeds United's board advertised the job, believing they needed an experienced hand with a big personality capable of leading a team packed full of international players through the forthcoming 1974/75 European Cup campaign. Revie's legacy was immense, and his successor would need broad shoulders to carry the weight of the empire he had created.

Sir Alf Ramsey fitted the bill. So too did Freddie Goodwin, the former Leeds United player who had impressed in the lower leagues at, of all places, Brighton & Hove Albion (signing Eddie Spearritt and Peter O'Sullivan, among others), before moving up the ladder to take charge at Birmingham City. Nobody mentioned Brian Clough's name because Brian Clough, as he was fond of reminding people, despised almost everything Leeds United stood for. His ongoing feud with Revie had become one of the game's great soap operas. Clough hated the boorish way his players went about their business; wasting time, haranguing referees, bullying teams with excessive physical force, overreacting to challenges. Then there were the widespread accusations – never proven, it should be said – of match-fixing which followed Leeds around. Clough was convinced that Revie sought to influence opponents and officials with bribes. 'They angered and offended me to such an extent that I took every opportunity to condemn their cynicism which, for me, devalued so much of what they achieved and the marvellous football of which they were capable – a high level of skill that I, like millions, admired,' Clough wrote in his first autobiography. 'Leeds, in those days, cheated – and I was more than happy to draw people's attention to the fact.'

Clough's anti-Leeds tirades included his August 1973 attack from the pages of the *Sunday Express* calling for Revie to be fined and United demoted to the Second Division, having been found guilty of 'persistent misconduct on the field' while playing Birmingham City. It had been that article which led to the FA charge of 'bringing the game into disrepute', thus drawing him into the unlikely orbit of Brighton & Hove Albion, the out-of-work Clough urgently needing employment in case the hearing found against him. Remarkably, considering everything he had said and written about them, Leeds United were now about to make an audacious attempt to take him away from the Goldstone.

It was Manny Cussins, the Yorkshire club's chairman, whose decision it was to seek out their nemesis. He had been impressed by the show of loyalty from Derby's players and supporters towards Clough following his resignation as County manager in October 1973. 'It has to be a special person to inspire devotion like that,' said Cussins, who believed Clough could win hearts and minds at Leeds providing he turned on the charm and played down his previous criticism of the club. By 16 July, a shortlist of four people had emerged – Clough,

Jimmy Armfield, Motherwell manager Ian St John and Bobby Robson. Clough, it was understood, was the board's first choice. 'His forthright approach is a quality which has more than once made him an unpopular and controversial figure in the world of football,' acknowledged Don Warters of the *Yorkshire Evening Post*. 'But it is also one which some people can admire, especially Yorkshiremen.'

By mid-July, the vast majority of football clubs, then as now, will have long since resumed pre-season training in readiness for the rigours ahead. In 1974, Albion were no different. There was, however, still no sign of Clough around the Goldstone. While the players went to work shedding those extra few pounds accumulated during the summer, their manager remained in Cala Millor on a family holiday. Once word reached Clough of Leeds United's interest, he returned immediately to England to speak with Cussins. 'I saw what went on when you left Derby,' United's chairman told him. 'I want the kind of manager whose players are prepared to go on strike for him.'

'Those first words from Cussins were brilliant,' Clough later admitted. 'They told me what I wanted to hear.' But there was more to it than Cussins simply massaging Clough's ego. This wasn't Iran – it was Leeds United, the opportunity to inherit a team of talents preparing to strut their stuff in the European Cup. The way in which Derby County had been eliminated from the competition at the hands of Juventus during the 1972/73 season amid rumours of bribery and corruption left a scar on Clough. 'I wanted another crack at it as soon as possible, and Leeds offered me that chance on a plate,' he said. 'The club had already qualified by winning the league championship the previous season. It was too good an opportunity to miss.'

On the morning of Monday 22 July, Clough, Mike Bamber

and Albion vice-chairman Harry Bloom met Cussins together with Leeds director Bob Roberts at the Courtlands Hotel to put the finishing touches to a deal that had been provisionally agreed late the previous evening. Peter Taylor, who Clough and Cussins both presumed would also be moving to Elland Road, made it a six-sided affair. An annual salary of £40,000 was offered to be split between the two men, with £22,000 going to Clough (£10,000 more than he was getting at Brighton). Taylor, however, was still in two minds about quitting for Leeds. Prior to the meeting, Bamber had taken him aside and asked if he would be prepared to stay on in sole charge at the Goldstone. Taylor was interested but still went into the meeting with his options open.

If anything, the way the negotiations went only convinced Taylor that his future lay in Sussex, not Yorkshire. 'Cussins was asking us to pack in the south coast and move up there at our own expense,' he later complained. 'That was no good to me. I said if he wanted us that badly, there had to be more than a flat wage. His answer astonished me: "You're in Europe next season. What more do you want?" What a way to talk to people. That finished me.'

As Clough shook hands with Cussins on a deal, Taylor informed those present that he would be staying put. Clough and Cussins were furious. The meeting broke up in confusion with the six men adjourning from their meeting room in the hotel's basement. While ascending the stairs, United's chairman tried discreetly to ask Bamber whether he thought Clough could handle the Leeds job on his own. At which point Clough, clearly spooked by events, decided to take matters into his own hands.

'He realised that his dream chance could be slipping away,'

reflected Bamber on what happened next. 'Suddenly he nipped past us into the waiting arms of the press and television. Before anyone else could get a word in, he announced to the whole world, "Gentleman, I've just been appointed manager of Leeds United." It was an amazing thing to do because nothing had been finalised. Cussins found himself with a fait accompli.'

'When I said I wasn't going with him, Leeds were ready to call the whole thing off,' Taylor maintained. 'Only Brian could have got away with a thing like that. Once he'd made the announcement, Cussins could hardly contradict it, could he?'

For the time being, the waiting media (alerted by Clough, ever the opportunist, to the location of what were meant to be secret negotiations) remained oblivious to the discord that had arisen as the deal came to its supposed conclusion. Brian Clough was Leeds United's new manager, with Peter Taylor remaining at Brighton & Hove Albion – that was the story. Clough certainly wasn't about to let on how close things had come to breaking down. There was simply too much at stake for him personally. For years he brushed aside any suggestion that Taylor's decision to remain almost scuppered the whole deal. In his first autobiography, published in 1994, Clough wrote, 'Cussins and Roberts were a bit taken aback when I told them Taylor was not coming. But there was never any hint of them developing cold feet or pulling out. Cussins insisted, "You're our man – you are the one we want."' By the time his second autobiography was released in 2002, that dismissive air towards Taylor had made way for a more combative edge, Clough appearing keen to shift the blame for some of his own career faults. 'Just as it was his initial instinct for us to walk away from all we had created at Derby, it was Pete who broke up our partnership. I went; he stayed down south.' Then there were the financial jibes. 'I discovered Mike Bamber had offered him more money to stay and I always knew Pete fancied a crack at management in his own right,' he wrote. 'Money would have got Pete to Leeds. It might have cost their chairman Manny Cussins a few grand but money could have lured him to Elland Road.'

Had Taylor gone to Leeds, then he would in fact have virtually doubled his improved salary at Brighton & Hove Albion. Anyhow, it was never just about the money. Taylor had put down roots in the Brighton area. He loved living by the coast. His daughter had got a job as a journalist on a local paper. Then there was the question of loyalty, not so much to the club, but to Bamber. 'Nothing had been pre-arranged between myself and the Brighton board, as Brian believed, but I felt the job was only half done and that we owed loyalty to Bamber for signing us under the shadow of a disciplinary commission,' he wrote in *With Clough By Taylor*.

> Not only that, but he had kept his promises; cash for transfers, no interference, accommodation in the best hotels, a new Mercedes coach for team travel. Brighton treated us wonderfully and I wasn't prepared to discard them even for the champions of England, but I could read Brian's ambitious mind. He saw himself jumping straight from the Third Division into the management of a European Cup side. He saw himself leading out Leeds United at Wembley in the following month's Charity Shield match against Liverpool. He was bitter when I said, 'Count me out.' After nine years, the partnership was over.

Taylor's decision to go it alone was the culmination of a resentment that had been simmering for years. It began early in 1971, when the indigestion he had occasionally been experiencing turned out to be a heart murmur. Although Clough arranged for him to be admitted to Derby Royal Infirmary, he visited Taylor just once during his six weeks convalescing. Later that year came the discovery of Sam Longson's alleged secret £5,000 pay rise for Clough. Taylor felt massively betrayed. 'Brian told me nothing about it, nor did Sam Longson. I saw the contract by accident on [Derby assistant secretary] Stuart Webb's desk. I took Sam out into the middle of the pitch before a league match and asked him to explain. All he could say was, "How did you find out?" I told him that was a disgusting question. How could he reward Brian and not me when I'd suffered a heart attack running the club while he was away doing his television shows? Brian apologised and helped make sure I got a rise as well. He promised to make it up in other ways but the damage was done. I'd thought I could trust him with my life but already I was having doubts.'

Brighton & Hove Albion could so easily have represented a new start for the pair of them. Instead, they ended up rarely seeing each other. Taylor had his scouting work to do; Clough was rarely around other than on match days, and even then his presence was never guaranteed. Clough sensed Taylor 'was not quite as full of himself as usual, or particularly happy in his work'. He criticised the quality of Taylor's recruits. 'The players you're saddling me with down here can't fucking play at all,' Clough raged at one point, possibly in an attempt to apportion blame for Albion's inconsistent form. Taylor became hurt and disappointed by the way his old friend was treating the club as much as himself. 'I realised that he wasn't the person I thought,' Taylor later confided. 'He was walking all over Bamber, who couldn't do a thing about it. Brian should have repaid his loyalty. The chairman had taken us on with the FA inquiry hanging over our heads. Brian shouldn't have accepted the job if he didn't want it.'

After a series of minor tremors, the ground between Clough and Taylor had finally cracked as a result of the first major earthquake in their relationship. In later years, having initially built bridges at Nottingham Forest, there would be further minor tremors followed by a second big one. The relationship then became poisonous, irreconcilable. In July 1974, it hadn't got to that stage. They were going their separate ways professionally but would continue, very occasionally, to talk privately while referring to one another civilly in public.

Bamber had pulled off a coup in persuading Taylor to stay. However, it wasn't long before the atmosphere around the Courtlands Hotel began to turn sour. No sooner had Clough used his initiative and spoken to the media than Bamber declared Albion's intention to sue the Yorkshire club for 'enticement and withdrawal of an agreement by the two Leeds directors'. In a terse statement, Bamber announced:

> Leeds United Football Club, through their chairman Mr Manny Cussins, made an illegal approach for Brian Clough last Friday week and they had a secret meeting last Monday. Brighton football club did not know of any of these events until I received a phone call on the Saturday evening asking me to meet Brian Clough and Manny Cussins at London Airport on Saturday lunchtime. This I refused to do, informing them to come to Brighton if they wished to see me. They came yesterday evening. The board of Brighton directors did not wish to release Brian Clough from his contract which had approximately four years and three months to run. But after long negotiations between Manny Cussins, Bob Roberts, Brighton vice-chairman

Harry Bloom and myself, a compensation figure of £75,000 plus a friendly match with Leeds to be played sometime at the Brighton ground was agreed on. The two Leeds directors have subsequently withdrawn from the above agreement and have announced that Brian Clough is their new manager. Brighton have instructed their solicitors to issue writs immediately.

When pressed further, Bamber's language became a good deal stronger. 'I shook hands with Mr Cussins on the compensation deal last night but he withdrew just one hour later. I did not shake hands with him or Mr Roberts this morning. They are not the sort of men whose hands I would like to shake. I am amazed that a club of Leeds' standing should act like this.'

As Bamber spoke, so Clough, standing nearby, was doing his best to answer a barrage of questions from journalists. Ever the propagandist, he also took time to field a phone call from the *Yorkshire Evening Post*, aware perhaps of the need to extend an olive branch in the direction of the county's largest city. 'I'm prepared to discuss the team, the backroom staff – a wonderful bunch, and that's a great comfort – indeed anything relevant to my job, but my wage is my own business,' he told the newspaper's sports editor Mike Casey. 'What I want to impress on you is that I'm coming home to Yorkshire. I was born in Middlesbrough, the same as Don Revie, and I'm coming to do a job. That job is to keep Leeds at the top of the tree. I know there's been a lot of anti-Clough talk in the West Riding, but it doesn't worry me. Alright, I've spoken my mind more than once, but that's because I'm honest. I like to get things out in the open. That's the way I live. I can't change that. But what my critics forget, or overlook, is the good things I say about people. Only the other week I described [Leeds captain and Scotland international] Billy Bremner as the star of the [1974] World Cup. I've praised [goalkeeper] David Harvey, [utility player] Paul Madeley and United's often brilliant play last season, but no one remembers to thank me for that. But enough of the past. What matters now is the future, and as far as Leeds United and myself are concerned it couldn't be brighter.'

Clough also made time for one last chat with John Vinicombe. 'I am going to Leeds as from now and Peter Taylor stays at Brighton & Hove Albion,' he told the local newspaperman. 'I am absolutely and unbelievably sad at the final breaking up of something that has lasted since our playing days twenty years ago. There will be real compensation for Brighton as they have Peter Taylor as manager. Peter and I have brought Brighton from obscurity into the limelight. Mike Bamber has said they have had £1 million of publicity and I think we can claim we have done a superb job for this club.'

Never a man comfortable in the spotlight, Peter Taylor did however also seek out Vinicombe to give his version of events. 'There was an offer made to me to go to Leeds, a lucrative one, by Manny Cussins, the Leeds chairman,' Taylor said. 'After a great deal of talk with my chairman Mike Bamber and Brian that went on into the early hours of this morning, a decision was made. Of course I'm sad at parting with Brian, but let's not kid ourselves – the break started at Derby. Brian was bitter about the Derby episode and I think it affected his performance at Brighton. Last night Brian and myself were confronted with his desire to get into the big time but there was also the important moral aspect of the Albion. We were both concerned about the situation at Brighton, but if you analyse the outcome both Brighton and Leeds have benefitted. At the time I spoke with Brian last night there was no turning back for at least one of us. In actual fact the compromise was that Brighton and Leeds have both been satisfied. We have been showered with respect from the Brighton board and the public and now I'm happy to say that Brighton and Leeds will not miss out. I was not present when Brian made his statement about going to Leeds. I didn't turn my back on him, but I just had to get out.'

Clough may have been wrong about many things, but his inkling that Taylor always 'fancied a crack at management in his own right' was bang on the mark. In the weeks leading up to Leeds United's approach, several Albion players sensed a change in the weather when it came to who was in charge of the team. Suddenly Taylor seemed to be the one having meetings with Mike Bamber, conducting interviews with the local media, and generally making or breaking individual players' futures. John Templeman couldn't help but notice how Albion's chairman had referred to Taylor as 'the manager' while discussing his proposed transfer to Exeter City. John Vinicombe also picked up on a subtle recent shift in Taylor's language. The traditional 'we' had disappeared, usurped by 'I' as in the first person. It wasn't 'we' who had signed Ricky Marlowe from Shrewsbury Town, taking Albion's spending under Clough and Taylor to almost £250,000. It wasn't 'we' who enticed coach Gerry Clarke to the Goldstone from Chesterfield. Instead it was 'I' as in Peter Taylor. There was no mention of Clough whatsoever.

'I knew that a split was inevitable,' he confessed in *With Clough By Taylor*. So too, if truth be told, did Bamber, who observed first-hand the underlying tensions between the two men and how Taylor seemed committed to the club in a way Clough patently wasn't. It was, Bamber came to realise, a question of *when* the latter would leave, not *if*. Come the moment, come the chairman's very own Plan B: offer the job to Taylor.

That moment duly arrived at the Courtlands Hotel on Monday 22 July. Taylor's decision to accept, along with Bamber's proclamation to sue Leeds United, proved there was more to Albion than many had suspected. Here was a club prepared to stand firm, one that was serious in its intention to climb from the third to the first tier of English football. Appointing Brian Clough as manager hadn't been a publicity stunt. There really was a serious, long-term plan in place. Clough might not have recognised that, but Taylor most certainly did.

It was several years before Bamber opened up publicly about the extent of his misgivings over the way Clough conducted himself while managing Albion. 'I thought it was wrong for the manager to slop around in a tracksuit all day,' he told Tony Francis in 1987, during the research process for the book *Clough: A Biography*. 'How could he do that and tell the players off for not wearing a tie? His behaviour with the television crews was entirely wrong as well. I permitted Brian to keep his contract with LWT but the poor cameramen were kept hanging about for hours. Even then, they could never be sure that he would turn up. Brian and I got on very well socially, but he was a different animal as soon as there were a group of people in the room. Then he became the showman. He'd have half a pint of beer in public, but as soon as we were on our own again he couldn't wait to get at the champagne. I had a moan at him only twice: once when he didn't level with me over the Iran national team offer – I thought it was a stunt, but he never admitted it; the other occasion was on a club tour to Majorca. Brian was sun-worshipping by the pool all day with two blokes waiting on him hand and foot. I found out they were his friends who'd come out with us. "This is a bit off, isn't it Brian?" I said. But he didn't seem to care.'

Right up until the last, Clough's ability to amaze, confound and frustrate – sometimes all at the same time – left Bamber at a crossroads between wanting to laugh, scream and shake his head in disbelief. Leeds United's players had already returned from their summer holidays for pre-season training when news of Clough's appointment broke. Naturally Bamber assumed his now ex-manager would be heading straight from Sussex to Yorkshire to meet them. Instead, Clough, while in the process of saying goodbye, divulged that Manny Cussins was taking him to Heathrow, whereupon he'd be catching a plane to Majorca to resume his family holiday. 'I told him he was mad,' said Bamber. 'He had a duty to be at pre-season training and he shouldn't mess about with a club like Leeds. Typical Clough – he wouldn't listen. I think that was one of the biggest mistakes he made, but he was too arrogant to see it.'

Before even setting foot in Leeds, Clough was sowing the seeds of his own downfall by failing to learn from his transgressions at Brighton. United's international thoroughbreds, however, would prove to be a far more unforgiving lot than Albion's bunch of local heroes. And they wouldn't waste any time in letting him know.

10

UTOPIA

'I'd get through London and then see a sign that read: "Brighton, fifty miles". My heart always sank.'

Brian Clough returned from Majorca seven days after his impromptu decision to inform the world that he had been appointed manager of Leeds. Having missed the start of pre-season training, he then turned up two hours late for United's annual pre-season get-together, an important social event in the calendar for the players, their families, directors and indeed everyone at the heart of the club. He arrived late for his first actual day at work and continued to be late for training on most mornings thereafter. On Friday 2 August, Clough went and compounded this rapidly lengthening charge sheet by beginning his now-infamous first team talk with the words:

'Gentlemen, the first thing you can do for me is throw your medals and your pots and pans in the dustbin because you've never won anything fairly. You've done it by cheating.'

Johnny Giles later insisted that he actually started with 'Right, you fucking lot…', before going through the squad one by one addressing their various strengths and weaknesses, often in the most brutal of terms ('If you'd been a racehorse you'd have been shot,' to winger Eddie Gray, whose career had been dogged by injury). But the finer details are almost immaterial. The damage had been done and Clough, despite having only been in post a matter of days, was already on borrowed time. The 72-mile commute to Elland Road from his home in the Allestree area of Derby was beginning to feel every bit as tortuous as those last fifty miles on the road to Brighton.

That, however, was of little concern to Brighton & Hove Albion's players, who were still coming to terms with what had happened at the Courtlands Hotel over the course of Sunday night and Monday morning, 21–22 July. Almost to a man, they had seen it coming. Even the ones who had served under Clough before leaving the club either voluntarily or involuntarily during the previous nine months were far from surprised.

'I think we all knew that he wasn't going to be there long,' says Norman Gall. 'Maybe a year, possibly a bit longer. He just didn't really seem to get Brighton. I don't just mean the club, but the place as a whole. He always seemed to be away or at home. That's not the way to get to know a club, a town or its people. You've got to get in there during the week, not just when a football match is on. That way you'll find out what people think about you, what people think about the team, and by doing that you will get to know the town and what it stands for.'

'I wasn't surprised to hear that he'd left Brighton, but I was surprised to hear where he was going,' says Ian Goodwin. 'I thought, "He won't last at Leeds, not with that lot. No way." You can't go in there and say, "Throw your medals in the bin, you cheating bastards" – not to the Billy Bremners and Johnny Gileses and Norman Hunters of this world. They're the kind of pros who had been there, seen it, done it. They'd all won far more than he ever had as a player. He could get away with that attitude with guys like me and some of the other Brighton players, but doing it at Elland Road when you're surrounded by established pros is another thing altogether.'

'As soon as I left Brighton I got tapped up to go and manage at Southwick,' adds Brian Powney. 'That suited me because I lived along the coast at Seaford, I had my vending machine business on the go and I was quite happy to take on a local side in a local league. We were doing pre-season training there and somebody came up to me and said, "Cloughie has gone." I said, "What do you mean, he's gone?" And he said, "He's gone to Leeds United and Peter is staying." Straight away I thought, "Oh that's a bad move, that's a really bad move," because there was no way the Bremners and Hunters of this world were going to put up with his way of doing things. And they didn't.'

'To be honest I was surprised he even came [to Brighton] in the first place because of where we were,' says Peter O'Sullivan. 'It wasn't just that we were in the Third Division – we were a Third Division club in the south of England. I don't think he would have even managed in London. Anywhere below Derby was too far south for him. We were all southern softies as far as he was concerned, even me – and I'm from north Wales! He wasn't in it for the long term. And you know what? He was too good for us anyhow, at least at that point in time. I think a very big financial incentive probably had something to do with it, but only he and Mike Bamber probably know the truth about how he ended up down here.'

Less of a surprise to many of Albion's current and now former players was Peter Taylor's decision to stay. 'He was around more than Clough,' says Harry Wilson. 'He loved the climate down there. He had a superb seafront apartment. His wife liked it. His daughter liked it. You could see him thinking, "Why move?

I've got enough money. I've got all the contacts I need. I can make this work on my own." I for one was jumping for joy when I heard he [Clough] had left. I don't think he liked me. He might have done, but the way he treated me, calling me the worst full-back he'd ever seen in his life, you certainly wouldn't have known it. I regarded him going and Taylor staying as a fresh start for me.'

'When Lammie and I left, it was Peter Taylor doing the work behind the scenes,' says John Templeman. 'I think Brian had already made up his mind then that he wasn't going to be there much longer. Maybe Pete got wind of that and thought, "I've got an opportunity here." We'd already reported for pre-season training at Exeter when we heard Brian was going to Leeds United. We were both quite taken aback, but when you consider how little time he spent in Brighton and how little he helped the players when we needed support and confidence having just been relegated from the Second Division, maybe we shouldn't have been.'

Lammie Robertson's immediate reaction was that Clough departing and Taylor remaining amounted to some kind of grand scheme concocted in secret by the two men. 'I always saw them as a double act, even when they were apart. Nothing, absolutely nothing, surprised me about them. I thought, "Anything can happen here." Suddenly they had control of two clubs. They had a feeder club [Albion] and they'd do deals between them. That was my take on it. Of course, we didn't have time to find out if that was the case because he [Clough] was only there a few weeks, but I could see something evolving along those lines.'

There was also a feeling among some of Albion's class of 1973/74 that the club might in fact be better off under Taylor, free now to implement his own management style and ideas, whatever they may be. 'I'd already left Brighton by then, but I did think keeping hold of Taylor was a shrewd move, one that would work out well for those who were still there,' adds Ian Goodwin. 'I always thought he was the brains of the organisation. He was aloof in many respects, but he was clearly a thinker. You'd sit next to Cloughie and he'd be screaming and shouting at people. I'd stopped listening to him anyway. It would go in one ear and come out the other. But Taylor would sit in the stand and analyse the game. I've always wondered whether Peter should have put his flipping hand up Cloughie's arse and operated him like a dummy, because he was the one who talked the most sense.'

'They were very different characters,' says O'Sullivan. 'Clough was the extrovert. Pete was the introvert, standing back and listening with his cigar or Campari in hand, looking intelligent. But you'd think, "He knows what he's doing." He wasn't big on tactics. In fact, neither of them were. Coaching was average then, not like it is today with all the high-tech stuff. You'd go out on Saturday or whenever and if anyone got injured then they would put someone else in the same position. It was more a case of buying players that fitted certain key positions, much like they did at Nottingham Forest. Under Pete, we started to buy the right players.'

Unsurprised, relieved, disappointed – those were the overriding emotions doing the rounds in Albion's dressing room once news of Clough's defection broke. The disappointment cut especially deep with the newest arrivals at the club. Ian Mellor, signed in March from Norwich City, hadn't even played a competitive game under Clough, likewise Fred Binney, Steve Govier, Andy Rollings and Ricky Marlowe. There was, however, consolation of sorts for Mellor. 'He [Clough] made me the club's record signing,' Mellor said when we spoke in 2005. 'I'm really proud of that, that he thought enough of me to pay that kind of money.'

'I was absolutely gutted,' says Rollings. 'I'd joined Brighton to play first-team football, but also to play under him. Having Brian Clough as your new manager, saying, "You're going to be the new Roy McFarland", was just incredible. It might have all been talk, him trying to impress and make me feel good about myself, but it worked. Everyone knew what he'd done at Derby and now I was going to be playing for him. I thought he could only enhance my career. Then you find out all of a sudden that he's gone. Yeah, I was gutted alright.'

As indeed were many Albion supporters, particularly the younger element who had unreservedly bought into Clough's star quality. 'I was really upset,' recalls lifelong fan Ralph Harrison, a ten-year-old regular at the Goldstone Ground in 1974. 'We'd started stabilising over the course of the season and weren't getting thrashed like we had against Bristol Rovers and Walton and Hersham anymore. We had this massive name at Brighton. It wasn't so much that we *could* do something under Clough, but that we *would* do something. Then suddenly he's gone to Leeds. I'll always remember walking along behind the West Stand before one game and I spotted Clough surrounded by a big group of people who I presumed were reporters. He broke away from them to get inside the ground and I was standing there, right slap bang in his way. I didn't have a pen or paper on me to get his autograph, which I think is what he was expecting. So instead he came up, ruffled my hair, and walked on by into the ground. It all happened so quickly, and I was really taken aback – but it was marvellous. Nobody believed me at school when I told them what had happened. I've never forgotten that and I never will.'

Clough's departure came less than four weeks before the start of the 1974/75 season. The fact that the majority of the players, not to mention Taylor himself, saw it coming meant there was no falling apart behind the scenes at the Goldstone. Quite the opposite. Majorca had given everyone time to bond in the sun. On their return for pre-season training, the sun continued to shine as Glen Wilson and Gerry Clarke put the team through its paces, alternating between using Hove Park and Sussex University with the occasional workout at one of the many nearby beaches. Chris Carter, the locally based middle-distance runner who had competed for Britain in the 800 metres at the 1964 and 1968 Summer Olympics, came by on several occasions to help break the monotony and offer specialist coaching. It was, so many of the players remember, a happy, positive place to be both inside and outside the dressing room.

'For the majority of my time playing for Brighton, we had a great team spirit,' says O'Sullivan. 'We all used to go out together. Saturday nights we'd be out after games, often as many as a dozen of us with our wives and girlfriends in some Italian restaurant until 1 o'clock in the morning. We'd run special trains to away matches where the players and the fans would mix. There was this great togetherness, and that started when Pete was manager. Mike Bamber had a lot to do with it, the way he ran the club, but under Pete the players began to gel more socially. I'd been there through some of the bad times when dear old Pat Saward and Cloughie had been in charge. That's why I noticed the change more so than the others. Back then I used to go to the Italian restaurants on my own!'

'I'd grown up in a mining village in County Durham and I'd

never seen anything like Brighton and the area around it,' adds Harry Wilson. 'There were people all over the place, restaurants all over the place, shops all over the place. You had two piers to walk on. Brighton beach was made up of stones but many of the others were sandy. If you didn't want to go to the beach you had the South Downs to go walking on with the views over the coast and the surrounding countryside. And it would all look even better in the summer when the sun was out. You'd think, "How the hell did I end up here?" I loved it from day one, but I loved it even more once Clough went and Peter Taylor took over. It was a happier place to be. People think of him [Taylor] as this dour person with a low profile – and he did have a low profile compared to Clough, but he was in fact a very funny guy with an excellent sense of humour.'

On the evening of Monday 12 August, five days before Albion's opening league game at home to Crystal Palace, Taylor sat down in his apartment overlooking the sea to compose some words for the match programme. Clough had barely given anything of himself to the club programme, strange, perhaps, considering his loquacious nature. Taylor, infinitely more comfortable writing words down than saying them in public, chose to be different. The programme was an easy way of conveying messages to supporters without actually having to engage in conversation. Taylor's notes for the Crystal Palace programme amounted to a personal manifesto, one that somehow managed to be bold, inspiring, informative, naïve and uncharacteristically arrogant all at the same time.

'Since the last league match was played by the Albion there have been a lot of changes at the Goldstone,' he declared.

My long-time friend and partner Brian Clough left to take over at Leeds and I stayed to manage Brighton. But all this is old news and in the past. Today's match against Crystal Palace, one of the best teams in the division, marks the start of a new era in football for Brighton. Eleven new players have been signed, as well as our new coach Gerry Clarke from Chesterfield, and from today we will all be put to the test. Success is the only thing I'm interested in – for myself, the team, the board and the fans. But not success at any price. When – and I say when, and not if – we win the Third Division title, we will have got there playing skilful football. Anyone can annihilate the opposition by brute strength and dirty play, but we will annihilate them with pure football. There will obviously be bad times and setbacks and you, the fans, will wonder what I was talking about. But we will weather it because we have a good, young, skilful side who are desperate to win. And we won't be seven-day wonders either. We will have a team who can get Brighton into the Second Division and keep them there. But the players, although the most important part of the club, aren't the only part. The public can also have a big say in our success and, judging by the loyalty you showed during the bad times last season, I'm sure I can count on your support this year.

Over the course of the mid-to-late 1970s, a rivalry developed between Brighton & Hove Albion and Crystal Palace which became increasingly more unpleasant with every game played between the two clubs. The bitterness really took hold as a result of events which unfolded during a 1976/77 FA Cup first-round second replay held at Chelsea's home of Stamford Bridge. The match was settled 1–0 in Crystal Palace's favour but only after referee Ron Challis disallowed two seemingly legitimate Albion goals: one supposedly for handball; the other a successful penalty which had to be retaken and was subsequently saved. However, the fuse had in fact been burning since Saturday 17 August 1974. Stoked by soaring temperatures, Albion and Palace fans fought each other before, during and after the match in scenes reminiscent of the mods versus rockers clashes in Brighton of May 1964. Hooliganism, the scourge of British football in the 1970s and 1980s, had touched down in Sussex.

That was the bad news.

The good news, at least from an Albion perspective, was that Peter Taylor's charges prevailed on the pitch in his first match as manager, Ian Mellor scoring the only goal of the game in the second half. For the first time since 1964, Albion had a victory to celebrate on the opening day of the season. 'We've beaten the most skilful side in the Third Division,' boasted Taylor afterwards.

But that wasn't all.

Having failed to attract a single 20,000-plus home attendance during Brian Clough's tenure as manager, Taylor's inauguration drew an impressive 26,235 paying punters to the Goldstone. Inside Albion's boardroom, the sound of champagne corks popping just about drowned out the police sirens drifting in on the late afternoon breeze from the neighbouring streets of normally genteel Hove.

Meanwhile, up in Leeds, it wasn't so much a case of the glass being half empty, more of the glass not existing at all. Having managed to offend a fair chunk of United's squad with his first team talk, Clough continued to ruffle feathers around Elland Road over the days that followed. His relationships with coach Syd Owen ('truculent and obstructive') and Don Revie's former assistant Maurice Lindley ('a master of the art of looking busy at all times') were non-existent. Revie's desk and other office furniture was dispensed with, causing the ex-manager's secretary to resign in protest. Despite United scout Tony Collins advising him not to make too many changes too quickly, Clough drew up plans to offload several members of the squad (which he'd labelled the 'Over-Thirties Club'), including Giles, Hunter, goalkeeper David Harvey and left-back Terry Cooper. The in-joke at training became 'Who's leaving today?' as players got wind of those supposedly surplus to requirements via the local media.

Confused over what they were hearing and worried that club favourites were about to be sold, supporters also began making their feelings known. Season-ticket holder George Hindle started a petition against Clough, collecting 400 signatures at the city's Merrion Centre shopping complex on a Thursday evening. One of the four charter trains booked to convey supporters to London for the Charity Shield against Liverpool on Saturday 10 August was cancelled due to insufficient interest. What had been a stable, happy family under Revie appeared to be rapidly coming apart at the seams.

It wasn't so much that Clough sought change; all new managers want to stamp their authority on unfamiliar surroundings. It was the way he went about it: the impudence, ridiculing players, riding roughshod over the feelings of backroom and support staff, turning up late if at all for training, the lack of preparation for games, pretty much everything that had caused such angst behind the scenes at Brighton. History was repeating itself, except now his every move was open to the kind of scrutiny which comes with managing the champions of England. Issues that might have festered behind closed doors at the Goldstone simply couldn't be contained within Elland Road. Or, indeed,

Wembley. When Clough led Leeds out beneath the now sadly demolished twin towers to face Liverpool in the traditional curtain-raiser to the forthcoming season, the body language of the men walking behind him spoke volumes. Whereas their opponents strode proudly in the wake of Bill Shankly, taking charge of Liverpool for the last time before retiring, United's players moved with the surliness of a dozen schoolboys held for detention at the behest of a headmaster they despised.

'I needed help,' Clough admitted in his first autobiography. 'I needed friendly faces, people I could trust and whose support I could count on. Without my mate, I was more vulnerable than ever before.' His mate was, of course, Taylor. Five days after the Charity Shield and two days before the beginning of the regular league season, Clough reached the absolute low point of his spell in charge of Leeds United. It was late at night at the Dragonara Hotel in Leeds (now the Hilton on Neville Street). Clough was in his room and unable to sleep, rattled by the horrible truth of the situation he found himself in. As the clock ticked round to 2 a.m. on Friday morning, he picked up the phone and dialled Taylor at his apartment in Hove. Taylor's wife, Lill, answered.

'Brian was crying and in a terrible state,' she recalled. 'He said he'd give his right arm for Peter to join him. I felt really sorry for him. Peter was still asleep and Brian said not to wake him. He just blurted it all out, how the players were ganging up on him and making his life a misery. Between sobs I could hear him say he'd made a terrible mistake going to Leeds. He was convinced there was a conspiracy to get him out.'

Eventually Taylor woke up and took hold of the receiver. 'He begged me to go back with him, said we'd crack it together, but he had no chance on his own,' Taylor once said of the conversation that followed. 'I must have been one of the few people who didn't realise what he'd been going through. There was no point kidding him. I didn't consider it for a second. I was committed to Mike Bamber and the Brighton board. It was Utopia down there. Brian wouldn't take no for an answer. He told me to name my own price and asked me to come up the very next day. He was bitterly upset when I turned him down.'

Less than forty-eight hours later, as Albion were beating Crystal Palace, so Leeds lost their first league game of the season 3–0 away to Stoke City. Four days later, Queens Park Rangers came to Elland Road and won 1–0, David Harvey allowing a thirty-yard effort from Gerry Francis to slip through his fingers and over the line. A team meeting was subsequently called to discuss the dip in morale and results. Duncan McKenzie, signed by Clough from Nottingham Forest, was amazed to hear Syd Owen's clearly audible comment of 'What rubbish' coming from the back of the room as the manager spoke. John McGovern, another new recruit who had previously played under Clough at both Hartlepools United and Derby County, could barely believe the difference in atmosphere between the Baseball Ground and Elland Road. 'When he [Clough] spoke to us at Derby, players would stop in their tracks and listen,' McGovern said. 'At Leeds they just walked away and ignored him. The respect had gone.'

'A manager hasn't a prayer of succeeding if he doesn't carry the players with him,' Clough would later argue in his defence. 'You can't laugh, you can't train, you certainly can't win matches, and you would have trouble assembling everybody for a squad photograph. I didn't carry the Leeds players. I never gained their confidence or support. Instead of unity and common purpose there was animosity, unrest and suspicion. I have never experienced anything like it before and would never wish such dreadful circumstances on my worst enemy. It was like trying to swim against the tide, in hot tar.'

In *Walking on Water*, Clough pinpointed his predicament at Leeds more precisely. 'Leeds had done it all. They were the kings of English football. They weren't threatened, any of them, because they felt they were bigger than me. When I went to Derby and Brighton, everybody looked up to me. When I went to Leeds, the boot was on the other foot. I was the one looking up because they were the stars, internationals wherever you cared to look, on the team-sheet and off it.'

On 24 August, a second-half strike by Allan Clarke gave Leeds a 1–0 victory at home over Birmingham City. Four days later, United played well but were held 1–1 away by Queens Park Rangers. Another good performance on the final day of the month couldn't prevent a 2–1 defeat across the Pennines to Manchester City. That made it three defeats from five league games, hardly the stuff of champions. When Luton then drew 1–1 at Elland Road, large sections of the crowd booed not only Clough but also John McGovern, damned by his close association with the manager. Almost unthinkably, Leeds were in the relegation zone.

By now the discord had spread to the boardroom, split three to two in favour of Clough (chairman Manny Cussins, Bob Roberts and Sydney Simon being for; Sam Bolton and Percy Woodward against). When Roberts, Cussins's closest ally, went to Majorca on holiday, Bolton and Woodward took advantage of the moment to call on the chairman to sack Clough. Meetings between various directors were arranged in secret with no minutes being taken. On Tuesday 10 September, the entire United squad was summoned to a meeting in the players' lounge at Elland Road prior to training. The decision to fire Clough had, according to Cussins, already been taken, the suggestion being that the meeting was deliberately engineered by Bolton in an attempt to make it look as though player power was afoot. Bolton started by asking the players to enlighten the board about the unrest in the camp. Some had their say, others kept quiet. At one point, Johnny Giles suggested that he didn't think it was right to be talking about the manager in his presence. Clough duly exited the room, ready in his own mind to resign.

By all accounts, nobody spoke up in Clough's defence. It was Paul Madeley, the quiet strength and reason within United's squad, who delivered the killer blow. 'What the lads are trying to say, Mr Bolton, is that he's no good,' declared Madeley, straight-faced. Bolton and Cussins concluded proceedings by saying they would look into the players' concerns. In reality, Clough's fate had already been determined. On 12 September, it was announced that Leeds were parting company with their manager just forty-four days after he had taken charge; fifty-three since his official appointment.

'They say Cloughie was at Leeds for forty-four days but in reality it was more like twenty,' David Harvey told Phil Rostron, author of *We Are the Damned United*, echoing his regular absenteeism while in charge at the Goldstone. 'He was there so rarely that no one really had the chance to get to know him, and, from what I saw of him throughout his career, I'm at least grateful for that small mercy.'

A little after 6 p.m., a grinning Clough appeared on the steps outside Elland Road, cracking jokes as Cussins shuffled about awkwardly while being peppered with questions from journalists. Clough's demeanour was much the same an hour or so later as he took his place under the studio lights at Yorkshire Television to be probed by presenter Austin Mitchell, with none other than Don Revie also present in front of the cameras. There was good reason for Clough to seem so upbeat. Not only was his Leeds United nightmare at an end, but he was walking away with a big fat compensation cheque in the process. Despite failing to sign his four-year contract, Leeds decided to honour it. A pay-off of approximately £25,000 had initially been agreed. Incredibly, David Somersall Creasey from the Leeds law firm Jobbings, Fawcett and Grove, acting on Clough's behalf, then managed to increase the figure to around the £98,000 mark after tax. He also got to keep the Mercedes Leeds had given him. The lesson he'd learned while at Derby – never resign – had paid dividends. Clough was made financially for life, and he knew it.

Barely able to believe his good fortune, Clough drove back to Leeds from Derby the following morning having been told the quickest way to get a cheque through the system was to present it at the issuing bank. In time he would pay off the mortgage on his house in Allestree before moving to a substantially larger property in the nearby village of Quarndon. 'I came out of Elland Road a little crestfallen professionally but quite rich,' he wrote in *Walking on Water*. 'I was financially secure for the first time in my life and I knew that whatever job came my way, I would be able to do it with complete peace of mind.'

In September 1974, it didn't appear quite as straightforward as that. True, Clough was rich, but Austin Mitchell, not to mention the majority of Fleet Street's finest sports hacks, weren't convinced he would get another job that easily. 'What's going to happen now to Brian Clough?' Mitchell asked during the Yorkshire Television interview. 'Oh, a million things will happen to Brian Clough,' he replied, before claiming, with a flick of a hand in Revie's direction, that he might even apply to coach England's youth team. Back came Mitchell: 'Well, aren't you going to be in a very difficult situation, because after the argument with Derby you left Brighton under a cloud, and now this with Leeds? Who's going to touch you with a barge pole, as it were?' Clough replied that 'many, many people would', claiming the seven weeks he had been in charge at Leeds 'is not enough time to even find out where the local butcher's shop is', but it was a pertinent question. Having resigned from two clubs and been sacked by another within the space of eleven months, there was a feeling that Clough was damaged goods.

Mike Bamber didn't watch the interview. Being a Yorkshire Television production, it was only screened in its entirety in that part of the country. But already his brain had sprung into action. Since defeating Crystal Palace on the opening day of the season, Albion's form had been patchy at best. Victory at home over Chesterfield came sandwiched between away defeats to Peterborough United and Blackburn Rovers. Their League Cup campaign had stumbled at the first hurdle, Reading winning 3–2 at the Goldstone in a third replay after the previous games finished 0–0, 2–2 and 0–0. Not so much a crisis, then, as a slight reality check.

Was it really worth telephoning Clough to see if he would come back? Bamber appears to have thought long and hard about this throughout mid-September. He kept it to himself without so much as a word being uttered to Peter Taylor, the players or even the club's directors. Only Harry Bloom second-guessed the chairman's thought processes, promising to remain tight-lipped.

Ultimately, for several reasons, Bamber felt it wasn't worth the gamble. First, there was everything that had gone before during Clough's nine-month term in office: the flirting with other potential employers; regularly going absent-without-leave; promising to move to Sussex without ever bothering to do so; abusing the chairman's trust and generosity; upsetting players with his bluntness. Second, Albion were in the process of suing Leeds United regarding the circumstances surrounding Clough's departure from the Goldstone. The lawyers could always be called off, but only if and when it ever reached the point where Clough was seriously interested in returning. Third, the cost. Clough had raised Albion's profile immeasurably, but it came at a price. The double whammy of inconsistent form and disappointing attendances meant the projected income based around crowds of over 20,000 hadn't materialised. If results didn't improve then there was no guarantee attendances would rise even if Clough did return. In fact, they could even go the other way, a degree of anger remaining at the way Albion's ex-manager seemed to use the club as little more than a port in a storm.

Above all else, Bamber felt it necessary to repay Taylor's loyalty. He could so easily have accompanied Clough to Leeds on a more substantial salary. Instead, Taylor had bought into Bamber's vision of raising a habitually underperforming football club from the depths of the English Third Division. Bamber thought it could be done. Taylor thought it could be done. Clough, judging by his actions and words, didn't think it could be done. More to the point, he wasn't even interested in trying.

And so Bamber chose to stick rather than twist. The win and the attendance against Crystal Palace had given Albion's chairman real cause for optimism. Results since then had been mixed but Taylor deserved the opportunity to fly solo over a prolonged period of time and show what he was capable of. Whatever move Brian Clough made next, it wouldn't be a return to the Goldstone.

11

PROMISES, PROMISES

Almost a year to the day after taking over at Brighton & Hove Albion, Brian Clough sat down with the renowned broadcaster David Frost to record an interview for the BBC in front of a studio audience. It turned out to be one of the most open, honest interviews that he ever gave. Clough was relaxed, entertaining, polite, philosophical even, but there was no doubting recent experiences had left him feeling wounded – something Frost was keen to explore from the beginning. Asked if he would like to rewrite the last twelve months, Clough replied, 'No, it would take me many, many, many, many years. It's been a nightmare on a lot of occasions, obviously, and after twelve months to find yourself out of work is not very pleasant.' Frost questioned whether he thought of himself as out of work. 'Oh, literally, of course,' said Clough. 'My profession is managing a football club and at the moment I'm not doing that, so obviously I'm out of work.'

From there, Frost steered the conversation onto Clough's sacking by Leeds, the £98,000 so-called 'golden pay off' and his predecessor at Elland Road, Don Revie. 'I'm loath to mention him, you know, and if we can refrain from doing it we'll do so,' said Clough, breaking into a smile. 'You hate to mention him why?' asked Frost. 'Because he's a very talented man and I don't like him,' Clough responded. 'Don't ask me why. He's a very, very talented man and his record is unsurpassable. And I just don't happen to like him, and I don't like the way he goes about football either. Football is a game of opinion. There are people in your profession who perhaps don't like the way you do your bit. It makes the game go round. There's half the country don't like a Labour government. It just happens the other half do.'

In jumped Frost, keen to explore the Clough-versus-Revie theme further. 'Why don't you want me to ask why you don't like him?' he probed. 'Because I can't tell you,' replied Clough. 'It's impossible. We'd get closed down, David.' Cue much laughter from the studio audience and Frost, who jokingly challenged his interviewee to experiment. 'No,' said Clough with a smirk, before moving on to the legal ramifications of him taking the Elland Road job in the first place. 'I've got Brighton suing Leeds for breaking [a] contract that I'm supposed to have broken, which I did obviously in certain aspects, but it was between Brighton and Leeds. It was rather over my head. I felt like one of these people that were sold many, many years ago in the market. I was under contract to Brighton, Leeds came in and they were trying to settle compensation. It didn't quite work out, and then there's something going on in the background at the moment court wise, so it makes it rather difficult.'

Credit to Frost, whose instinct told him it was worth dipping into the less well-charted waters of Clough's relatively recent history, namely Albion, besides touching on more widely reported events at Derby County and Leeds United. 'Do chairmen have the same characteristics or were they three very different men to deal with?' he asked of Sam Longson,

Mike Bamber and Manny Cussins, perhaps anticipating the answer. 'A couple have had the same characteristics because they were elderly gentlemen,' Clough replied. 'Michael Bamber was a little bit different. He was more in my age bracket. He was more the one who thought my way or wanted to get on my way, because you've got to have communication between the people you work with. I don't know whether you know your gaffers intimately, but if you don't then you'd better watch out because you've got to know their problems. When people get to sixty-nine, seventy, seventy-one, seventy-two, seventy-three, seventy-four and you're perhaps not quite forty yet, then you tend to see things differently. So the older chairmen, mostly, are the same. The younger ones are a little bit better and a little bit more on your wavelength.'

'Looking back now, do you wish you'd tried to hold on at Derby?' asked Frost. 'I've had many, many regrets at leaving Derby but, having left, and having made a decision, I wouldn't for one second tell you I'd made the wrong one,' said Clough, choosing his words carefully. 'Would you tell yourself you'd made the wrong one?' countered Frost, spotting the kink in his answer. Without so much as a pause, back came Clough: 'I've asked myself many, many times, "Have I made the wrong one?" And sometimes, depending on the mood, I've come up and said, "Yes, you did," and sometimes, most times, I've said, "No," because at that time you do believe in doing things that you believe you're right in doing. When you get to about forty-five, fifty... how old are you, David?' Frost replied that he was thirty-five. 'Good lad, but you've got another ten years to go, and then you might feel, you know, that you perhaps have to calm down a little bit.'

For his follow-up question, Frost referred to a previous

conversation the pair had shared in the canteen at London Weekend Television. What surprised Frost, post-Derby, was how quickly Clough 'leapt into another job with a Third Division team at Brighton' rather than waiting for bigger fish to come calling. 'Was that a mistake?' he asked. 'It was a mistake perhaps jumping in so quickly – but I daren't tell you the very, very words I said to you at that particular question – but I couldn't bear sitting out of work, being unemployed, and sitting on my backside,' said Clough. 'I used a different word [than sitting] to you, in actual fact. I couldn't bear the thought of it, having been involved so long. This word 'unemployment', you know, sends a shadow, a thing, down my spine of great fear.'

It wasn't exactly the most ringing endorsement of Brighton & Hove Albion, but at least Clough was being honest. Frost had cracked the code. While a handsome pay-packet and an FA disciplinary charge unquestionably played their parts, unemployment – the scourge of Clough's native Middlesbrough during the recession-hit decade of his birth – had been at the root of his decision to take over at the Goldstone Ground. Now, sitting beneath the BBC's studio lights, Clough once again found himself unemployed.

'What's the dreadful thing about being – you said it's terrifying as well – but out of a job, unemployed, you were saying you are at the moment,' asked Frost later in the interview. 'Well, the rejection for a start was terrifying having been sacked,' acknowledged Clough. 'That's hard to bear. Irrespective of how much you tell them they are wrong, you tell yourself they are wrong, it's still hard to bear. The feeling of being out of the one thing that you feel you can do best, that's a terrible fear.' Was the fear, Frost wanted to know, that he wouldn't get back into management? 'No, not only that, because I'm thick enough to believe I'll get back,' said Clough. 'Either thick enough or talented enough, one of the two.'

'How many football matches have you seen since you left Leeds?' Frost asked, having covered a diverse range of other subjects including politics, the importance of family and Clough's career-ending injury as a player with Sunderland.

'One,' came the reply.

'Only one?'

'One. I went to Amsterdam. I wanted to get away for a few days. I went to Amsterdam with Stoke City when they played Ajax, and I had four beautiful days in Amsterdam. The weather was gorgeous. The sights were just as… how long is it since you've been there?'

'A couple of years.'

'A couple of years. It's just the same. Absolutely gorgeous. Everything about the place is magic.'

'But you haven't seen a single match in England. Why is that?'

'I just can't bring myself to go along. I want a period out of it. I want to cool down. I want to sit back and look at it.'

'You'd find it painful to go to a match today?'

'I would find it very painful at the moment, yes.'

At the other end of the scale, Peter Taylor had never been busier. For the first time in his career, the former goalkeeper was now in sole managerial charge of a Football League club. With that, his responsibilities changed. Forget about plying the highways and byways of England in search of untapped talent. Now, more than ever, Taylor needed to be actively engaged at the coalface. And he couldn't do it alone. At the start of September 1974, Brian Daykin resigned as manager of the Midlands Counties League side Long Eaton to become Albion's assistant manager. In time, Ken Gutteridge, manager of Burton Albion, would also come south to the Goldstone as a trainer, replacing Gerry Clarke who returned to Chesterfield only a matter of months after leaving the Derbyshire club. Like Taylor, Daykin and Gutteridge were walking encyclopaedias on non-league football, particularly in the Midlands. They could now undertake the kind of scouting missions which had previously been Taylor's preserve, leaving the manager to concentrate on matters closer to home.

* * *

'When – and I say when, and not if – we win the Third Division title, we will have got there playing skilful football.' How those words, crafted by Taylor for the match programme versus Crystal Palace, came back to haunt him as the 1974/75 season wore on. By mid-October, Albion had slumped to twentieth in the table after a run of eight games without a win, the absolute nadir being a 6–0 away defeat at the hands of Walsall. Several of the new recruits signed during the 1973/74 campaign simply weren't cutting the mustard. In addition, Taylor was underwhelmed by the contributions of certain more established players who he believed weren't pulling their weight, among them Peter O'Sullivan. On 28 September, Sully was dropped for Bury's visit to the Goldstone, having made 194 consecutive appearances for the first team. Tired of all the managerial comings and goings, Third Division football and even his adopted Sussex, O'Sullivan responded by asking to go on the transfer list. Two months later, he asked to come off it again. The reasoning behind his about-turn is revealing.

'I could see that Peter Taylor's heart was in it,' he says.

'Cloughie had left and I think it was a case of "Is he [Taylor] going to stay or is he going to go as well?" They'd always worked together as a pair. Once I realised he was serious about staying, I thought I may as well too. So I decided to knuckle down and get on with it. We had some good players. And, let's face it, there are worse places to live than Brighton. I think I was out for six or maybe seven games, got back in the team, then played another 200-odd games, by which time I was almost too old to go anywhere else!'

Underwhelmed by results, not to mention the absence of club stalwart O'Sullivan from the starting XI, crowds started to dip as the feel-good factor generated by the opening-day win over Crystal Palace evaporated. 'Supporters must already be wondering whether my methods are right,' said Taylor after a 2–1 defeat at Charlton on 24 September. 'My answer is that we shall astonish people with what can be done at the Goldstone. Hang on, it's going to be worth waiting for.'

Alas, football supporters are not renowned for their patience. Two weeks later, Albion found themselves 2–0 down at home against Wrexham in front of a paltry attendance of just 8,900. Although they recovered to force a 3–3 draw, calls for Taylor to go were clearly audible from the vociferous North Stand. They were there again on 19 October, when Preston North End won 4–0, the improved gate of 16,413 being down to ex-England and Manchester United legend Bobby Charlton's presence as the Lancashire team's player/manager rather than anything the home side had to offer. By the end of November, Albion had sunk to twenty-third in the Third Division, one place off the bottom of the table.

Fortunately, Taylor had two things going for him: the backing of his chairman, and an understanding of where the problems lay. Having largely rebuilt Albion's squad along with Clough during the 1973/74 season, Taylor realised further surgery was necessary in order to stave off the threat of relegation to the Fourth Division. By the end of 1974, Paul Fuschillo, Ken Goodeve, Steve Govier, Billy McEwan and Ronnie Welch, all brought in under the Clough/Taylor regime, had either departed the Goldstone or played their last games for the club, making way for several new arrivals destined to become firm favourites on the terraces. They included experienced centre-back Graham Winstanley, bought from Carlisle United for £20,000, Yorkshireman Ken Tiler at right-back, and a pacey bank clerk from the Nottinghamshire market town of Newark.

'I'd worked in the local branch of NatWest for five years since leaving school while playing semi-professional football,' says right-winger Gerry Fell. 'I played for a team called Stamford in the United Counties League. Late in 1973 we played Long Eaton, who were managed at the time by Brian Daykin, in the FA Cup. Brian then made an approach for me at the end of that season and I joined Long Eaton in the summer of 1974, playing about five games for them. That was when Brian left and went to Brighton as Peter Taylor's assistant. Within a fortnight of him leaving, I got the call. Apparently, Brian had recommended me to Peter, who watched me a couple of times, and that was it. I gave in my notice at the bank and signed. In fact, I gave in my notice before I signed my contract at Brighton, can you believe? If I'd been on my own at the time, then I don't know if I would have had the guts to go through with it. I've got my wife, Diana, to thank. She pushed me into it! I think I probably would have, but I'm not sure. She's always been really supportive. She's the strong one out of the two of us.'

Living relatively close to Derby and being a keen football

fan in general, Fell had kept a close eye on events surrounding Brian Clough and Peter Taylor over the previous couple of years. 'They'd won the league at Derby, he [Clough] had had the ruck with Sam Longson, and then all of a sudden they go down to a club like Brighton. Of course it made headline news. I just thought it was strange. You saw this flamboyant chairman, Mike Bamber – who was a star, an absolute star – and you're thinking, "Crikey O'Reilly, there's a club that's going to be on the up." And then there I am all of a sudden signing for them! To be honest I can't remember much talk about him [Clough] at all. That was in the past. Peter was running the show by then and putting together more or less a new team. He was a very straight-talking guy and always good with me. He said, 'You've got a great chance here.' I'll always be grateful to him for giving me that chance, him and Brian Daykin, because let's face it, he just put me straight out there from playing local football.'

It was Ken Gutteridge who was responsible for unearthing another rough diamond from the East Midlands hinterlands. Peter Ward had left school a week before his fifteenth birthday, becoming an apprentice engine fitter with Rolls-Royce in Derby on £3 per week. In his spare time, he played up front for Borrowash Victoria in the Derby Combination League. Burton Albion, managed by Gutteridge and then one of the superpowers of non-league football in the Midlands, subsequently took Ward on, offering him a semi-professional contract after he scored a hat-trick in a 4–1 win over Tamworth.

He was small, almost too small to be a professional footballer, but there was something about Ward's close control and ability to turn opposing players that mesmerised Gutteridge. On moving to the Goldstone, he wasted no time telling Taylor about him. Taylor sent Daykin to see Ward in action, but the assistant manager was unimpressed. Gutteridge then asked Taylor to take a look for himself. This he did, journeying to Burton for an FA Trophy match against Buxton in which Ward was closely marshalled by the former Sheffield Wednesday and England defender Peter Swan. Burton lost but Taylor saw potential in their teenage centre-forward.

Four days later, both Taylor and Daykin watched Ward play at Maidstone. The pitch was bad, Burton were poor and Ward wasn't much better, but he showed some nice touches. Taylor offered £4,000, a considerable sum for a player Burton had acquired for nothing and failed to pay a penny in wages until after his hat-trick against Tamworth. Burton took the cheque and Ward moved into digs overlooking the sea in the Brighton suburb of Rottingdean. Unlike Gerry Fell, the young striker was deemed too raw to put straight into the first team. However, when the time was right, Taylor knew he had the potential to make one hell of an impact.

For now, Taylor's squad remained in or around the Third Division relegation zone, while the players he had recently acquired gradually gelled with the best of what was already there – talents such as Tony Towner, Steve Piper, Peter Grummitt, Harry Wilson, the inexperienced but promising Andy Rollings and the revitalised Peter O'Sullivan. They were working hard, Taylor could see that, but had yet to enjoy the fruits of their labours and lacked conviction when playing away from the Goldstone. 'I am absolutely confident that in the very near future some team is going to catch a packet from us,' he said after the 1–0 defeat at Halifax on 30 November, Albion's tenth defeat on the road out of eleven league matches. 'We are building up in the way I had hoped and I have said all along that the process can only be gradual if it is to achieve a lasting effect.'

Fortunately, at home, notwithstanding the Preston North End result, Albion were far more of a force, winning six, drawing five and losing just one of their twelve league games up until the end of 1974. There had also been first- and second-round wins in the FA Cup at the Goldstone against Aldershot and Brentford respectively. When Albion were then paired against non-league Leatherhead in the third round, few people, least of all Taylor, expected lightning to strike twice following their capitulation to Walton and Hersham in the same competition the previous season. 'Magnificent,' was the manager's reaction on hearing the draw. 'The main thing is that we are at home again.' Yet the omens weren't entirely in Albion's favour. Walton and Hersham had been a decent enough team brimming with experienced amateur players, some of who had once played the game professionally. Ditto Leatherhead. By some uncanny coincidence, three members of the Leatherhead team – Colin Woffinden, Dave Sargent and Willie Smith – had featured in the Walton and Hersham side that had humiliated Albion fourteen months earlier. Buoyed by victory in the second round over Colchester United, another Third Division outfit, Leatherhead certainly fancied their chances despite being the away team.

On Saturday 4 January 1975, twenty coaches laden with supporters rolled out of Leatherhead during the late morning and headed south along the A24 bound for Sussex, swelling the crowd inside the Goldstone to in excess of 20,000. Taylor insisted Albion had prepared for the tie as if Liverpool were the opposition, yet it was Leatherhead who looked the sharper side during the first half, with their lively winger Chris Kelly (dubbed the 'Leatherhead Lip' for his outspoken nature) twice going close to opening the scoring.

Midway through the second period, Kelly, playing his first full match since undergoing a cartilage operation in November, collected the ball near the centre circle and set off towards Albion's goal. On he surged, beating a couple of defenders before calmly placing the ball beyond the reach of Grummitt and into the net. Albion rallied, but to no avail. For the second season in succession they had crashed out of the FA Cup at home to Isthmian League opposition from Surrey. 'We were outfought, outplayed and have no excuses,' admitted Taylor. 'We didn't play five minutes' football and we couldn't string two passes together.'

Among the players there was a sense that Albion, to borrow comedian Eric Morecambe's famous line, were 'playing all the right notes, but not necessarily in the right order'. The talent was certainly there in the squad; the preparation, however, was all too often lacking. Peter Taylor's strengths lay in scouting, not coaching. Brian Daykin and Ken Gutteridge came from non-league environments and weren't used to working full-time with professionals. 'I still to this day don't know what Brian Daykin's background was,' says Andy Rollings. 'Everybody used to say that he "delivered the eggs", which I guess was a bit of a put-down because he was a pretty average coach.' Harry Wilson goes further, accusing Daykin of 'not knowing the game'. As for Gutteridge? 'I've been with better,' is his diplomatic response.

'I just always felt with Pete that he was probably the best number two in the country, but he was not the best manager,' adds Rollings. 'Pete created teams but the day-to-day effect around the place under him was a bit lacklustre. Personally, I didn't find him motivating enough, although we did have a few run-ins. There was one occasion when I was out of the first team and playing in the midweek reserve side. One weekend the first team were away. I didn't have to go with them, so I went home to see friends and family in Bristol. Anyway, they lost quite badly. Pete called a training session on the Sunday and had a practice match to eliminate some of the things that had gone wrong. I got back on the Monday morning, Pete called me into his office and says, "Where were you yesterday? You weren't here. We couldn't get hold of you." Obviously this was before mobile phones and what have you. I apologised but he said he'd have to fine me a week's wages, which was a lot of money back then. At that very moment, Brian Daykin walked in with his tracksuit on. He dropped his tracksuit bottoms and he had the biggest stud mark you've ever seen right from the top of his thigh down his shin. Apparently, he'd had to take my place in training in the reserve team because I wasn't there, and Peter O'Sullivan had gone right through him. It was funny because that was the first time I saw the lighter side of Pete. I was sitting there trying not to laugh, and I looked over at Pete and he's trying really hard not to laugh as well. It was quite surreal.'

For all his faults as a manager, by and large the dressing room was willing to fall in behind Taylor because they could see – as Peter O'Sullivan observed – that his heart was in the job. Andy Rollings recalls one incident that encapsulates not only the pros and cons of Taylor's management style, but also his passion, so rarely evident in public, and unpredictability. 'We used to have lots of meetings. Every other Friday up in the boardroom, yet another meeting. Heaven knows what we used to talk about, and some of us would switch off when he started waffling on, but there would be a fair bit of him trying to make us realise how lucky we were to be footballers. "Yes, we know that, Pete!" This one time, Kenny Tiler was sat in a corner. Pete used to have this seafront apartment, and apparently he'd seen

Kenny walking past one day looking a bit dishevelled. So Pete had a little go about how he'd been dressed. "You're a pro footballer, you should set an example" – all that kind of stuff. Pete then starts to move on to someone else and Kenny suddenly goes, "Oi, boss, you've had that same pair of shoes on for the last eight months." Pete sort of stopped dead in his tracks, then went, "That's what I want! That's exactly what I want, a bit of fire! That's what I'm after. I want that throughout the team." You'd be half asleep one minute, then that would happen.'

Following their dead-of-night exchange over the telephone five days after Leeds United's Charity Shield appearance at Wembley, it is believed Clough and Taylor didn't speak another word to each other throughout the remainder of 1974. Not that they were at loggerheads. Taylor was simply busy at the Goldstone while Clough, as alluded to in the David Frost interview, had all but turned his back on football for the time being, living the life of a semi-recluse at home. Bruised by events at Leeds but cushioned financially courtesy of the £98,000 'golden payoff', he could afford to wait and see what, if anything, materialised. At the beginning of 1975, the club that had half-heartedly made an enquiry regarding employment a little over fourteen months previously, only to be beaten to the line by Albion's concrete offer, got in touch again. That club was Nottingham Forest.

Sir Walter Winterbottom, the first full-time manager of the English national football team from 1946 to 1962, once described Forest as the club that everyone wanted to manage. In the seven years prior to January 1975, it sometimes seemed as if everyone got the opportunity, as no fewer than five different managers came and went from the City Ground. In 1967, Forest had pushed hard for the First Division title under

Johnny Carey's guidance, eventually having to settle for second place behind Manchester United. That same year only Tottenham Hotspur stood between them and an appearance at Wembley in the FA Cup final, Jimmy Greaves scoring the London side's opening goal in a 2–1 semi-final win at Hillsborough. When Carey left in 1968, so Forest's fortunes went into decline. Relegated from the top flight in 1972, they had yet to make a return when Clough agreed to become manager, assuming his responsibilities on 6 January.

That's not to say Forest were on a life-support machine. The season beforehand they had finished seventh in the Second Division under the previous manager, Allan Brown, coming within a whisker of reaching the last four of the FA Cup (leading 3–1 away to Newcastle United in the quarter-finals, when the match was abandoned with twenty minutes remaining due to home fans invading the pitch, Newcastle eventually progressing after two replays). Like Albion, there was a touch of the Eric Morecambe about Forest. Many of the right notes were already there – Viv Anderson, Ian Bowyer, Martin O'Neill, John Robertson and Tony Woodcock would all go on to achieve great things at the City Ground under Clough – but their potential wasn't being anything like fulfilled. 'Nottingham Forest were a big club with a small attitude,' is how Brian Powney remembers them around that time. He was right. Crowds had fallen to the 12,000 mark as the expected push for promotion during the 1974/75 season failed to materialise. However, afforded the right leadership, Forest were a success story waiting to happen – even with the benefit of hindsight.

'There is only one thing in the club's favour now, and that's me,' said Clough on arrival, playing up to his 'Big Head' image while at the same time playing down the relatively solid foundations of what he was inheriting. He couldn't do it alone though. Almost immediately, Jimmy Gordon, who had served alongside Clough at Derby County and Leeds United, came back on board in a training capacity. But, as at Elland Road, Clough's old mate would be conspicuous by his absence.

These days it is almost taken as read that Peter Taylor reunited with Brian Clough as soon as the latter set foot in Nottingham. All Clough had to do was whistle (or, for comedic purposes in the screen adaptation of *The Damned United*, kneel and grovel) and his sidekick, tired of life in the Third Division with Albion, came running. Not so. Not so at all. Taylor was out to prove that he could go it alone. So, it appears, was Clough, who didn't even bother asking Taylor if he wanted to join him. For some considerable time to come, English football's most formidable managerial partnership remained on hold. In all honesty, had Taylor quit to join Clough at that early stage, then there would have been more than a few Albion supporters willing to buy him a one-way train ticket to Nottingham. Mired in the relegation zone and dismissed from the FA Cup by Leatherhead, the champagne atmosphere of that opening-day victory over Crystal Palace had long since gone flat. If Taylor's first stab at solo management in the Football League was going to end in anything other than ignominious failure, then the green shoots would have to appear soon.

As long as their home form held up, then Albion had every chance of beating the drop to the Fourth Division. After crashing to Leatherhead, Taylor's evolving side regrouped and won eight of their remaining eleven league fixtures at the Goldstone, drawing two and losing just one. They became tighter defensively, built around the sturdy pillars of Peter Grummitt in goal, Ken Tiler and Harry Wilson at right and left-back respectively, with Steve Piper partnering captain Graham Winstanley in the centre-back positions (Piper, having started the season at right-back, switched positions on Tiler's arrival, edging Andy Rollings out of the starting XI). The training methods under Taylor, Daykin and Gutteridge may have left much to be desired, but those key rear-guard pieces of the jigsaw puzzle developed an understanding which gave Albion something to build on.

Elsewhere it was more of a mixed bag. Gerry Fell learned quickly and, along with Tony Towner and Peter O'Sullivan, became the focal points on which Albion launched their attacks. To the frustration of his teammates, the experienced Ernie Machin, bought from Plymouth Argyle for £30,000, declined to relocate from his native Coventry, making him unavailable to train with the team during the week. Ian Mellor took time to settle and at one stage went on the transfer list, having only found the target four times since his debut goal versus Crystal Palace. Fred Binney proved to be more successful yet fell well short of the twenty-plus-goal haul that supporters had expected from him. Ricky Marlowe was undoubtedly quick but his finishing could be horribly wayward, meaning the likeable Scot was out of the side as much as he was in it.

As the season built towards its climax, Albion's wretched away form kept them tethered dangerously close to the relegation zone. Besides a 4–2 win at Chesterfield and 2–2 draws against Colchester and Plymouth, they conspired to lose every match on the road from Boxing Day 1974 until the end of the campaign. Only the 3–0 reverse at Crystal Palace on 18 March came by more than a one-goal margin, but narrow, often unfortunate defeats don't win any consolation points. With seven games remaining, Tranmere Rovers and Huddersfield Town were all but doomed on 27 and 28 points respectively.

Above them sat Bournemouth (32), Watford (34) and Albion (35), with no fewer than thirteen teams clubbed together in the 36 to 44-point bracket. Four sides would go down to the Fourth Division. Albion were far from cut adrift in the lower reaches of the league table, but they were also far from safe.

All of which made the manager's increasing absences from the dugout on scouting missions a source of mounting frustration. Right now, Taylor needed to be with his team, issuing instructions, changing formations when things went wrong, substituting the right player at the right time, barking reprimands and providing encouragement. Instead both he and Daykin were regularly missing games in order to watch potential signings, leaving their precariously placed team in the inexperienced hands of Ken Gutteridge. Albion supporters, understandably, were less than impressed. 'Why does Taylor and his assistant need to be away watching other teams when Brighton are at home?' asked Sid Green of Billingshurst in the letters page of the *Evening Argus* after Taylor and Daykin were nowhere to be seen when Gillingham came to the Goldstone on 5 April. 'They, or specifically he [Taylor], need to be here. He is a manager now, not a scout, and the manager's job is to manage.'

Taylor could always have used the *Evening Argus* as a right of reply, had he not fallen out with the newspaper following the 2–2 draw at Plymouth on 29 March. Throughout the season the manager had penned a regular Wednesday column under the title 'Taylor Talks', expressing his various thoughts on all things Albion. When the newspaper, in his opinion, 'failed to give the team sufficient praise for drawing at Home Park', Taylor not only stopped writing the column but ceased co-operating with the *Evening Argus* full stop. 'I fully accept the consequences of my decision,' he declared at the time. As far as Taylor's detractors were concerned, his stand against the main source of Albion information in the local community merely became another stick to beat him with.

With so much at stake and his critics starting to sharpen their knives in readiness for a full-on assault, Taylor had little option than to be present for Walsall's visit to the Goldstone on Wednesday 9 April. The match went ahead in blizzard conditions, Albion literally struggling to see the ball throughout the first half as Walsall dominated possession without scoring. After the break, with the wind at Albion's backs, it was a different story. In the seventieth minute, Wilson crossed from the left flank towards Towner, who controlled the ball before drilling a shot beyond Walsall goalkeeper Mick Kearns, sealing a 1–0 win in the process. With results elsewhere going their way, Albion had some breathing space.

Three days later, Towner scored again, this time away to Wrexham, as Albion slipped to a lacklustre 2–1 defeat. Once again, results elsewhere were favourable, meaning they remained two places above the relegation zone. However, the following Wednesday even their impressive home form deserted them when a well-organised Halifax Town side came to the Goldstone. Unable to break the visitors down, Albion's supporters grew restless to the point where slow handclaps rang out around the ground during the second half. Had Town's Bobby Campbell found the net with seven minutes remaining instead of blazing the ball horribly wide of Grummitt's goal, then Taylor's fitful team would have come away with nothing. Instead, a point from a 0–0 draw was enough to keep Albion clear of the bottom four.

With the trap door looming, Taylor nevertheless maintained an air of supreme confidence. Albion would, he insisted, not only beat the drop but surprise everyone with their form during the 1975/76 campaign. 'It has all happened to us this season,' he declared after the Halifax game, 'but next year will be different. We will get the players we want.' Writing in the *Evening Argus*, John Vinicombe struck a more cautious tone. 'I hope he is right. Many of the 10,309-crowd last night will need convincing, although Taylor had a good point that there have been some very entertaining home matches. Last night was not one of them.'

At least Albion's destiny lay in their own hands. Four games of the 1974/75 season remained: the first two at home against Huddersfield Town and Peterborough United; the second two away at Preston North End and Port Vale. Beat Huddersfield and Peterborough and they would be safe, the results of the final two games becoming purely academic. Against Huddersfield, when Albion once again struggled to make headway against well-organised yet limited opposition, the crowd turned their frustrations on the players, with one in particular, Ricky Marlowe, attracting the lion's share of the flak. Marlowe had failed to convert a number of opportunities during the first half and cut a disconsolate figure in the dressing room at the break. 'It's ridiculous the way they are going on,' Steve Piper said by way of consolation, draping an arm around his teammate's shoulders. 'No, it isn't,' replied Marlowe. 'I am playing badly.'

In the seventy-eighth minute, O'Sullivan delivered a pin-point cross towards Marlowe, who went some way towards conquering his demons by heading a goal that finally broke the tension, Gerry Fell adding a second during the closing stages to secure a 2–0 win. Four days later, a penalty by Harry Wilson and a long-range howitzer from O'Sullivan either side of half-time manufactured another 2–0 victory at Peterborough's expense. With the spectre of relegation now banished,

Taylor immediately resumed his wanderings in search of new talent, leaving Gutteridge in charge of the first team for the trip to Preston. Not even the identity of Taylor's supposed target – a certain former England international by the name of Geoff Hurst – could fully appease the manager's detractors. 'I'm not renewing my season ticket of £30 until there is either the signing of a striker in the Geoff Hurst class or, far more important, a clear-out of the whole management set,' wrote Mr K. Gibbons of Woking in the *Evening Argus* letters page, one of a number in a similar vein echoing general discontent at poor results, broken promises over winning the Third Division title, questionable team selections and a management/coaching structure lacking Football League pedigree.

'Peter Taylor's first season of [Football] League management when left to his own devices by the departure of Brian Clough to Leeds United contained much that was good and a lot that left room for criticism,' wrote John Vinicombe in his *Evening Argus* review of the 1974/75 campaign.

> The players hardly kicked-off in a relaxed atmosphere with promises, promises ringing in their ears. Frequent changes on the training and coaching staff early on could not have helped with the departures of John Sheridan and then Gerry Clarke in a matter of months. With the arrival of so many new faces, and then staff comings and goings, it was not surprising that results did not go according to plan.

The good referred to by Vinicombe came in the guise of Albion's home record: fourteen wins, seven draws and just two reverses from twenty-three league fixtures. However, defeats in the final two games of the season at Preston and Port Vale, both by 1–0, merely underpinned their already dreadful away form. 'On their travels Albion just could not put it together and they managed a paltry 7 points, one of the worst away records in the Third Division,' added Vinicombe, reflecting on two wins, three draws and a whopping eighteen defeats. 'Taylor's explanation was that the team lacked know how. Accepting that luck evens out in the course of a season, Albion's final placing of nineteenth with 42 points, one less than last season, was about right.'

In Nottingham, Brian Clough wasn't exactly pulling up trees either. His first match in charge, an FA Cup third-round replay at Tottenham Hotspur, had produced a surprise 1–0 win, raising expectations of what was to come. It proved to be a false dawn. Forest garnered just 14 points from their sixteen remaining Division Two fixtures to finish the season sixteenth in the table. Fulham beat them in the fourth round of the FA Cup after three replays. There would be no silverware, no promotion and precious little to smile about for Forest supporters during the spring of 1975. As Clough recalled in his first autobiography, 'Forest could have been relegated, the season I took charge, for one basic reason. We were crap.'

The following season saw a marginal improvement in Forest's fortunes under Clough. His old mate, on the other hand, was about to embark on the most successful year of his entire solo management career, one that would fundamentally change the character and direction of Brighton & Hove Albion.

12

THE TURNING POINT

Pity poor Mr K. Gibbons of Woking. There was no signing of a striker in the Geoff Hurst mould during the summer of 1975. Furthermore, there was no clearout of the management set either. Despite Peter Taylor declaring that Albion would 'get the players we want' in the wake of April's lacklustre 0–0 draw at home to Halifax Town, everything remained pretty much as it was around the Goldstone Ground. Other than Joe Kinnear, Phil Beal and Neil Martin, a trio of old hands brought in specifically to add experience and provide cover in defensive, midfield and attacking positions respectively, the faces that resumed pre-season training in June were the same ones that had crawled over the finishing line at Port Vale on the last Monday of April.

Did Mr Gibbons follow through with his threat not to renew that £30 season ticket? If so, then he missed out – big time. Like one of those Etch A Sketch children's toys so popular during the 1970s, Albion's players yearned to wipe the slate clean and start all over again. The summer months gave them the opportunity to reboot, with another club trip to the Majorcan sun doing wonders for morale. At long last, Eric Morecambe's notes were about to get played in the right order.

The 1975/76 season began on Saturday 16 August, and once again there was trouble between rival supporters. This time, rather than being limited to one or two isolated incidents, such as the Albion versus Crystal Palace match twelve months previously, acts of hooliganism were reported the length and breadth of the entire country. In Southend, Sheffield Wednesday supporters ran amok among holidaymakers along the seafront, damaging shops and smashing kiosks. In Wolverhampton, fourteen people were stabbed as Manchester United fans turned the streets around Molineux into a battleground. From London to York, Ipswich to Burnley, Magistrates' Courts threw open their doors to deal with hundreds of arrests made before, during and after football matches. Even Brian Clough got involved, jumping from the dugout at the City Ground to prevent so-called supporters climbing over a perimeter wall onto the field of play as Nottingham Forest took on Plymouth Argyle. 'We have seen nothing like it,' commented a police spokesman in Wolverhampton. 'It must have been bottling up inside them all through the long hot summer.'

Unlike 1974, there were no reported incidents in or around the Goldstone, probably because the opposition for Albion's opening game was Rotherham United from distant Yorkshire and not Crystal Palace. The attendance was down, with only 10,138 spectators bothering to come through the turnstiles compared to 26,235 the year beforehand. Albion's lowly finish the previous season had tempered expectations among their fan base and, with Peter Taylor wisely steering clear of any lofty predictions, the hot air remained in the ozone rather than warping the minds of players, management and supporters alike. 'I have picked this team on merit and considered carefully how each player has come through a hard training programme,' said Taylor prior to kick-off. 'The whole month has impressed me with the application of the players and in this department I have seen a vast improvement.'

Albion began purposefully and were ahead after just two minutes through Fred Binney. Nine minutes later, Ernie Machin rammed a free kick high into Rotherham's net to double their advantage. Shortly before half-time, Tony Towner delivered a tantalising cross in Neil Martin's direction, the 34-year-old veteran striker twisting in mid-air to head a majestic third. Had it not been for the second-half heroics of Rotherham goalkeeper Jim McDonagh, then Albion could well have doubled their margin of victory – and them some – instead of having to settle for a 3–0 victory.

Four weeks later, Albion did manage to hit their opponents for six, Fred Binney and Gerry Fell both scoring twice as Chester were battered without reply at the Goldstone. However, at this relatively early stage of the season there was still an inconsistency about the team. Seven days after hammering Chester, Albion produced what Taylor described as the worst performance of his two years at the club in a 2–0 defeat away to Colchester United. 'Of all the matches I've seen since I've been here, the one at Colchester hit me more than any other,' he fumed. 'I thought our preparation had been absolutely right. Afterwards I told them [the players] in no uncertain terms what I felt. I was absolutely staggered at their performance. It can't happen again. It was a diabolical display from the start.'

Within the dressing room, there was frustration, once again, over Taylor's managerial naivety. Albion started against Colchester with a 4–2–4 formation, which allowed the Essex side, without a win in six matches, to swamp the midfield. The formation could and should have been changed once it became clear Albion were struggling, but wasn't. John Vinicombe, sensing the players' displeasure at been publicly hung out to dry for a defeat caused as much by poor tactics as individual performances, made a discreet reference to it in his match report. Adopt that formation for the next fixture against top-of-the-table Crystal Palace and the opposition 'will punch holes through the two-man midfield', he wrote. Fair play to Taylor, who, on listening to the opinions of a handful of senior players, decided to go with a 4–4–2 formation for the trip to Selhurst Park on Tuesday 23 September.

Appearing up front that evening was a man who would play a brief but important role in Albion's 1975/76 season. Barry Butlin was an experienced striker who had graced English football's top flight with both Derby County and Luton Town. To his cost, he also knew all about Brian Clough. 'Brian had originally sold me from Derby to Luton,' recalls Butlin. 'He'd already transferred me in his mind when he came to the club, so that was that. Off to Luton I went. In September 1974, I was transferred from Luton to Nottingham Forest when Allan Brown bought me. In December, Allan was sacked. Then, in January, Brian came in and I was literally out of the side overnight. He'd sold me once before so obviously he was looking to do it again. But I soon came to terms with it. It's all a matter of opinion. I wanted to play first-team football on a regular basis and that meant going somewhere else to do it.'

That somewhere else proved to be Brighton & Hove Albion on a one-month loan deal arranged between Clough and Taylor. Installed at the Courtlands Hotel along with his wife Jackie and two young daughters, Sally and Lisa, Butlin went straight into the team for the match at Colchester and kept his place in the revised 4–4–2 formation against Crystal Palace. 'It didn't worry me that Brighton were in the Third Division,' he adds. 'To be honest with you, Brighton had a decent team and it just seemed strange to me that they were languishing midway down the Third Division. Neil Martin had also gone from Nottingham Forest to Brighton, so having someone that I knew around the place obviously helped. Being a northerner, I didn't understand the intensity of the rivalry between Brighton and Crystal Palace. To me Crystal Palace was in London and Brighton was on the south coast. That didn't automatically say to me, "This is a local derby." Then when I turned up and walked out it took my breath away. It was a full house. I'd suddenly come across this local rivalry that I wasn't at all prepared for. Sure enough, it proved to be quite an intense experience.'

In front of 25,606 spectators, Crystal Palace's largest home attendance in over two years, Albion began as if determined to make up for the Colchester debacle. In the third minute, Fell provided a low cross which Binney deliberately dummied, allowing the ball to run through to Butlin, arriving at speed at the far post. The on-loan striker's first-time shot was an unstoppable one and Albion had the lead. Although Crystal Palace gradually worked their way back into what proved to be an ill-tempered affair, they were unable to find a way past Peter Grummitt. It finished 1–0 to the visitors, with Malcolm Allison, Crystal Palace's flamboyant Fedora-wearing manager, unable to hide his frustration around the corridors of Selhurst Park afterwards. 'They marked us very tight and they kicked us,' he complained bitterly. 'For football, we slaughtered them. How many shots did Brighton have? Three? Four? We were beaten by frustration. You can outplay a side and not beat them.

That is what happened to us. I was told Brighton didn't fight very hard. Well, you saw them tonight. The teams that go up from this division will be those who fight every week, not just here and there.'

Allison meant it as a dig, not a compliment. Unlike Albion, he believed Crystal Palace had what it took to remain in the promotion frame. Standing within earshot, Taylor refused to take the bait, choosing to be more contrite after his outspoken words following the Colchester match. 'I was delighted by the result but I have talked too much this week,' he said. 'The lads did the talking out there tonight.' John Vinicombe agreed. 'Indeed they did,' he wrote in the following day's *Evening Argus*. 'It was a performance that could well herald the much promised revival. This was no ordinary league match. The exchanges were conducted in a cup tie atmosphere and the cut and thrust carried through with the zest of deadly rivals.'

The Crystal Palace match did prove to be a turning point. Between 23 September and 24 February 1976, Albion won sixteen of their twenty-four league fixtures to soar up the Division Three table, moving into second place during mid-November. Some of the football they played, particularly at home, was scintillating. Aldershot were thrashed 4–1, Colchester 6–0 and fellow promotion hopefuls Hereford United 4–2, the revitalised Ian Mellor (now off the transfer list), Fred Binney and Neil Martin flourishing in an environment that encouraged attacking football. As the wins clocked up, so too did the attendances at the Goldstone – 10,000 became 12,000, 12,000 became 14,000, 14,000 rapidly became 18,000, the apex arriving on 24 February, when 33,300 witnessed the 2–0 win over Crystal Palace. More supporters wanted to watch the team playing away, leading to the introduction of club charter trains to far-flung corners of the country, often featuring vintage Pullman coaches from the Brighton Belle service which had ceased its daily runs between London and the south coast in 1972. At long last, Mike Bamber's long-held vision for Brighton & Hove Albion was starting to crystallise.

'Playing at the Goldstone, cor, we used to pack them in,' says Tony Towner. 'And you've got to remember we got the crowds without relying on season-ticket holders. It was just people who rolled up and paid on the turnstiles in all weathers. Being a local boy who'd been there all those years, right the way from being an apprentice, it was lovely for me to see. You'd play at places like Bury or Halifax and there would be 3,000 or maybe 4,000 people there. Then you'd come back to the Goldstone and it would be rammed. That's why we were so strong at home. You wanted to play well in front of your own fans.'

December 1975 also brought about an added bonus for Albion in the form of a cheque from Leeds United. Ever since Clough's departure in July 1974, Albion had been chasing damages from the Yorkshire club for enticing their manager into breaking his contract, which still had approximately four years and three months left to run. The matter rumbled on for the better part of a year and a half, until Leeds finally agreed to pay a sum of £35,000, considerably less than the £75,000 Bamber had initially demanded. Still, something was better than nothing. It does, however, beg the question of what Clough's ill-fated forty-four day spell at Elland Road ultimately cost Leeds. Take Albion's compensation figure, solicitors' fees, the £98,000 'golden pay-off', Clough's wages for the period he was in charge plus various other sundry expenses (such as the Mercedes he kept after his sacking) and there's unlikely to have been much, if any, change out of £150,000. 'We don't know the exact amount, it is subject to taxation,' declared Manny Cussins after the Albion settlement became public knowledge. He did, however, admit that Clough's brief tour of duty had been 'an unsatisfactory investment'. Even if Cussins was aware of an exact or approximate figure, he certainly wasn't about to let on.

Clough was quick to recognise Albion's resurgence under Taylor. Eight wins, seven draws and eleven defeats in the league meant Nottingham Forest entered 1976 looking down the Second Division table rather than up it, Peterborough United of Division Three putting them out of the FA Cup in a third-round replay. Keen to make his transfer to Sussex a permanent one, Barry Butlin instead found himself being recalled to the City Ground as Clough searched for solutions.

'Brighton made me so welcome, but Forest weren't doing very well at all,' recalls Butlin. 'They struggled badly. When I came to the end of my loan period, Brian got me straight back up to Forest and I had a real purple patch during which I played really well. We had this team meeting before one game and Brian said, "If sending you down to Brighton gives you that impetus, then I'd better start sending some more players down there!" I'd seen the seafront and the wonderful countryside and thought it was the prelude to us staying there as a family, but it wasn't to be. I was disappointed, to say the least. To the best of my knowledge he [Clough] was still on decent terms with Peter Taylor at the time and he'd definitely picked up on what was going on at Brighton, not just in terms of how well I'd done down there but the club as a whole. You could tell it was starting to go places.'

If Clough felt a degree of envy over Taylor's relative success at the Goldstone, especially in light of his inability to spark any kind of revival at Forest, then he chose not to show it.

Somehow, despite his deficiencies as a manager, Taylor was starting to make headway. From a distance, Clough observed in silence. As Forest continued to struggle, so the penny began to drop: in order to recapture his old enthusiasm and have any chance of genuine success, he needed Taylor back on board. But there was a catch. With Albion looking more like shoe-ins for promotion with every passing week, Clough needed Taylor way more than Taylor needed Clough.

And so Clough continued observing on the off chance that Albion's bandwagon just might come off the tracks. In the event of such a train wreck, maybe Taylor would be open to the prospect of a reunion?

* * *

On Saturday 6 March, Albion recorded their fourteenth straight home league win by thrashing Peterborough United 5–0, consolidating second place in Division Three behind Hereford United. No sign of any derailment yet. For the first time in several years, competition for places at the Goldstone had assumed healthy levels of ferocity. In accordance with the old sporting mantra that everyone wants to be on a winning team, some players were having to deal with the disappointment of not making the side every week, those being the days when only one substitute was permitted. Steve Piper, a regular starter since breaking into the first XI as a teenager, now found himself relegated to the reserves. Piper wasn't happy about the situation. Then again, a manager's job is to find the right blend on the pitch and encourage his players to fight for positions, not necessarily to fret over their happiness or lack thereof.

'I'd played the majority of the games during his first season in charge, but then the following year he wanted to bring other players in,' says Piper. 'Graham Winstanley had arrived, then a guy called Dennis Burnett who had played for Millwall, and of course we also had Andy Rollings as a centre-back. I played about twenty games here and there over the course of the [1975/76] season but Andy played in my position most of the time. He [Taylor] just didn't fancy me for some reason. I just had to go with it. I didn't necessarily agree with it, but that's all down to opinion. You learn that, the longer you are in the game. Different managers have different opinions and sometimes those opinions can change from season to season, month to month, or even week to week.'

Strong in defence, Albion were equally gifted in attack, where Fred Binney, Ian Mellor and new signing Sammy Morgan (replacing the out-of-favour Neil Martin, dropped after a disagreement with Taylor over the number of strikers at the club) found themselves peering nervously over their shoulders at Peter Ward, the former Rolls-Royce apprentice who had been scoring goals for fun in the reserves. However, Taylor still felt something was missing in midfield. Larger attendances at the Goldstone equalled more money being available to strengthen the side. And so, with Mike Bamber's permission, Taylor made a stealth-like bid to sign Port Vale's captain Brian Horton – somebody he regarded as one the finest midfielders in England outside the First Division – from under the noses of Albion's arch rivals.

'I'd been at Port Vale for six years and that season we had a good little team who were hot on the heels of the likes of Brighton, Palace and Millwall,' recalls Horton. 'I'd been rejected by Walsall as a kid which, in a roundabout way, ended up being the best thing possible for me. I went out to work in the building trade, built myself up physically to the point where I was probably fitter than many players in the Football League, played non-league for Hednesford Town, then came back into the professional game as a 21-year-old with Port Vale. When they made it clear they were prepared to sell me to raise some much-needed cash, a few clubs were interested, but, as far as I'm aware, Crystal Palace and Brighton were willing to go higher than the others.'

On Tuesday 9 March, Port Vale travelled to London to face Crystal Palace at Selhurst Park. Shortly before kick-off, Horton was told 'not to do anything stupid', as Crystal Palace were gearing up to buy him. Sure enough, once the game finished, Port Vale's manager Roy Sproson told his captain that a deal had been done while the match was in progress. 'Only it wasn't Palace I was going to – it was Brighton!' says Horton. As the rest of the Port Vale team boarded a coach for the journey back to Staffordshire, Horton stepped into a limousine sent by Bamber which spirited him away to Brighton. There he was met by Taylor, who, over a beer at the plush Metropole Hotel on the seafront, sold the club to him. The following evening, Horton watched Albion take on Shrewsbury Town at the Goldstone in front of over 21,000 spectators. The morning after, he signed.

'The size of the crowds at Brighton did play a big part in my decision,' adds Horton. 'The offer was a very good one compared to what I was on at Port Vale and Pete told me I would be captain, but I'd always enjoyed playing down there because of those big crowds. Port Vale would be getting four or five thousand through the gate and you'd go to Brighton and there would be eighteen or twenty thousand at the very least. The pitch at the Goldstone Ground was always lovely thanks to dear old Frankie Howard. The team was doing well. Who wouldn't want to be a part of all that?'

Horton's debut the following Saturday coincided with a disappointing 1–0 defeat away to Preston North End, after which Albion bounced back to win consecutive home games against Grimsby Town (4–2) and Swindon Town (2–0). Prior to the latter, two late Sammy Morgan goals transforming what seemed destined to end in a draw, Taylor had noticed something which alarmed him. With the finishing line in view and promotion within their grasp, the players suddenly appeared horribly nervous. 'I have never seen them so tense,' said Taylor. 'They were white-faced before the match. Even at lunchtime, I knew something was up. Players can do nothing when they are so tense. I suppose it is understandable. It was not a physical match. It was more of a mental task for us. I am not making excuses, but these facts have to be faced.'

With a trio of back-to-back away games coming up against Hereford United, Rotherham United and Chesterfield, Taylor chose to make a key team change to try to ease the pressure. Sir Alex Ferguson once said that the first time he saw Ryan Giggs in action, the then thirteen-year-old 'floated over the ground like a cocker spaniel chasing a piece of silver paper in the wind'. Twelve years previously, Taylor had felt a similar surge of excitement while watching Peter Ward play for Albion's reserve team. He didn't say anything in public at the time, for fear of unsettling the youngster or alerting other clubs to his tremendous potential. But, come March 1976, it was getting to the stage where Ward simply had to be blooded on a bigger stage. The striker was confident, cocky even, but in the right sense of the word. Taylor hoped some of that youthful zest would rub off on Albion's increasingly edgy dressing room.

On the last Saturday of the month, Taylor went with his instinct and dropped Binney in favour of Ward for the match at Hereford. In 1976, it wasn't unusual for the BBC or ITV to televise recorded highlights of important league matches in the second, third or even fourth tiers of English football, giving armchair supporters an insight into the world beyond the top flight. With Hereford first and Albion second in Division Three, the BBC opted to feature the top-of-the-table clash on its *Match of the Day* programme. What better way for Ward, fuelled by a pre-match drop of whisky in the dressing room to calm the inevitable nerves, to announce his arrival on the league stage?

With just fifty-one seconds on the referee's watch, Ward turned a defender and struck a shot past Hereford goalkeeper Kevin Charlton to give Albion the lead, becoming only the third player ever to score in the first minute of his league career. Throughout the remaining eighty-nine minutes plus injury time, Albion played by far the better football but were ultimately held 1-1, television pictures confirming that Dixie McNeil had in fact punched Hereford's second-half equaliser into the net. That, along with skirmishes between both sets of supporters after the match leading to numerous arrests, ensured there was more than enough for the assembled media to get their teeth into. But it was Ward who still managed to steal the headlines.

'It was a shit goal, to be honest,' Ward once admitted to me. 'I turned the defender well and hit more of a cross shot. Sammy [Morgan] went in putting the keeper off and it crept into the corner. He even said he'd touched it, so I didn't know if it was mine. The unbelievable thing was that this all happened on *Match of the Day*. They only had one or two games on every show then, but for some reason had decided to cover this one. We stopped the coach somewhere that night on the way back to have a drink and watch the game and it was proved it was my goal. That was it. I'd started. The last eight games I got something like six goals.'

'He was top quality, right from the beginning,' says Andy Rollings of Ward. 'On the field he was electric with his close control, incredible balance, terrific pace and ability to turn players. It was a real case of "What have we got here?" But he was also quite something in the dressing room, totally confident in himself and his own ability. He exuded this "I'm the best player" attitude – and he was. You marvelled at his skills and what he meant to the team. You always knew when you were out there that he had a goal in him, which, when you're 1–0 down and up against it, is priceless. His was natural ability, the kind you can't coach.'

Ward did in fact score six goals over the course of Albion's last eight games, going on to become the top marksman in the entire country the following season with thirty-six strikes in the league and cup competitions. However, not even his sharpshooting during what remained of the 1975/76 campaign could prevent Taylor's men from suddenly losing their way. Nerves, the kind that surfaced for the first time ahead of the Swindon match, had much to do with it, as did Millwall and Cardiff City's relentless pursuit of both Hereford and Albion. While Hereford kept their heads, so Albion began to lose theirs, particularly when playing away from the Goldstone. The creditable draw at Hereford was followed by disappointing trips to Rotherham (another 1–1 draw) and Chesterfield (a 2–1 defeat). Although a 3–0 home win over Horton's old club Port Vale followed, anything less than a point at Millwall on Good Friday would, to all intents and purposes, spell the end of Albion's promotion push.

The Old Den, Millwall's home until 1993, was never exactly the most welcoming of places. So it proved that day as thousands of people, mainly with Millwall loyalties, descended on a ground hemmed in by railway lines and Dickensian rat-runs, the kind of urban environment just perfect for ambushing away supporters. Many gave up trying to get inside long before kick-off as dangerous levels of congestion built up around the turnstiles, the records declaring that 23,008 – Millwall's largest attendance for four years – did somehow manage to gain admittance. On the field, Albion failed to live up to the occasion against a well-oiled side unbeaten in their previous twelve league matches. First-half goals by Trevor Lee and John Seasman put the Londoners in control, Terry Brisley's crisp strike on the hour ending the game as a contest. Although Binney, who partnered Ward up front throughout, scored with six minutes remaining, it proved to be no more than a consolation.

The following day Albion played out a dour 1–1 draw away to Aldershot. Mathematically, promotion was still a possibility. That was until Gillingham's Danny Westwood scored with his team's only shot on target at the Goldstone on Easter Monday, Joe Kinnear capping a miserable holiday period on a personal level by missing a second-half penalty (his underhit back pass at the Old Den having led directly to Millwall's second goal). Ward's equaliser two minutes from the end of normal time salvaged some pride in the form of another 1–1 draw, but the promotion dream was over.

On 24 April, a crowd of just 11,859 – Albion's lowest at home since the previous September but still the highest in the division that weekend – watched Taylor's side conclude their fixture programme against Sheffield Wednesday with a third successive 1–1 draw. The atmosphere was peculiar to say the least. Promotion had been denied, hence an undeniable air of anti-climax. And yet there existed a genuine belief, in the dressing room as well as on the terraces, that Albion were onto something – providing they kept hold of the majority of the side that had got them this far. Prior to kick-off, Brian Horton led the team around the perimeter of the pitch, the players applauding the fans and the fans reciprocating with warmth. Afterwards, the majority of Albion's squad went for an Italian meal washed down by multiple beers, wines and spirits. 'We'd missed out this time, but we'd come really close,' recalls Harry Wilson. 'Next time, we'd make sure that we didn't miss out. That was the feeling among us. I never drank alcohol until I was twenty-five and after that I only ever drank wine, not pints of beer, but I still went out. The team spirit among that group of lads was spot on. If one went out, you all went out – win, lose or draw.'

Amid the gallows humour and a keen sense amid the players of wanting the 1976/77 season to come around as soon as possible, one man struggled to put a brave face on Albion's misfortune.

Their manager.

After drawing with Sheffield Wednesday, Taylor fulfilled his post-match duties around the Goldstone with grace. He talked to his players, sponsors, supporters and the media, batting away one or two mischievous suggestions that Albion, a Third Division outfit for the vast majority of their existence, didn't really want promotion. 'The public who supported us so wonderfully know that isn't true,' he insisted. 'Any ideas or talk like that is ridiculous, but we didn't deserve to go up on our away record.

And, although it might sound contradictory, we were the best potential side in the division, certainly towards the end. But we didn't have enough consistency. We played some great stuff and some poor stuff, sometimes in the space of a week. I'm not shifting blame from me to the players. I take full responsibility.'

For the first time, Taylor also publicly praised Ward, someone he had done his level best to shield from any hype. 'He is the hottest property in English football,' Taylor declared. 'I would not dream of listening to any offers for him. He is that good he would get in Derby's side tomorrow.' And with that Taylor was gone, the silence which filled the corridor outside the manager's office eventually being broken by John Vinicombe. 'I do wish he would just forget about Derby,' quipped the *Evening Argus* reporter, eliciting a few chuckles and nods of agreement among the press pack.

Taylor took Albion's failure to secure promotion badly, and personally. Against all expectations, little Hereford United finished as champions with Cardiff City and Millwall also securing promotion berths, Albion trailing in empty-handed in fourth place. Once again, the first team, together with their manager, backroom staff, Bamber and the club's directors, were scheduled to go to Spain for some rest, relaxation and friendlies during the first week of May. After that, Taylor decided he would stay on in Majorca and ponder his next move. Had he taken Brighton & Hove Albion as far as he could? That was the question which bothered him – one only he could answer.

'He did what he'd done before at times of crisis,' Brian Clough wrote in his first autobiography. 'He buggered off to his villa by the sea, just around the coast from our favourite haunt, Cala Millor. He'd gone there with a sense of failure, having missed promotion, with a heavy if not broken heart. We had not been in touch very often since parting company on the south coast, but he could see that progress was being made at Forest, his hometown club, the one Pete always wanted to manage. He was Forest daft!'

Once again, Clough was being economical with the truth. Progress around the City Ground had been steady at best, Forest managing to haul themselves up to an eighth-place finish in Division Two on the back of eight straight home league wins. But, sixteen months into the job, Clough was still far from setting the banks of the River Trent alight. He did, however, have one reason to feel optimistic. Albion's promotion bandwagon was lying in tatters at the side of the tracks, and Clough had a pretty good idea how that wreck would affect Taylor's state of mind.

One afternoon in late June, his suspicions were confirmed when Maurice Edwards, a postmaster who had scouted for Clough and Taylor, got in touch. On a flying visit to the Midlands from Majorca, Taylor dropped by Edwards's post office in Burton-on-Trent and the two men fell into conversation. Taylor was in low spirits and frustrated by the backroom set-up at the Goldstone, believing he could no longer rely on the club's non-playing staff for adequate support. Out of the blue, he then offered Edwards the assistant manager's position at Brighton & Hove Albion. Edwards turned him down before suggesting that Clough would probably welcome the opportunity to reunite with Taylor – not at the Goldstone, but at the City Ground. According to Edwards, Taylor said he would willingly work with Clough again, but was reluctant to make the first move. By contacting Clough, Edwards was making that first move for him.

A couple of days later, Clough telephoned Stuart Dryden,

vice-chairman of Nottingham Forest, asking to meet for a drink at Widmerpool Cricket Club where he was playing in a testimonial match. As they sat outside the pavilion, Dryden trying to second-guess what was on Clough's mind, Forest's manager suddenly announced that he was going to Majorca the very next day 'to fetch Taylor'. Twenty-four hours later, Clough arrived unannounced on the Spanish island, tracked Taylor down, and popped the question: 'How do you fancy coming to Forest?' Clough's recollection is that Taylor tried stalling for a while, but he could detect a twinkle in his eye. 'He couldn't ever hide his enthusiasm from me, no matter how hard he tried – and he tried again on that occasion,' said Clough.

'I was surprised to see him,' admitted Taylor. 'We arranged to meet at a café and Brian talked me into joining him. His timing was brilliant. He had read the situation perfectly. I'd shot it at Brighton and he had a two-bob team at Nottingham. We both knew we were banging our heads against a brick wall on our own. Together we could do any job. There was no point delaying any longer.'

Except that delay they had to, at least for a week or two. Clough telephoned Dryden from Majorca to say he 'had done what I came for, but we must let things die down for a while'. That's because Taylor had yet to inform Mike Bamber of his decision to quit as Albion's manager – an obligation he was absolutely dreading. Bamber, however, was already anticipating some kind of showdown. Just three days before the start of pre-season training, Taylor had got in touch from Majorca to say he would be spending another week on the island. 'I hadn't heard from him all summer, which was unusual,' Bamber recalled several years later. 'Normally he'd be rushing around looking for players. I knew something was afoot.'

On the morning of Friday 16 July, a day of violent electrical storms across Sussex, Taylor made his way to the Goldstone and told Bamber he was resigning. Even then he resorted to white lies. 'I have no plans at all, except to take the dog for a walk,' Taylor told the gathering press, who, on learning Clough had also been in Majorca, were already putting two and two together. 'There is no significance in the fact that Brian Clough was on holiday at the same time as me,' maintained Taylor. 'He was one of many footballing people who were in Majorca. It was the worst holiday I have had in my life. It was a very hard decision to make because Mike Bamber and the board have been so good to me. It's been a manager's utopia.'

Through what he later confessed to be 'a daze', Bamber read the resignation letter Taylor had composed. 'Having been with Albion for two years and not having achieved Second Division status, which was my goal, I now consider the time has come to part company with the club,' Taylor stated. 'During my period as manager I have always had from yourself and the board of directors complete backing and respect which has been unique in management.' In that regard Taylor was echoing sentiments Clough would make in both his autobiographies, describing Bamber as 'the nicest and best chairman I ever worked for' in the first book and 'the pleasantest and finest chairman who ever employed me' in the second. Not that such compliments prevented either man from walking out on him.

In *With Clough By Taylor*, published four years after he left Albion, Taylor went deeper into the circumstances surrounding his resignation while continuing to praise Bamber as a chairman. 'I had stayed with Brighton for the right reasons and, in my opinion, I left them for the right reasons,' he wrote. 'A change is required at times, and I think both of us needed one.

Mike Bamber had been wonderful to me. I could have anything – a new car, money for players, a salary increase. I took a long holiday in Majorca, then returned to resign. After keeping them clear of relegation in 1974/75, I had missed promotion in 1975/76 by losing an Easter match at Millwall. From that day, my doubts grew. I told Bamber "I'm going, I'm a failure," and he said "If you call this failure then I want more of it," which was a nice note to leave on.'

Bamber wasted no time appointing a successor, moving so quickly that the new incumbent was in position before the majority of the players were even aware of Taylor's departure. In January 1973, Albion had played Fulham at Craven Cottage and lost 5–1. During the first half, Fulham's ex-England international Alan Mullery punched teammate Jimmy Dunne in the face for not paying enough attention to the player he was supposed to be marking. Far from being outraged, Bamber was most impressed. Anyone who wanted to win that much clearly cared, he reasoned. By coincidence, the incident had returned to Bamber in a dream just days beforehand. When Taylor resigned, Albion's chairman knew instinctively who he should appoint. Mullery, still registered as a player, had been hoping to step into Alec Stock's shoes as manager of Fulham during the summer of 1976. When Stock decided that he wanted to continue in the post, Mullery was left in limbo. Despite his having no managerial experience, Bamber felt he was the right man for the job. Mullery said yes almost immediately.

'I was disappointed when I heard the news about Peter because it was him who had given me my chance in league football eighteen months or so beforehand,' says Gerry Fell. 'You think, "Crikey, this is my job. What's going to happen now?" It was the first time something like that had happened to me because I'd only been there such a short period of time. But then we heard more or less straight away about Alan taking over. That's when I realised, "Ah, that's what I'm supposed to do. I just carry on playing." These things happen in football and you adapt.'

'I think he [Taylor] was very, very disappointed that we didn't make it that year,' adds Horton. 'He felt that we could, and perhaps should, have won promotion. But we didn't and that's when he chose to go back with Brian. My big concern at the time was the man who was replacing him. Alan Mullery had seen it all and done it all for England, Spurs and Fulham and he played in my position. We'd heard that he might be coming as player/manager. I thought my days at Brighton were numbered before I'd even really got started. But that's not what happened. We started the season and we kept winning, and kept winning, and at some stage he obviously thought, "We've got a good side here. I'm going to let them get on with it." And he did.'

Thirty-three and a half months after it had begun, the Clough/Taylor era at the Goldstone was over. A week after resigning as Albion's manager, to nobody's great surprise, Taylor was unveiled as Brian Clough's right-hand man at Nottingham Forest. At that stage nobody could possibly have imagined what heights lay in store for that club under the pair's stewardship. Mind you, courtesy of the foundations they had laid at the Goldstone between 1973 and 1976, from firing up the public relations machine to player recruitment, Brighton & Hove Albion wouldn't do too badly either.

13

RISE AND FALL

In 1977, under Brian Clough and Peter Taylor's guidance, Nottingham Forest won promotion from the Second Division. In 1978, they finished top of the First Division, the equivalent of the modern-day Premier League, capturing the League Cup as a bonus. In 1979, Forest then went and won the European Cup, defeating the Swedish side Malmö 1–0 in the final in Munich. They also managed to retain the League Cup the same year. Taylor was right. Together he and Clough really could do any job. Well, almost. The FA Cup remained elusive but, heck, there's only so much silverware a cabinet can take.

Brighton & Hove Albion's progress, along with that of most other British football clubs besides Liverpool, was more sedate. But there was progress all the same. In May 1977, having led the Third Division for almost the entire season before easing off after achieving their goal, they were promoted as runners-up to the Second Division. The following year Albion were desperately unlucky not to win promotion to the First Division, an inferior goal difference denying them on the final day of the 1977/78 campaign. Twelve months later, they made up for it by reaching the top flight for the first time in the club's history. The

Skegness donkey, as Clough once labelled Albion, had reached the big time within six years of Mike Bamber becoming the club's sole chairman.

'The framework of the team was already there,' says Andy Rollings. 'Brian Clough had made some signings and got the media interested. Then Peter Taylor laid the foundations. It just needed somebody to step in, tweak it a bit more, and we'd be up and running. And that somebody was Alan Mullery. The season we went up from the Third Division we used pretty much the same players who'd played under Peter – myself, Kenny Tiler, Tony Towner, Gerry Fell, Peter O'Sullivan, Brian Horton, Ian Mellor, Peter Ward, Peter Grummitt, Graham Winstanley, Harry Wilson – guys like that. One or two new faces then came in like Chris Cattlin and Mark Lawrenson, but he [Mullery] really didn't change it that much. He moved Steve Piper from defence into midfield which proved to be an inspired bit of management, but other than that it was pretty much business as usual. And we just flew.'

'I think Mullery maybe had a bit more about him than Taylor,' says Peter Brackley, still at the microphone for BBC Radio Brighton throughout Albion's ascendancy. 'The players liked the fact that he had only just finished playing himself. People like Brian Horton responded to that. Taylor had signed Horton, but Horton more or less became Mullery on the pitch as Brighton came up through the divisions. They had a similar playing style. Horton would never stop talking while he was out there, just like Mullery in his playing days. Horton was a massive signing for Brighton, no question, every bit as important as Peter Ward, who scored most of the goals.'

Between August 1975 and April 1979, Albion won sixty-eight of their eighty-eight league fixtures at the Goldstone Ground, losing just six. Such dazzling form meant the crowds kept rolling in, ensuring money remained available to pay generous wages and fund whatever team rebuilding Mullery saw fit. When Preston North End made it clear they were prepared to sell their promising young centre-back Mark Lawrenson, Albion moved swiftly to outbid mighty Liverpool with a cheque amounting to the peculiarly round sum of £111,111. In fact, Albion's sizeable attendances, often in excess of 30,000 punters, became the envy of many English clubs further up football's traditional food chain. 'To think that as a player I was watched by 30,000 people at Notts County but I couldn't get 30,000 to come and watch Forest even in a semi-final of the European Cup,' moaned Clough, for whom disappointingly low attendances during Forest's glory years became a source of immense frustration.

Albion's rise from the Third to the First Division meant that, as of August 1979, the Seagulls, as they had become known, were dining at the same table as Nottingham Forest. However, while Clough and Taylor basked in the afterglow of their European Cup success, Albion's players, with only a handful of top-flight appearances between them, struggled for form during the opening months of the 1979/80 season. By the end of October, they were bottom of the league, a 3–0 defeat to Arsenal at Highbury on 3 November segueing into a 4–1 home loss to Liverpool, which in turn made way for a 4–0 whipping in a League Cup replay back at Highbury. Albion weren't just dead in the water but sinking fast, a rapid return to the Second Division on the cards unless some kind of shot in the arm could be administered quickly.

On Friday 16 November, Albion's squad travelled north by train ready to face Nottingham Forest the following afternoon.

Unbeaten at the City Ground for fifty-one matches stretching back to April 1977, the odds on Forest not making it to fifty-two seemed about as slim as Clough taking a vow of silence – and sticking to it. One of the fifty-one had been a League Cup quarter-final tie in December 1978, Forest defeating Albion 3–1 in the first match between the two clubs since Clough and Taylor's respective defections from the Goldstone. The encounter was tighter than the score line suggests, Forest's manager commenting afterwards how impressed he was by the club's progress since his tenure on the south coast. Nevertheless, Clough believed his European champions would steamroller the league's bottom-placed team and, prior to kick-off, let his players know as much, describing Albion as the 'biggest load of rubbish' he had ever seen in the First Division. Albion's players heard his every word drifting down the corridor, the door to the increasingly stuffy away dressing room having been left wide open. 'Brian Clough did our team talk for us,' Alan Mullery later admitted. 'That was all the incentive we needed.'

To everyone's surprise, Albion came out faster than a John McEnroe serve. In the twelfth minute Lawrenson's cross was headed down by centre-forward Ray Clarke (transferred from FC Bruges the previous month) in the direction of Gerry Ryan, another Mullery signing acquired from Derby County during Albion's 1978/79 promotion season. Ryan kept his head to squeeze a right-foot shot past Forest's England international goalkeeper Peter Shilton and the visitors had a deserved lead.

From that point on Forest dominated, yet somehow Albion's defence managed to hold out even when the home side were awarded a penalty, goalkeeper Graham Moseley (another Mullery signing from Derby) diving low to his left to save John Robertson's spot kick. 'The longer the game went on, the more apparent it was that Brighton would win,' wrote James Kirk of the *Sunday Telegraph*, who, along with other members of the assembled media, could barely believe what he was witnessing. The final whistle was greeted by scenes of elation among the players and visiting supporters. Albion's first ever away win in the top flight had come at the expense of the mighty European champions, breaking their long unbeaten home run in the process.

'Even though it was against Clough and Taylor, I still went in thinking of it as just another game,' says Peter O'Sullivan. 'It was nothing to do with revenge or anything like that. Life's too short and, anyway, I'd enjoyed playing under them. But it was nice to win, even if it was a bit like the Alamo. I seemed to be playing left-back most of the game, so God knows where Gary Williams [signed by Mullery as a replacement for Preston-bound Harry Wilson] was – probably in the crowd behind our goal I would think. We couldn't get any deeper. After we scored, I don't think we got out of our half. It was the biggest robbery ever, but we managed to get away.'

Back in the dressing room, Mullery went from man to man grabbing every one of his players by the face 'like he was going to kiss us', according to centre-back Peter Suddaby, making his Albion debut that day. 'Which, fortunately, he didn't.' All around was revelry, the kind that comes with winning a major trophy rather than a regular league match. Until, that is, Clough suddenly stuck his head round the door, at which point the air fell horribly silent. Rather than berate Albion's players, Forest's manager told them they were 'bloody fantastic' and 'a credit to their shirts'. Three of them – Moseley, Ryan and Peter Ward – were also minor miracle workers, having broken a Friday night curfew to head for pubs on the far side of Nottingham where, by Ward's reckoning, 'nobody would have a clue who we were'. On entering the first hostelry the trio walked slap-bang into a large group of Albion supporters. What happens on the far side of Nottingham clearly stays on the far side of Nottingham as news of the breakout failed to reach Albion's management. Considering Forest's formidable home form, maybe a strong nightcap wasn't such a bad idea after all. Clearly, it didn't appear to do them any harm.

Over the weeks that followed, Albion rapidly made up ground on the clubs above them, losing just three of their next nineteen league fixtures to banish all talk of relegation. By now the majority of the players who had taken the club this far – Ian Mellor, Ken Tiler, Steve Piper, Tony Towner and Gerry Fell among them – had moved on, to be replaced by talents such as Lawrenson, Ryan and future England internationals John Gregory and Gary Stevens. Andy Rollings, a towering figure in the centre of defence for five years, found himself playing second choice to Steve Foster, another England international in waiting signed from Portsmouth. Other members of the old guard, however, flourished at a higher level. Peter Ward scored with such regularity that he became the subject of international speculation involving England and transfer speculation surrounding Nottingham Forest. Brian Horton, always regarded by Peter Taylor as one of the finest midfield players outside the First Division, held his own against the likes of Arsenal's Liam Brady, Glenn Hoddle at Tottenham Hotspur and the rapidly emerging Bryan Robson of West Bromwich Albion.

And then there was Peter O'Sullivan, 'Sully', the man who had joined Albion on a free transfer in April 1970 and outlasted everyone, managers as well as players.

'Sully was a great individual player and a great team player,' says Ray Clarke, who lined up alongside and against the very best that Europe had to offer during the mid-to-late 1970s while wearing the shirts of Sparta Rotterdam, Ajax and FC Bruges. 'He was also a very natural player. There was me, slogging my guts out in training trying to get super-duper fit, and he just does it naturally. I never met another guy like him. Really, really annoying! But he was a great lad, fun to play with and fun to be around.'

'Peter O'Sullivan was such an important player for us,' adds Andy Rollings. 'The word legend gets overused these days but that's exactly what he was for a number of years. He should have played at the top level all the time, he was that good a player. He had natural ability and great fitness. Why he didn't play at the top level before we got there that season, you'll have to ask him. I think he just loved Brighton, loved the club, loved the people, and was quite happy so long as he was playing football. What he did at this club was incredible, and as an individual player he was one of the best I've ever played with.'

'Yeah, that's about spot on,' says O'Sullivan, when told the reasons put forward by Rollings as to why he chose to remain with Albion in the lower divisions. 'Mind you, you've got to remember I was on the transfer list at some point under every manager I had at Brighton, except for one – Brian Clough. If I had wanted to go when he was in charge, he'd have kicked me out. But I was too frightened to ask!'

Success is relative. Nobody can seriously compare Albion's rise through the divisions during the late 1970s with what Clough and Taylor achieved at Nottingham Forest over the same period. Yet, given that the building blocks essentially existed at Brighton & Hove Albion – a loyal and supportive chairman, players of considerable potential, a sizeable fan base, the funds to strengthen the team – it is only natural to wonder how far Clough and Taylor could have taken the club had the former been prepared to commit for the long haul.

Except, despite some fairly half-hearted protestations, he was never going to do that.

Not in a million years.

'We're from the north, Pete. What do we care about Brighton? Bloody southerners. You can't manage a team that's not your own people.' Clough never actually uttered those exact words – they're taken from the film adaptation of *The Damned United* – but it's easy to see how he might have done. The poet William Blake may have regarded Sussex as 'the sweetest spot on Earth', but Clough was having none of it. 'People go to Brighton for various reasons,' he wrote in his first autobiography, published in 1994, the year after his retirement. 'For a holiday, for a day trip, for a place to retire, for a Tory Party conference. Or for a dirty weekend. With all due respect to the club and its fans, you don't go there for the football. Brighton is not a big-time club and is never likely to be.'

Alan Mullery, a Londoner, felt differently. Brighton & Hove has often been described as London-by-the-Sea, and he warmed to the place immediately in the same way that a Lancastrian or Yorkshireman might be drawn to Blackpool or Scarborough. 'I was thirty-four years old and the best five years of my football life were about to begin,' Mullery wrote in his 2006 autobiography of becoming Albion's manager, quite an acknowledgement for a former England captain with multiple domestic and European honours to his name at club level. Brighton & Hove wasn't built for Brian Clough. Nottingham, however, was. And that turned out to be Mullery's good fortune. You don't have to come from the north to be sport-obsessed or to harbour a deep sense of pride in your surroundings. Mullery appreciated that. Clough, with his apparent aversion to the south and its people, didn't. What's more, he wasn't prepared to listen to anyone who thought otherwise. In the cold light of day, it's a wonder Clough stayed at the Goldstone for as long as he did.

Forest had long since given up hope of catching Liverpool at the top of the First Division by the time the return fixture in Sussex came around on 29 March 1980, although their quest to retain the European Cup remained on track. In the eighty-sixth minute, substitute Gary Stevens won a tackle just outside Albion's penalty area before passing to Horton, who in turn found O'Sullivan striding down the left flank. O'Sullivan played the ball to Ward, standing with his back to Forest's goal, who then laid it off in the direction of Gary Williams. 'Hit the fucking thing!' screamed Horton. And so, from a considerable distance, Williams did just that. Peter Shilton may have been the finest goalkeeper in the country at the time, if not the world, but he had no chance of preventing the ball from entering the top right-hand corner of Forest's net. Only Justin Fashanu's oft-replayed effort for Norwich City versus Liverpool topped it in the annual goal of the season competition on the BBC's *Match of the Day* programme. Against all odds, Albion had done the double over Nottingham Forest and their former managerial duo.

This time, Clough wasn't so gracious in defeat. 'Fluke, absolute fluke,' stormed Forest's manager as he prowled menacingly through the corridors of the Goldstone's West Stand. 'When a fella scores like that from thirty-five yards it can only be a fluke.' The shot may have carried an element of fortune (Williams has since admitted he was trying to hit the ball as hard as possible rather than aiming for the top corner), but there was nothing lucky about the result. 'They [Albion] generally outshone the visitors and exuded an almost tangible will to win,' wrote John Nicholls in *The Times*. 'That one was nothing to do with the Alamo,' adds O'Sullivan. 'We played bloody well that day and scored a bloody great goal. If anything, that stands out more than the win at the City Ground because of the overall team performance. We deserved it.'

'He wasn't happy about that at all, I can tell you,' recalls Mullery of Clough's reaction at losing twice to Albion in the space of a single season. 'There's that line he came out with comparing being at Brighton to asking Lester Piggott to win the Derby on a Skegness donkey. Well, we proved him wrong. But, hey, who am I to argue with everything he achieved over his career with Peter? What did used to bother me, though, was I couldn't work out how he did it. His attitude to football was getting a group of lads to play together, but the coaching and fitness side was something nobody had ever seen before because they didn't do anything. Yet they won games over and over again. Some of his players were grossly overweight and didn't seem to look after themselves. I even caught one – and I won't name him – drinking a glass of Scotch in the Langfords Hotel in Hove the day before we played them. You can't win with players like that – but they did! You can never, ever, find anybody else who did it the way that he did. If I look at Bill Shankly, if I look at Bill Nicholson, if I look at any of the top-class managers at that time, they were always doing the coaching. But Brian never did. It's a mystery to me, a complete mystery.'

Two months after losing 1–0 at the Goldstone, Nottingham Forest won the European Cup for a second time thanks to John Robertson's goal against Hamburg in Madrid. By then Albion's players were on the beach, having comfortably secured their

First Division status, finishing sixteenth in the table out of twenty-two clubs. Forest's achievement made news on a global scale; Albion's barely raised a headline beyond Sussex. In their own ways both were remarkable achievements. No doubt about it, the summer of 1980 was a good time to be a Nottingham Forest or a Brighton & Hove Albion supporter.

* * *

Unbeknown to all – managers, assistant managers, chairmen, vice-chairmen, players, club secretaries, supporters, even the media, who like to think they can spot a change in the weather before everyone else – the beginning of the end was approaching faster than anyone could possibly have anticipated.

In Nottingham, the publication of Peter Taylor's autobiography, *With Clough By Taylor*, shortly after Forest's second European Cup win sent Clough into apoplexy. It was, to quote the former *Nottingham Evening Post* reporter Duncan Hamilton, 'Taylor's book, but indisputably Clough's story.' Clough only heard about its impending release through word of mouth, not from Taylor himself – a betrayal he regarded as unforgivable. As if that wasn't bad enough, the text itself contained some cutting judgements on Clough's character. He was, according to Taylor, insecure and lacking in self-belief with anxieties that stemmed from failing his eleven-plus exam at school. Having repaired the damage caused by the first major earthquake to hit their relationship with Clough's defection from Albion to Leeds United, so the ground between the two men now split again. Rather than working in tandem, they began to think and act as individuals, talking behind their respective backs and briefing against one another as if part of some Shakespearian tragedy. The team, almost inevitably, began to suffer, exiting the 1980/81 European Cup competition in the first round. Taylor's sense of humour deserted him. He became paranoid, appearing to Hamilton to be on the verge of a nervous breakdown. Ultimately, the stress proved too much for a man with a history of heart problems. In May 1982, Taylor resigned. Even then they couldn't agree, Clough maintaining that he helped secure a £31,000 pay-off for Taylor while Taylor insisted he did all the negotiating himself, with the fee actually being £25,000.

In Brighton & Hove, cracks were also beginning to show. Having reached the Promised Land, Mike Bamber wanted to expand the club off the field by making improvements to the Goldstone, including building sponsors' lounges. Alan Mullery was adamant that team strengthening should remain the priority. The two men began to clash. So long as Harry Bloom was on hand, the pair had a buffer for their frustrations. Bamber valued Bloom's opinion and would listen to him, as did Mullery, who came to regard the club's vice-chairman as a father figure. On Saturday 18 October 1980, Harry Bloom died of a heart attack on board a coach as it prepared to transport the players, directors and backroom staff from Stoke-on-Trent railway station to a nearby hotel ahead of a match at the Victoria Ground, Stoke City's pre-1997 home. A vital if unseen cog in Albion's rise to prominence, not to mention a thoroughly decent man, was no more.

From that point the relationship between Bamber and Mullery was, in effect, doomed. The latter resented the way the former kept going behind his back regarding players' contracts. As Albion's form dipped, causing attendances to fall, so money increasingly became an issue. Bamber asked Mullery to make cuts in his backroom staff. Mullery resisted. However, both men agreed that if cash had to be found then the easiest way of raising it was by selling the club's prized asset, Mark Lawrenson. In the summer of 1981, with Albion having narrowly avoided relegation to the Second Division by winning their last four league games of the season, Mullery got in touch with Manchester United manager Ron Atkinson and the pair agreed a fee of £400,000 for Lawrenson plus two United players, shaking hands on the deal at a football dinner in London. The following day, Mullery informed his chairman – only to be told that Bamber had already arranged Lawrenson's transfer to Liverpool for £900,000. Mullery was livid and another argument ensued. This time, Mullery resigned.

In the aftermath, Brian Horton, aghast at the departure of a manager he both liked and respected, was traded to Second Division Luton Town by Mullery's replacement Mike Bailey. Peter O'Sullivan was sold to Fulham. John Gregory went to Queens Park Rangers. And Lawrenson completed his transfer to Liverpool, the club Albion had beaten to his signature back in 1977. By now Peter Ward was also a memory, Peter Taylor persuading Brian Clough to take him to Nottingham Forest in October 1980 as a replacement for the Manchester United-bound Gary Birtles. Andy Rollings, surplus to requirements, found himself at Swindon Town. The last remnants of the Albion teams that played under Clough and/or Taylor before rising through the divisions under Mullery had gone. Only Mike Bamber remained, like a ship's captain nervously surveying shifting ice floes from his bridge, along with Glen Wilson on the backroom staff and Frankie Howard, still tending his beloved turf.

'I did find the speed of it all upsetting,' admits Horton. 'The gaffer went. Then I went. Then everyone else seemed to go. My biggest regret is that I didn't get the chance to say goodbye to the fans, who had been amazing throughout those years. We played Leeds at home on the final day of that season and needed a win to stay up, which we got. There was a really great buzz about the place afterwards. Little did I know that would be my last game. I never had the opportunity to say cheerio because I didn't know what lay just around the corner. That was hard.'

The following season, Albion finished a creditable thirteenth in the First Division, yet off the field all remained far from well. Attendances continued to drop, as few as 12,857 witnessing the 1–0 win over Leeds on 2 March 1982. Many supporters blamed the overly defensive tactics employed by Mike Bailey for the fall. Whatever the reason, Bamber was now struggling to meet the bills. Albion had been paying players unrealistic salaries, with some being awarded ten-year contracts – sheer financial folly for a football club of any size, let alone one outside the English elite. In December 1982, Bailey was sacked, the three-month delay in appointing a permanent successor creating a malaise among the squad which contributed to the club's relegation to the Second Division at the end of the season.

On the flip side, Albion's performances in the 1982/83 FA Cup contrasted markedly to their disappointing form in the league. Victories over Newcastle United, Manchester City, Liverpool, Norwich City and Sheffield Wednesday meant that, on Saturday 21 May 1983, Albion walked out to face Manchester United at the old Wembley Stadium in the club's first ever FA Cup final. 'Even a dark cloud can sometimes have a silver lining,' remarked Bamber, in a nod to the club's Jekyll and Hyde form over the previous few months.

The very same day as Albion were going toe to toe with Manchester United in north London, Brian Clough was raising money for charity by taking part in the 100-mile Centurion Walk across the Pennines. His relationship with Peter Taylor, if it could still be called that, had by this time taken a bizarre new twist. Six months after announcing his retirement at Nottingham Forest, Taylor was back in business just a few miles down the A52 trunk road as manager of Derby County, the very club where the pair had forged their reputations. To add fuel to the fire, the draw for the third round of the FA Cup that season paired the two clubs against each other, Derby triumphing 2–0 in a match bristling with rancour. With the very last tie of that season's competition in progress at Wembley, Clough and his group of walkers stopped at a pub for a breather. At some point Clough called home to speak to his wife Barbara, who relayed the jaw-dropping news that Taylor had gone and signed John Robertson, Forest's talismanic winger, behind his back.

'Peter Taylor could not be as close to someone as he was to me for all those years and expect to get away with the Robertson signing without even giving me a call,' Clough wrote in his first autobiography. 'Just a courtesy call to say "How's the walk going? Glad to hear you've got the club doctor with you – you could need him, silly bugger. Are you carrying oxygen? By the way – I've signed John Robertson." That would have been classic Taylor. Lead them up the garden path, or the Pennine Way, then hit them with the real reason for the call. He didn't ring and I never forgave him.'

On hearing the news from Barbara, Clough returned to the bar and told Alan Hill, his trusted backroom confidant at the City Ground, that he was finished with Taylor and would never speak to him again (he was true to his word; when Taylor died in 1990 the pair hadn't exchanged so much as a word for seven years). Instead, the two men set about tarnishing their respective names through the media. Clough in particular was often vicious in his choice of words, once claiming he would run his erstwhile partner over should he see him hitch-hiking on the A52. 'No one will know how my wife and daughter suffered over those remarks,' Taylor retorted, adding that he would never forgive Clough 'for the misery he has caused'. It was hard to believe they had ever been friends at all.

Despite the verbal brickbats, Clough and Taylor continued to be held in high esteem throughout the wider football world long after their partnership had descended into acrimony, their names forever carved in stone by supporters of Nottingham Forest and Derby County.

Which is more than can be said for Mike Bamber on the south coast of England.

Albion's relegation from the First Division after four seasons in the top flight was somewhat sugar-coated by the club's appearance in the 1983 FA Cup final, Manchester United winning 4–0 in a replay after the first match ended 2–2. With so many gifted players still on the payroll, such as Jimmy Case, Steve Foster and Gordon Smith (whose failure to convert a last-minute opportunity in the initial Wembley final saw him enter FA Cup folklore), there was every reason to believe the club would bounce straight back the following season. When the expected challenge for promotion failed to materialise, so supporters began to take their frustrations out on one man. 'Bamber out!' became a familiar chant on the terraces as fans openly questioned where the money was from the run to the FA Cup final, the insinuation being that the chairman had lined his own pockets. In reality, nothing could have been further from the truth. The money went towards servicing existing debt and paying the wages on those crippling ten-year contracts, ones that Bamber had admittedly instigated. If the chairman was guilty of anything, it was negligence brought on by letting his heart rule his head, rather than any form of criminal behaviour.

The time had come to cut Albion's cloth accordingly. Over the course of the 1983/84 season, many of the club's big earners were sold. Free transfers, bargain signings and developing young local talent became the order of the day. 'Events over the last decade have perhaps moved too quickly,' Bamber admitted in December 1983. 'It has been very much like being on a rollercoaster. Quite honestly, we probably had our success too fast and there was no time to consolidate. The solid foundations and right base from which to progress long term wasn't established, so we have decided to build for the future. In other words, we are making a completely fresh start, and this is going to be done with the right structure and the right basic organisation here at the football club.'

There would be no long-term future for Mike Bamber at the Goldstone, however. In the summer of 1984 he was replaced as chairman and ousted from the board. The match programme for the first Albion home game of the 1984/85 season didn't so much as mention Bamber's name, let alone express any gratitude for what had been achieved on his watch. It was a shoddy way to treat a man who had dared to dream and, as a consequence, steered his local football club to previously unknown heights. Within four years, the 'pleasantest and finest chairman' who ever employed Brian Clough would be dead.

14

AN UNLIKELY LEGACY

Long after Brian Clough had vacated Albion's dugout, and even while he was still there, the players who had served under him at the Goldstone Ground came to regard Old Big Head as the 'Hotel California' of football managers – you could check out anytime to ply your trade elsewhere, but he never really left you.

Some came to resent his spectral presence in their lives.

Whispers of Clough's liking for a 'bung' – whispers that he always denied, it should be said – had circulated for years. 'So what?' was the opinion of many. Clough was a central figure in the game before the Premier League's giant cash cow walked among us. The wages of managers and players, who lived on the same streets as the supporters who idolised them, as opposed to within expensive gated communities, bore no semblance to today. In a working-class sport, making a bit of boot money on the side was almost the norm. 'It was seen as no great crime,' Alan Mullery once said of players who sold FA Cup final tickets on the black market for corporate or business use. 'Everyone knew it was going on.'

But there were limits.

'After I left Brighton to work at Rolls-Royce, I thought I'd go and play part-time somewhere,' says Ian Goodwin. 'I spoke to a guy at Nuneaton, Geoff Coleman, who'd played at Northampton Town for a while. Geoff asked me to sign and I said that he had better speak to Alan Leather, Brighton's club secretary, just to make sure. I'd been told that I couldn't go back and play in the Football League because I was still technically on the books at Brighton, but that playing non-league would be fine. Then on the Thursday night word came through from Geoff that I couldn't play on Saturday because Cloughie wouldn't let me. He wasn't going to release me, even to play semi-pro. That was until £350, God's honest truth, was folded, put in a plastic bag and driven from Nuneaton to Burton-on-Trent. And I played for Nuneaton on the Saturday. That pissed me off, that he took £350 off a little non-league club. That was all wrong.'

Then again, Peter Taylor wasn't exactly spotless either.

'When I was at Exeter City I became very good friends with Nicky Jennings, a winger who also played for Plymouth and Portsmouth,' says John Templeman. 'We lived around the corner from each other. Nicky had been given a testimonial match because he was going to retire at the end of that [1978/79] season, and he heard that Nottingham Forest were looking for a friendly. A game was arranged because, although there was a lot of snow around the country at the time, we were snow-free in Exeter. We were all set up for this particular evening and the day beforehand Nicky received a phone call from Peter Taylor threatening to call the game off if Nicky didn't give him half the proceeds. Nicky couldn't believe it. He came straight round to my house saying, "What shall I do?" Nicky had a cousin who was a solicitor based in Yeovil, and he phoned him up and made him aware of it. Nicky was being told by Peter Taylor that he wanted him to phone back and give him his response. When Nicky phoned him back and explained that his cousin was a local solicitor and would be dealing with it in the event of it being cancelled, he [Taylor] backed down on the threat. Nicky was only going to get £10,000 or so out of it, which would still have been quite a lot of money at that time, something to help with his retirement because he'd had some serious injuries. Whether Clough knew about it, I don't know. I doubt very much whether anybody was aware of it other than Peter Taylor because it was him on the phone to Nicky. That was very naughty of him, quite shocking in fact.'

'They were very conscious about money,' adds Brian Powney. 'They talked about money a lot. They seemed very money conscious – a score here, a score there. I actually think the whole move [to Brighton & Hove Albion] was about money. Even in the film *The Damned United* you've got Taylor saying, "Brian, this club's got a lot of money." That was about right.'

For Peter Ward, who emerged at the Goldstone after Clough's departure but still ended up signing for him at Nottingham Forest, money had nothing to do with it. At the City Ground, Ward failed to replicate the outstanding form he had shown up front for Albion. In October 1982, he found himself back at the Goldstone on loan. Ward wanted to stay, especially with Albion making headway in the FA Cup. After a 2–1 win at Anfield in the fifth round, Liverpool's first home defeat in any cup competition since 1974, he returned to Forest and approached Clough about the possibility of signing permanently for Albion, or at least extending his loan period. 'Son, I've never been to an FA Cup final,' Clough told him. 'Neither will you.' Ward was devastated. Instead, Clough sent him out again on loan, this time to Seattle Sounders in the North

American Soccer League. Two months later Ward watched on television as his former Albion teammates played Manchester United, the club he had supported as a child, beneath the twin towers at Wembley. 'It was like he was doing it purely out of spite, the pillock,' Ward once told me of Clough's belligerence.

Yet, behind the ruthlessness, the pettiness, the downright nastiness and any financial jiggery-pokery, Clough undoubtedly had a heart the size of Derby, if not Brighton & Hove. Stories of his generosity towards charitable causes, society's underprivileged and the elderly – a modern-day Robin Hood fighting the cause of the underdog – are legion. His players rarely witnessed this side of him; they needed to be managed, coached and disciplined, not indulged or pampered. Steve Piper was one of the rare exceptions, and even then Clough's random act of kindness came at the very end of his career. Transferred from Albion to Portsmouth in 1978 and forced into retirement the following year by a knee injury, a testimonial game in his benefit was arranged between Portsmouth and Crystal Palace to be played on Tuesday 14 October 1980. Clough got wind of Piper's misfortune and, for the match programme, contributed the following words:

> Anybody who is interested in football knows the problems I had when I went to manage Brighton. At the time I'd gone from the top at Derby to a side struggling for survival in the Third Division. They were difficult times and Peter Taylor and I needed all the help we could get from the players. Unfortunately not too many of them really wanted to play for Brighton when we got there and after they had met us two the number got even less. But there were one or two we could really rely on, and none more so than Steve Piper who was one of the most honest and genuine lads, if not the most genuine, we had on the books.

I was only there five minutes before leaving for Leeds but in the time I was in charge I seem to remember Steve breaking his nose twice. That was typical of a player who didn't mind putting his head in where it hurts for the benefit of Brighton. His loyalty to me and the club was absolutely staggering. I was very sorry to hear that he's had to retire from the game because of injury. I know the feeling well, and I only hope that he gets the support he now deserves. Testimonials were made for the Steve Pipers of this world.

'That's not bad, is it?' says Piper, reading Clough's words again some thirty-seven years later while sat in the dining room of his home in Worthing. 'I didn't ask him to do it. The first time I saw it was when I read the programme. It's nice. I'll always keep that. It means a lot to me.'

For the players who were there, the 1973/74 season, when arguably the best manager in Britain and his trusty assistant came to manage the sixth-worst team in the Third Division, has now taken on an almost dreamlike sepia-esque quality. Did that really happen? Why us? What were Clough's real motives for coming? 'I've asked myself those questions and many more over the years,' says Brian Powney. 'Why did he do it? Why come here and show such little interest? He hated the south. "Bloody southerners" – that's what he used to call us. There wasn't a single thing I can think of which sent out a positive statement along the lines of "I want to be here, I want to be successful" – not one. I suppose if I were a kid at the time then maybe my perspective might be a bit different, but I'd played nearly four hundred bloody games by then so I knew a little bit about what was going on and people's attitudes. And it wasn't just Clough. I couldn't work either of them out, to be honest.'

'The FA have got sanctions against him. He isn't earning anything. He sees Mike Bamber waving a flag that's predominantly the colour of £50 notes, and he says, "We'll take the money." That's my personal opinion on why he came.' So says Ian Goodwin. 'I don't think he was interested in Brighton one iota. I don't think he gave a shit about Brighton. He's covered his backside, he can pay his bills, and he's still in the gang. He's still in the Football League. It's always said that it's easier to get a job when you've got a job than when you ain't got a job. He didn't have a job so he had to take whatever he could get, and that ended up being Brighton.'

'I don't think his heart or mind was ever in it,' admits Steve Piper, despite his fondness for Clough. 'He could have done what Eddie Howe did at Bournemouth and taken Brighton from the Third Division to the First if he had persevered with it. But then he had the call from Leeds and thought, "It's the big time again." I don't think he quite knew what he was jumping into down here. You look at his career otherwise and it's second to none, but all his connections were in the north-east and around Derby, not Sussex. We were just a stop-gap for him.'

'I played twelve years of professional football for Brighton & Hove Albion, making 488 appearances, and I can safely say that particular year was the strangest of them all by a mile,' adds Norman Gall, breaking into laughter. 'He was never going to stay, but I enjoyed working under him despite the way it all ended. It was a one-off year when so much seemed to happen. But I wasn't fit. That's what did for me. I'm glad to be able to say, though, that I played for Brian Clough, but Taylor… well, I couldn't care less about the man.'

'Only Brian knows the whole story of why he came down here, and he isn't alive anymore to tell us,' reflects Peter

O'Sullivan. 'He wasn't in it for the long term. That's why I think money had a lot to do with it. With Pete, it was different. Just look at the players he got in. And he wanted to stay, which is more than Brian did. You've got to hand it to Pete. He wasn't the best tactician, but he got us playing.'

'Brighton was the wrong place for Brian to go,' says the man tasked with following in Clough and Taylor's footsteps at the Goldstone, Alan Mullery. 'The chairman was very, very strong. The vice-chairman, Harry Bloom, was also very strong. I heard stories afterwards about what he [Clough] was like, how he went about his business, but he was never going to have it all his own way. I was blessed to go there, to be fair. I'd never even heard of three-quarters of the players, but as luck would have it there were some good ones, and this kid – Peter Ward – who scored goals for fun. I just made a few changes and that made the difference between Peter Taylor finishing fourth and us going up. I suppose you could say that Brian and Peter's loss ended up being my gain because I absolutely loved being there.'

Walk around the stands, concourses and corridors of the Amex Stadium, Albion's modern-day home since 2011 to the north-east of what is now the city of Brighton & Hove, and you will find no mention of Brian Clough. Or Peter Taylor, for that matter. There are no bars named after them, no 'Brian Clough Way' on the approach roads, no souvenir flags or scarfs on sale parading their faces in the same way as Anfield celebrates Bill Shankly or Old Trafford Sir Matt Busby. It's as if they never managed Albion at all. Given Clough's chequered incumbency, some may say that's no bad thing. And yet, paradoxically, his legacy, together with that of Taylor, is everywhere because of what happened to the club during the 1990s.

Albion had initially unveiled plans to leave the Goldstone as far back as the late 1970s. Despite its charm, the ground was wholly unsuitable for the 30,000-plus attendances which accompanied the club's rise through the leagues. With one eye on becoming a permanent fixture in the old First Division, Bamber made it clear that a new stadium would be built. It was just a question of where.

And therein lay the problem. Hemmed in by the English Channel to the south and the panoramic hills of the South Downs to the north, Brighton & Hove isn't blessed with copious amounts of spare land. A couple of potential sites were considered, but with team strengthening and players' wages draining the bank, moving home was never going to be a priority. When the team started malfunctioning during the 1980s, sinking back into English football's third tier in 1987, so the inevitable drop in attendances meant the item fell off the agenda altogether.

Until 7 July 1995, that is, when Sussex woke up to the news that Albion's board had sold the Goldstone, supposedly to pay off mounting debts. From the beginning of the 1996/97 season, the club would play its home games forty-eight miles along the south coast at Fratton Park, home to Portsmouth FC. In time, a 30,000 all-seater stadium would be built in an area north of Brighton called Waterhall, financed by profits from a new leisure development at nearby Patcham Court Farm. There was, however, one huge flaw in this proposal: Brighton Council had rejected plans for the Patcham Court Farm scheme two weeks previously. Those in charge of the club had sold the Goldstone without any concrete plans for a replacement.

Shaken from their summer hiatus, the supporters wanted answers. Some, smelling rank bad management bordering on corruption, turned detective themselves. One, a chartered accountant by the name of Paul Samrah, visited the Land Registry accompanied by local journalist Paul Bracchi. There they discovered that the club had sold the land occupied by the Goldstone to a property company called Chartwell, developer of retail parks, shopping malls and such like. The land was worth approximately £7 million. The club's debts were said to be around £4 million. The two Pauls considered who would benefit from such a sale. Scouring the small print, it became evident that Bill Archer, managing director of a DIY chain called Focus and Albion's new chairman, had gained control of the club for just £56.25, the equivalent of 5,625 shares being bought for one penny each. He had then reorganised the structure of the club by creating a holding company called Foray 585. To their horror, they then discovered that a single paragraph in the club's Memorandum and Articles of Association had been changed – one that would now allow Archer and the other shareholders in Foray 585 to benefit from the sale of the ground. Archer claimed this was an oversight, but the damage had been done. As far as Albion's supporters were concerned, the board had no plans whatsoever to return from Portsmouth.

Gloves off, those very same supporters went for Archer and chief executive David Bellotti, a former Member of Parliament for Eastbourne, launching a prolonged yet increasingly imaginative campaign that waged for the next two years. Pitch invasions, the boycotting of Focus DIY stores, a march through London, the burning of Archer and Bellotti effigies on Bonfire Night – it all happened, and much more. The campaign, widely publicised in the national media and backed by supporters of other football clubs, was enough to bring about a one-year stay of execution for the Goldstone, but that only delayed the inevitable. On 26 April 1997, by which time Albion had sunk to the very bottom of the fourth tier, the Seagulls played Doncaster Rovers in the last ever game at the ground before the bulldozers moved in, winning 1–0. Although their Football League status was ultimately preserved that season, ninety-five years of history had come to an end.

In September 1997, Archer finally signed a deal giving up his majority shareholding in the club, surrendering power to a consortium led by long-time supporter and former advertising guru Dick Knight. By that time, Albion were playing their home games seventy-five miles away in Kent, at Gillingham's Priestfield ground, an arrangement which continued until 1999 when the temporary lease of an athletics stadium in the Brighton suburb of Withdean was secured. The club survived – just – and, crucially, the reason it survived was its loyal and substantial fan base.

In November 1973, Brian Clough became Albion's manager, putting English football on notice that the club meant business. He brought in new players. Some of them proved to be successful signings, others less so. Clough left, Taylor stayed. He made more signings. The football improved and people came to watch in large numbers. Those supporters sustained Albion in the 1990s during the club's hour of need. The attendances may have dropped as events off the field started to affect the product on it, but the interest was always there in local communities throughout Sussex. People raised on the goals of Peter Ward, the doggedness of Brian Horton and the midfield artistry of Peter O'Sullivan still considered themselves to be Albion supporters. Fans of other clubs who remembered Albion's rise to prominence and the atmosphere at the Goldstone sat up and took notice. 'If it could happen to them, then it could happen to us' became a much-repeated phrase on radio phone-in shows and nascent internet forums. Had it not been for that fan base and Albion's relative stature within the English game, triggered during the 1970s by the presence of Clough and Taylor, then the club would almost certainly have perished and the Amex Stadium never been built.

'The Goldstone Ground was a bit different to here,' conceded Nigel Clough, on bringing his Burton Albion team to the Amex in 2017 and being reminded of watching Brighton & Hove Albion lose 8–2 at home to Bristol Rovers while sat in the dugout next to his father. 'I remember it being a big surprise and a big shock for any one of my dad's teams to concede eight goals. But sometimes you have to go through those things to benefit and move forward. The club's come such a long way in the last however many years. It's remarkable. It's a credit to everybody that's contributed to that.'

They didn't win any major trophies at the Goldstone. They didn't win any divisional titles or promotions. They showed remarkable double standards by turning their backs on the only chairman either of them ever really saw eye to eye with as managers. Brian Clough and Peter Taylor did, however, put Albion on the map. That's not a bad legacy to leave behind, even when some of those being left behind don't particularly like you.

Then again, as Clough himself once said, 'I like to portray nice things about myself. I feel we've all got this weakness. We all like to be liked. And yet show me somebody who's liked by everybody and I'll show you somebody who's wrong.'

AND IN THE END

MIKE BAMBER

After relinquishing the reins as Brighton & Hove Albion's chairman in the summer of 1984, Mike Bamber took a back seat from football altogether, the final months of his tenure having taken their toll health-wise. Diagnosed with cancer in 1986, Bamber died on 11 July 1988 at his home in Jersey. He was just fifty-seven years old. At that stage, sections of Albion's support still attributed the club's gradual decline during the 1980s to his financial profligacy, the wretchedly short tribute published in the first match-day programme of the 1988/89 season reflecting the split in opinion over Bamber's legacy. Dudley Sizen, Albion's then chairman, nevertheless stuck his neck out in memory of his predecessor. 'Mike was the most successful chairman we've ever had and the club enjoyed its finest hours under his leadership,' he acknowledged. 'I feel privileged to have known him as a personal friend and fellow director.'

HARRY BLOOM

Harry Bloom's death in October 1980 was felt by everyone at the Goldstone Ground. Often the first one there in the morning and the last out at night, Bloom was the quiet strength and reason in an often turbulent working environment, acting as confidant, negotiator, intermediary and all-round father figure. His passing, however, didn't end the family's association with the club. In 2009, his grandson, Tony Bloom, took over from Dick Knight as Albion's chairman, while Ray Bloom, one of Harry's four sons, has also been a board member for many years. The HB Restaurant at the Amex Stadium is named in honour of the club's late vice-chairman.

BARRY BUTLIN

Barry Butlin returned to Nottingham Forest following his loan spell at Brighton & Hove Albion before moving on to Peterborough United and then Sheffield United, retiring from football in 1981 following 'two or three nasty injuries'. He subsequently spent thirty-five years working in financial services and continues to keep fit and busy by providing a dog-walking service in his neighbourhood of Derby. 'The money's OK, the dogs don't answer back and the majority of them are lovely,' he says. Butlin is fondly remembered by Albion supporters of a certain age for his match-winning goal against Crystal Palace in September 1975. 'It still sticks with me, that one. It was the start of a cracking time down at Brighton. I only wish it could have gone on a little longer.'

BRIAN CLOUGH

Nottingham Forest remained a force in the English game under Brian Clough throughout the 1980s and early 1990s, although they never again scaled the heights of their 1978–80 pomp. However, as Clough's health went into decline, and his management style became more erratic, so the club's fortunes began to suffer. On the first day of May 1993, Forest were relegated from the top flight, Clough having already announced that he would retire at the end of that season. 'I might have stayed in management a shade too long,' he acknowledged. In the years that followed, he made the occasional public appearance and gave the odd interview, yet severed many of his links with football. In January 2003, determined to quit the booze for good, he underwent a liver transplant. 'I am a lucky man, an extremely lucky and appreciative man,' Clough wrote in an updated version of *Walking on Water*. 'To the family, apparently somewhere in Ireland, who donated my new liver I send my love and it goes without saying that if ever there is anything I can do for them.' He died on 20 September 2004 of stomach cancer, aged sixty-nine. The obituaries were warm and generous, though few bothered mentioning his association with Brighton & Hove Albion. Those that did tended to acknowledge it only in passing. Albion's match-day programme for the club's next home game carried a four-page tribute in which Peter Ward shared some of his memories – good and bad – with your author. 'Despite what some people seem to think, he was actually a very nice man,' said Ward, recalling his post-Albion spell at the City Ground. 'On every away trip he'd always come down the coach with a crate of beers for everyone. If anyone didn't want one, he'd sit down and talk with them until they eventually took one. He ruled, he was the boss, and of course there were times when he would bawl and shout. But then he had Peter Taylor who would always calm things down. They were a great double act.'

GERRY FELL

Gerry Fell went on to play for Southend United and Torquay United after leaving Brighton & Hove Albion before retiring from football in 1981. He became a financial advisor, returning to Sussex before moving back to his native East Midlands along the Nottinghamshire/Lincolnshire border, where he continues to live and work. 'It's a totally different environment up here, a very rural farming community,' he says. 'I miss my mates in Brighton but I keep in contact with a lot of the old bunch, and I've retained all my old clients from down south because I do all my business by phone and email. You can be anywhere to do that.' His best piece of financial advice? 'I've seen some absolute horrors when it comes to credit cards. Just don't borrow on them, full stop. It leads to nothing but trouble.'

NORMAN GALL

After retiring from the professional game at the end of the 1973/74 season, Norman Gall got a job as a rep for the Watney brewing company, continuing to play non-league football while also doing some coaching. He still lives in Sussex, his Newcastle accent very much intact. 'I got married down here, had two children, and I liked it,' he says. 'Life up there [in the north-east] had been quite hard whereas down here I had been successful as a footballer. I'd bought a house. I'd spent virtually my entire adult life here. It was home, and it's still home.' He continues to go and watch Brighton & Hove Albion play at the Amex Stadium whenever possible. 'My last year at the Goldstone was a disaster in some ways, but that was ages ago. Different things have happened. Different people are involved now. But there's one thing I would like people to know – I was so lucky to play for Brighton & Hove Albion.'

IAN GOODWIN

After turning his back on professional football, Ian Goodwin worked for Rolls-Royce before joining Peugeot, spending thirty-two years as part of the company's training department. Despite his fractious relationship with Brian Clough, he has good memories of playing for Brighton & Hove Albion. 'He was just one man and I didn't have a relationship with him anyway,' he says. 'I was happy there. It's where I married my wife and had some outstanding times. I'm basically bionic now, I had that many injuries and that many operations, but otherwise there's no complaints, no complaints whatsoever.'

BRIAN HORTON

Unlike the majority of those who served at the Goldstone Ground under Brian Clough and/or Peter Taylor, Brian Horton remained in football long after retiring as a player. He made the transition into management at Hull City before moving on to Oxford United, Manchester City and Huddersfield Town, eventually returning to Brighton & Hove Albion in February 1998 while the club was still in temporary residency at Gillingham. Ultimately the strain of trying to manage a Sussex football team playing its home games in Kent while living in Cheshire proved too much. In January 1999, with a return to Brighton from Gillingham in the pipeline but still to be confirmed, Horton left to manage Port Vale. 'That was without doubt the toughest decision I ever had to make in football,' he says. 'The date for moving to Withdean kept on getting pushed back which wasn't good for anyone associated with the club, let alone me. There seemed to be no end in sight to playing at Gillingham whereas Port Vale were a stable club. Some Brighton fans gave me a hard time about it but the vast majority have always been very good to me whenever I've gone back.' Horton has since had two spells in charge of Macclesfield Town, worked as assistant manager to Phil Brown at Hull City,

Preston North End, Southend United and Swindon Town, and was Paul Dickov's second in command at Doncaster Rovers from 2013 to 2015.

FRANKIE HOWARD

Frankie Howard continued working at the Goldstone until 1993, when, with the club venting money and under a new boardroom regime, he was cruelly made redundant at just a day's notice after forty years of service to Brighton & Hove Albion as a player and groundsman. He died in October 2007, aged seventy-six, with many former players attending his funeral at Woodvale Crematorium, Brighton.

ALAN MULLERY

Despite subsequent spells in charge of Charlton Athletic, Crystal Palace and Queens Park Rangers, Alan Mullery was never able to replicate the success that he enjoyed as Brighton & Hove Albion's manager between 1976 and 1981. He returned to the club in 1986, only to find the Goldstone Ground a shadow of its former self. Ordered to sell players and slash the wage bill, Mullery was sacked after just nine months with Albion fifteenth in the old Second Division. 'The rats are winning,' he declared. 'I've been stabbed in the back after being given five years to rebuild the club.' Time heals, however. Mullery now works as an Albion club ambassador and can usually be seen around the Amex Stadium on match days.

PETER O'SULLIVAN

After 491 appearances for Brighton & Hove Albion, Peter O'Sullivan joined Fulham in 1981 and was part of the side that won promotion from the old Third Division at the end of the

1981/82 season. A knee injury saw him lose his place in the side to a young Ray Houghton, after which Sully joined Charlton Athletic before spending brief spells with Reading, Aldershot and in Hong Kong. He retired from the professional game in 1983, continuing to play non-league football for several clubs across south-east England as well as representing the Sussex county side. O'Sullivan, who still lives in Sussex, remains one of the most popular players ever to have worn an Albion shirt. 'To be honest, I think I was probably in the right place at the right time,' he once told me. 'I got to play for a club that went from being a rank bad one in Division Three to a semi-decent one in Division One. When I first went there even the Goldstone made Rochdale look like Wembley. But I stuck it out.'

STEVE PIPER

Steve Piper remained a popular figure on the Sussex football scene long after retiring from the professional game, playing for a number of local clubs and representing the Sussex county side while working as a financial advisor. His death on Boxing Day 2017 at the age of just sixty-two came as a massive shock to those who knew him. The sudden pain that had shot through Piper's legs while playing a round of golf in September turned out to be the first symptoms of an aggressive, inoperable tumour in the left atrium of his heart. 'He may have been tough on the pitch but he was the perfect gentleman off it,' says Dawn Piper, his widow. 'He would do anything for me. My family always used to say, "You're so lucky to have someone like Steve," and I was. He was thoughtful, generous – always first to the bar – caring and very tactile. If the television was boring in the evening and I was on the internet, then he'd be there, stroking my feet, telling me he loved me. He'd say how happy he was to have me in his life, that he couldn't bear the thought of not being with me, and I'd say, "Well, you're always going to be with me. You don't have to worry about that." The moment he died, my heart was torn in two. He's left such a huge gap in my life, and in so many other people's lives.' Piper's funeral was attended by hundreds of mourners, including Gerry Fell, Norman Gall, Alan Mullery, Peter O'Sullivan, Andy Rollings, Tony Towner and John Templeman. 'It happened so quickly and took us all by surprise,' says Rollings. 'It was four or five days from finding out exactly what it was, and then that was it – he was gone. It knocked a big hole in me, I can tell you, and I know I'm not alone. Steve was just a gem of a guy and he'll be sorely missed.'

BRIAN POWNEY

On retiring from the professional game in 1974, Brian Powney successfully juggled his vending machine business with playing for and/or managing amateur football clubs along the Sussex coast. With 386 appearances in all competitions, he still holds the record for the most number of games played by an Albion goalkeeper. Powney was born in Seaford, continues to live in Seaford and between 1987 and 1991 managed Seaford Town. 'They'll have to get me out of here in a box,' is his humorous if brutally honest assessment of the ties that bind him to the small East Sussex seaside resort.

LAMMIE ROBERTSON

Lammie Robertson made nearly 150 appearances for Exeter City after leaving Brighton & Hove Albion, with a summer playing stateside at the Chicago Sting thrown in for good measure. He also had spells during the late 1970s with Leicester

City, Peterborough United and Bradford City before embarking on a second career in financial services. Already a qualified FA coach on moving to the Goldstone Ground, Robertson kept his hand in by scouting and occasionally coaching for John Duncan during the latter's managerial spells at Scunthorpe United, Chesterfield and Ipswich Town. Since retiring from the financial services industry he has worked as caretaker of the village hall in Goostrey, Cheshire. 'It keeps me busy, but I still like going to watch a game whenever I can,' he says.

ANDY ROLLINGS

Swindon Town 'just didn't work out' for Andy Rollings, and the strapping centre-back was transferred to Portsmouth in August 1981. A ruptured calf muscle brought the curtain down on his professional career in 1983, after which he turned out for Maidstone United (alongside Peter O'Sullivan), followed by several amateur clubs across Sussex, briefly finding himself back at Brighton & Hove Albion in 1986 playing for the reserves and coaching under Alan Mullery. Rollings continued to be a presence on the county football circuit until, aged forty-one, he heeded the advice of former Albion physiotherapist Mike Yaxley. 'I'd played two games in a week, wasn't feeling great, and he said, "I think you'd better stop otherwise your knees are going to be a wreck." I didn't want to but I'm glad I did, seeing how some former players have struggled to deal with old injuries after they retired.' Since then Rollings and his wife Judy have run the Chalet Café in Preston Park, Brighton. 'It's been the best thing,' he says. 'We were the generation that always had to go out and get another job after football, and to have something as stable as that has been brilliant.' He also works as a host at the Amex Stadium on match days.

PAT SAWARD

Having been sacked as Brighton & Hove Albion's manager prior to Brian Clough and Peter Taylor's arrival, Pat Saward resorted to working abroad, taking on coaching posts in the Middle East and Africa before turning his back on football altogether to run a travel business. He died in September 2002 after a long illness, aged seventy-four.

PETER TAYLOR

Despite returning to Derby County as manager in November 1982, Peter Taylor was unable to revive the financially stricken club as it teetered on the verge of relegation to the old Third Division. In April 1984, he resigned with two years of his contract left to run, never to return to management. On 4 October 1990, while holidaying in his beloved Majorca, Taylor died from pulmonary fibrosis (a respiratory disease in which scarring appears in the lung tissue, leading to breathing problems). He was sixty-two. When given the news over the phone by Nottingham Forest assistant manager Ron Fenton, it is said that Brian Clough silently replaced the receiver without saying a word. Slipping into the back of the church in Widmerpool, Nottinghamshire, to attend Taylor's funeral, Clough felt what he later described as a 'feeling of desolation' sweep over him. He came to bitterly regret the 'dreadful and needless waste' of their seven-year silence in the wake of the John Robertson affair. 'The reason seemed legitimate at the time but after all those years it was daft, stubborn and futile not to have made it up with Pete,' he wrote in *Walking on Water*, adding that 'time has helped to emphasise my guilt and the feeling of total regret.' The first of Clough's two autobiographies was dedicated to Taylor ('For Peter. Still miss you badly. You once said "When you get shot of me there won't be much laughter in your life." You were right.'). Two days after Taylor's death, Brighton & Hove Albion held a minute's silence at the Goldstone Ground prior to their game against Swindon Town, a wreath and a message of condolence being sent to his family from the club.

JOHN TEMPLEMAN

John Templeman made over 200 appearances for Exeter City after leaving Brighton & Hove Albion before finishing his professional football career with Swindon Town. He played non-league for Witney Town, managed a health centre near Newbury and became the personal fitness trainer to a Saudi Arabian princess – as you do. 'She lost about seven stone and her family asked me if I'd go back to Saudi Arabia with them to continue my work,' he says. 'So we did! We lived in a villa on the prince's estate with every luxury you could possibly think of and ended up staying there for a couple of years.' After Saudi Arabia, Templeman and his first wife briefly lived in Sweden (where she was originally from) before returning to the UK where he found work with the Prudential life insurance company. Their divorce, together with the death of his mother, 'left me in a bad place for three or four years' and he struggled with depression prior to meeting his second wife, Sue, whom he married in 2002. 'I had a bit of a mountain to climb and coming out the other side was a big personal achievement for me,' he says. Sue's death from liver cancer in 2006 came as another body blow – 'not least of all because she didn't smoke or drink' – as did the passing of his father two weeks later. In 2008, Templeman married again, this time to Emma, and the pair now have two children in Lois and Oscar, born in 2009 and 2012 respectively, in addition to his two grown-up children Kristina and Jonas. 'So here I am, in my seventieth year, doing it all again with five grandchildren in tow as well,' he adds, laughing. 'I've sometimes thought I should probably write a book about it all, if only I had the time!'

TONY TOWNER

Deemed surplus to requirements at the Goldstone Ground following the arrival of Gerry Ryan from Derby County in September 1978, Tony Towner went on to enjoy successful periods at Millwall and Rotherham United, coming second in a 2012 poll to find the latter's most popular player of all time. Shorter spells followed at Sheffield United, Wolverhampton Wanderers, Charlton Athletic, Rochdale, Cambridge United and various non-league clubs across the south-east of England before the boots were finally put out to pasture in favour of a career as a lorry driver. Towner now runs his own Brighton-based removals company, shifting loads anywhere from Shoreham to Slovenia. 'It only took me three decades to get into Europe,' he chuckles. 'I really enjoy it. I've been doing it quite a few years now and it keeps me fit.'

HARRY WILSON

Having joined Brighton & Hove Albion from Burnley, Harry Wilson left the Goldstone Ground during the summer of 1977 to return to Lancashire and sign for Preston North End. Six months later he survived a serious road accident when his Datsun was in collision with a transit van on the A59. Wilson remained in hospital for several weeks, having been told he would never play professional football again. Nine months later, he proved the doctors wrong by returning to Preston's first team. 'It happened at a bad time for me,' he says. 'I'd been playing well and Nobby Stiles [Preston's manager] had been geeing me up by saying [England manager)] Ron Greenwood was looking at me. But I suppose I was lucky to be alive. I lost a couple of yards of pace but then again I was never exactly the quickest of players!' Wilson went on to play for Hartlepool United, coach Burnley's youth team and work for the Football League, monitoring the youth development set-ups at clubs in the north-west and north-east of England. Now living in Burnley, he returns to Sussex whenever he can for player reunions.

PETER WARD

Having gone on loan from Nottingham Forest to Seattle Sounders in 1983, Peter Ward was sold later the same year to their Canadian neighbours the Vancouver Whitecaps for just £20,000. Besides the occasional friendly appearance and a handful of matches for non-league Hednesford Town during the autumn of 1990, he never played football in the UK again. Instead, Ward criss-crossed the United States turning out for Baltimore, Cleveland, Tacoma, Wichita and just about any club where he felt wanted. In 1989, he answered a call from former Albion teammate Mark Lawrenson, then player-coach of the Tampa Bay Rowdies, to join him on Florida's Gulf Coast. At the time of writing, he still lives there. As the man who spearheaded Albion's attack throughout what many supporters refer to as their 'glory years', scoring ninety-five goals in 227 appearances across three different divisions, Ward is widely regarded as the most popular figure ever to have played for the club.

ACKNOWLEDGEMENTS

This book would never have happened had it not been for the many former Brighton & Hove Albion players who willingly talked to me about what it was like working under Brian Clough and/or Peter Taylor between November 1973 and July 1976. I thank you all for sharing your stories – in your homes, over the telephone, in pubs – and for fielding my subsequent phone calls and emails during the writing process when facts needed to be checked and rechecked. You were a delight to listen to, every one of you. Courteous, informative, open, honest (often brutally so), funny and loquacious in a good way. I only hope I've done you justice in the final reckoning.

A big tip of the hat to Peter Brackley, who painted a vivid picture of what it was like dealing with both Clough and Taylor in a media capacity, and to Alan Mullery who did likewise regarding the managerial landscape he inherited at the Goldstone Ground. Thanks also to Paul Camillin, Tim Carder, Chris Cattlin, Paul Hazlewood and Luke Nicoli at the Brighton end of the country, who I was able to rely on for a combination of support, clarifying facts and generally pointing me in the right direction as I went about my research.

For supplying resource material and pictures I am heavily indebted to Andy Garth and Patrick Kneath at Brighton and Hove Stuff, Cardiff Central Library, The Keep in Brighton, Leeds Central Library, Nick Loughlin at *The Northern Echo* and Ian Hine, who oversees the marvellous website featuring scans of Brighton & Hove Albion programmes dating back to the Second World War and beyond (see www.seagullsprogrammes. co.uk). A labour of love indeed.

Thank you to Grant Burberry, Gareth Clarke, Ralph Harrison, Simon Higgins, Richard Levett, Chas Sargeant and the late Noel Tidy – all supporters of Brighton & Hove Albion who each contributed at various points along the road towards me being able to write this book. Closer to home, my partner Jane and children Rhiannon and Luca deserve medals for sharing their lives with a freelance writer and everything that entails. No burning of the midnight oil tonight, I promise.

Last but not least, Biteback Publishing (in particular Olivia Beattie and Victoria Godden), recommended to me initially by fellow writer and author Nick Szczepanik. I've worked with many different publishers over the years but never one that has 'got' the concept of a book quite so quickly before twisting my arm, in the nicest possible way, into going with them. If only it was always that easy...

ABOUT THE AUTHOR

Spencer Vignes is a freelance writer and broadcaster who lives in Cardiff, Wales. He has contributed to over 100 newspapers, magazines and media agencies across the world and is the author of seven books including *The Server*, longlisted for the 2003 William Hill Sports Book of the Year Award. Follow him @SpencerVignes or visit www.spencervignes.co.uk for more information.

BIBLIOGRAPHY

BOOKS

Beckett, Francis and Hencke, David. *Marching To The Fault Line* (Constable & Robinson, 2009).

Carder, Tim and Harris, Roger. *Albion A–Z: A Who's Who of Brighton & Hove Albion* (Goldstone Books, 1997).

Clough, Brian. *The Autobiography* (Transworld Publishers, 1994).

Clough, Brian. *Walking on Water* (Headline, 2002).

Edwards, Maurice. *Brian and Peter, A Right Pair: 21 Years with Clough and Taylor* (Derby Books, 2010).

Francis, Tony. *Clough: A Biography* (Stanley Paul, 1987).

Greaves, Jimmy and Giller, Norman. *Don't Shoot the Manager: The Revealing Story of England's Soccer Bosses* (Boxtree, 1993).

Hamilton, Duncan. *Provided You Don't Kiss Me* (Fourth Estate, 2007).

Hermiston, Roger. *Clough and Revie: The Rivals Who Changed the Face of English Football* (Mainstream, 2011).

Imlach, Gary. *My Father and Other Working-Class Football Heroes* (Yellow Jersey Press, 2006).

Mullery, Alan. *The Autobiography* (Headline, 2006).

Murphy, Patrick. *His Way: The Brian Clough Story* (Robson Books, 1993).

North, Stephen and Hodson, Paul. *Build a Bonfire: How Football Fans United to Save Brighton & Hove Albion* (Mainstream, 1997).

Palm, Carl Magnus. *Bright Lights, Dark Shadows: The Real Story of Abba* (Omnibus Press, 2001).

Redknapp, Harry. *Always Managing* (Ebury Press, 2013).

Rostron, Phil. *We Are the Damned United* (Mainstream, 2009).

Taylor, Peter. *With Clough By Taylor* (Sidgwick and Jackson, 1980).

Wilson, Jonathan. *Brian Clough: Nobody Ever Says Thank You* (Orion Books, 2011).

FILMS/DOCUMENTARIES

Brian Clough: In His Own Words (Hoppa Ltd, 2009).

Clough: The Greatest England Manager That England Never Had (ITV Sport, 2009).

The Damned United (BBC Films/Left Bank Pictures, 2009).

ONLINE RESOURCES

www.bbc.co.uk – for information regarding the political process and electoral events in the UK during 1974, see article dated 5 April 2005.

www.guardian.co.uk – for information on Lewes and its relationship with the Marian persecutions and Guy Fawkes Night, see article dated 4 November 2017.

www.independent.co.uk – for information on the radical nature of Sussex over the years, see article dated 2 August 2013.

www.independent.co.uk – for information on the political process and news events in the UK during 1973, see article dated 29 December 2013.

www.seagullsprogrammes.co.uk – the source of Brighton & Hove Albion match day programmes dating back to the Second World War and beyond, curated by Ian Hine.

www.youtube.co.uk – to view footage of (i) Brian Clough's appearance on ITV's *The Big Match*, broadcast on 2 December 1973 (ii) Edward's Heath's television address to the country, broadcast on 7 February 1974 (iii) Brian Clough's Yorkshire Television interview with Austin Mitchell, broadcast on 12 September 1974, and (iv) Brian Clough's BBC interview with David Frost, recorded in October 1974.

INDEX

Note: neither 'Brighton & Hove Albion' nor 'The Goldstone Ground' are listed, seeing as the vast majority of this book concentrates on the former with events taking place at the latter.

Abba 130, 139–41
Adamson, Jimmy 165
Ajax 203, 249
Aldershot 81–2, 93, 110, 117, 119–20, 209, 226, 235, 279
Ali, Muhammad 100–101, 117
Allen, Ronnie 61
Allison, Malcolm 225–6
Amex Stadium 267, 271, 274, 276, 278, 281
Amsterdam 203
Anderson, Viv 213
Andersson, Benny 141
Appleby, Bob 24
Archer, Bill 269–70
Armfield, Jimmy 165, 168
Arsenal 161, 245
Ashurst, Len 27
Aston Villa 10, 165
Atkinson, Ron 255
Atyeo, John 21

Bailey, Mike 255–6
Baltimore 285
Bamber, Mike 2
    ambitions for Brighton 8–10, 15–19, 98, 132, 144, 185, 226–7, 230, 244, 254, 256, 259, 273
    appoints Clough and Taylor 2, 39–48, 58
    appoints Mullery 241, 244
    becomes Brighton chairman 8, 10
    breakdown with Leeds over Clough's departure 173–4, 176–7, 227–8
    celebrities 18, 144
    Clough's departure for Leeds 169–73
    considers re-hiring Clough 195–6
    death 259, 273
    downfall as chairman 256, 258–9, 273
    managing Clough 66–7, 96–7, 100, 109–10, 122–4, 127, 196
    money 43, 46, 52, 82, 145, 181, 196, 241, 258
    opinions of Clough's period as manager 177–8
    personality 17–18
    relationship with Brighton players 134–5, 144–5, 158–60, 207, 237
    relationship with Mullery 254–5
    Ringmer restaurant 18, 144
    Taylor's departure as manager 239–40
Bannister, Bruce 68–9, 151, 153, 155
Bassett, Dave 62
BBC 129–30, 199, 202, 233, 251
BBC Radio Brighton 45, 73, 106, 146, 158, 244
BBC South Today 45

295

BBC World Service 45
Beachy Head 78
Beadle, John 115
Beal, Phil 221
Beamish, Ken 16, 60, 90, 92, 94, 99, 102, 119, 128, 131, 141, 158
Belgium 140
Bellotti, David 269
Big Match, The 69
Billingshurst 216
Binney, Fred 159, 161, 183, 215, 223, 225–6, 230, 235
Birmingham City 37, 166–7, 192
Birtles, Gary 255
Blackburn Rovers 118–19, 158, 195
Blackpool 250
Blackpool FC 11, 117–19, 131
Blake, William 250
Bloom, Harry 18, 19, 42–3, 47–8, 169, 174, 195, 254, 267, 273–4
Bloom, Ray 274
Bloom, Tony 274
Bolton, Sam 192–3
Bolton Wanderers 21, 165
Bond, John 147–8
Borrowash Victoria 207
Bournemouth 14, 94, 100, 216, 266
Bowyer, Ian 213
Bracchi, Paul 269
Brackley, Peter 45, 73–4, 106, 146, 244
Bradford City 281
Brady, Liam 248
Bremner, Billy 175, 180–81
Brentford 209
Bridges, Barry 3, 11, 60, 77, 110, 119, 127, 137–8, 143, 160
Brighton Belle 227
Brighton Council 268
Brighton Dome 130, 139–41
Brighton Pavilion 130
Brisley, Terry 235
Bristol 210
Bristol City 13, 21
Bristol Rovers 68–73, 75, 78, 82, 86, 94, 125, 151–5, 159–60, 184, 271
Brown, Alan 28, 89
Brown, Allan 213, 224
Brown, Jim 61
Brown, Mick 12, 101, 137, 155, 157

Burgess Hill 60
Burnett, Dennis 230
Burnley 222, 285
Burnley FC 12, 80–81, 165, 284–5
Burton Albion 27, 204, 207–8, 271
Burton-on-Trent 122, 127, 238, 262
Bury 11, 12, 21, 227
Busby, Matt 267
Butlin, Barry 224, 228, 274

Cala Millor 77, 110, 161, 168, 237
Cambridge United 100–102, 136–7, 154, 160, 284
Campbell, Bobby 217
Cardiff City 234, 237
Carey, Johnny 212
Carlisle United 160, 206
Carter, Chris 185
Case, Jimmy 258
Casey, Mike 174
Cattlin, Chris 244
Central Electricity Generating Board 59
Centurion Walk 257
Challis, Ron 187
Charity Shield 171, 189, 212
Charles, John 85
Charlton Athletic 13, 14, 95–7, 160, 205, 278–9, 284
Charlton, Bobby 205
Charlton, Kevin 233
Chartwell 269
Cheshire 277, 281
Chester City 57, 223
Chesterfield 46, 61, 82, 90, 92, 128, 142, 176, 187, 195, 204, 215, 232, 234, 281
Chicago Sting 280
Clarke, Allan 192
Clarke, Gerry 176, 185, 187, 204, 219
Clarke, Ray 246, 249
Cleveland 285
Clough, Barbara 32, 41, 257
Clough, Brian
    absences 64–7, 94, 97, 100–102, 104, 118, 127, 139, 196
    alcohol dependence 27, 105–7, 275
    appointed by Brighton 39–47
    attempts to lure Taylor to Leeds 190–91
    attitude to injuries 88–93, 136, 153

INDEX

barracking by opposition supporters 83
breakdown in relationship with Taylor at Brighton 172–3, 253
breakdown in relationship with Taylor at Nottingham Forest 253–4, 256–8, 282
bungs 261–2
David Frost interview 199–203
death 275
discipline 95–6, 138, 155–7
early relationship with Taylor 29–30
education 23
FA charge 37–8, 41, 44, 57–8
first meeting with Brighton players 1–5, 48, 132
Iran 120–25
legacy at Brighton 265–71
managerial style at Brighton 4–5, 51–3, 62, 64–5, 74–8, 80, 86–8, 98, 102–4, 111–13, 136, 138, 148, 153, 162–3, 264–5
managing Derby County 34–38
managing Hartlepools United 29–34, 36
managing Leeds United 179–80, 188–95
managing Nottingham Forest 212–14, 220, 224, 228–9, 237–9, 242–3, 245–50, 252, 262–4, 274–5
media work 36–38, 43, 69–71, 164
mood swings 73–4, 143–4, 146, 152–3, 275
move from Brighton to Leeds 168–78, 227–8
Nottingham Forest v Brighton (1979/80) 245–8, 251–2
origins of move from Brighton to Leeds 163–8
playing career 21–27, 48
politics 114–17
reaction at Brighton to leaving for Leeds 180–85
reflections on why he went to Brighton 202, 265–7
relationship with Mike Bamber 201, 240, 259
Robin Hood image 264
tempts Taylor to join Nottingham Forest 228, 237–42

Clough, Nigel 69, 113, 271
Clough, Simon 69
Colchester United 209, 215, 223, 225–6
Coleman, Geoff 262
Collins, Tony 189
Conservative Party 113–15
Cooper, Terry 189
County Durham 104, 185
Courtlands Hotel 97, 104, 143, 152, 169, 173, 176, 180, 224
Coventry 87, 215
Coventry City 10, 26, 87
Crabb, Ron 131
Crawford, Ray 65
Crawley 60
Crawley Town 9
Creasey, David Somersall 194
Crystal Palace 9, 13, 186–8, 191, 195–6, 204–5, 215, 222, 224–6, 230–31, 264, 274, 278
Curry, John 33
Curtis, George 135
Cussins, Manny 167–71, 173–5, 178, 192–3, 200, 228

Daily Mail 100
Damned United, The 41, 214, 250, 263
David, Anne-Marie 129
Dawes, Tommy 68
Dawson, Les 18, 144
Day, Billy 25
Daykin, Brian 203–4, 206–8, 210–11, 215–16
Dennison, Bob 25, 30
Derby 64, 74, 86, 101, 125, 139, 152, 180–81, 194, 206–7, 264, 274
Derby (horse race) 252
Derby County 34–41, 44–6, 53, 55–7, 77, 87, 89, 93, 103, 115, 117, 120, 126, 138, 148, 161, 167–8, 172, 175, 191–2, 195, 200–202, 214, 224, 237, 246–7, 257–8, 264, 282, 284
Derby North 115
Derby Royal Infirmary 172
Derbyshire 94, 97, 121, 204
Derbyshire West 115
Doncaster Rovers 270
Dougan, Derek 105, 107
Dragonara Hotel 190
Dryden, Stuart 238–9

297

Duncan, John 281
Dunne, Jimmy 241
Durban, Alan 126

Eastbourne 60, 269
Edwards, Maurice 238
England 22, 80, 93, 163–6, 195, 203, 205, 212, 242, 248, 285
Essex 223
European Broadcasting Union 129
European Cup 21, 33, 35, 53, 55, 62, 78, 88, 166, 168, 171, 243, 245, 251–4
Eurovision Song Contest 129–30, 139–41
Evening Argus 15, 19, 42–3, 58, 91, 101, 139, 140, 142, 153, 157, 216, 218–19, 226, 237
Exeter City 54, 159–60, 182, 262, 280, 283

FA Cup 54, 61, 63, 85, 95, 206, 209–10, 213–14, 220, 261
Fältskog, Agnetha 140
Fashanu, Justin 251
FC Bruges 246, 249
Fearnley, Gordon 68
Fell, Gerry 206, 208, 215, 218, 223, 225, 241, 244, 248, 275–6, 280
Fenton, Ron 282
Ferguson, Alex 232
Fleming, Charlie 21
Florida 285
Football Association 28, 37, 38, 41, 57, 126, 164, 167, 172, 266, 281
Football League 80, 88, 135, 165, 203, 262
Ford, David 111
Forsyth, Bruce 18
Foskett, Clive 63
Foster, Steve 248, 258
France 164
Francis, Gerry 191
Francis, Tony 115, 177
Fratton Park 268
Frazier, Joe 100, 117
Frost, David 199–203
Fulham 241–2, 255
Fuschillo, Paul 117–19, 206

Gall, Norman 11, 48–9, 51–2, 71, 75, 77, 94–5, 106, 111, 133–5, 141, 144, 152, 180, 266, 276, 280
Gatwick Airport 157

general election 114, 118, 120
Giggs, Ryan 232
Giles, Johnny 166, 179–80, 189, 193
Gill, Eric 22
Gillingham 160, 216, 235, 270, 277
Glenrothes and Buckhaven Technical College 127
Goldsboro, Bobby 7
Goldthorpe, Bobby 95
Goodeve, Ken 78, 206
Goodwin, Freddie 10, 166
Goodwin, Ian 10, 65, 85–8, 92, 106, 145, 180, 183, 262, 266, 276–7
Goostrey 281
Gordon, Jimmy 214
Gough, Bobby 128
Govier, Steve 147–8, 161, 183, 206
Gowling, Alan 131
Grand Hotel (Brighton) 140
Grand Hotel (Newcastle) 49
Gray, Eddie 180
Great Depression 38
Greaves, Jimmy 164, 213
Greece 129, 140–41
Greenwood, Ron 285
Gregory, John 248, 255
Grey, Alf 119
Grimsby Town 109–11, 154, 232
Grummitt, Peter 78–9, 94, 102, 111, 118, 125–6, 135, 208, 210, 214, 217, 225, 244
Gutteridge, Ken 204, 207–8, 210, 215–16, 219

Halifax Town 11, 12, 14, 15, 39, 111, 117, 159, 208, 217–18, 221, 227
Hamburg 252
Hamilton, Duncan 75, 253–4
Hardwick, George 28, 29
Harker, Chris 21, 27
Harris, David 128
Harrison, Ralph 184
Hartlepool(s) United 29–34, 36, 38, 54, 77, 88, 106, 191, 285
Harvey, David 175, 189, 191, 193
Haywards Heath 60
Heath, Ted 113–14
Hednesford Town 231, 285
Hereford United 42–43, 85, 120, 226, 229, 232–4, 237

INDEX

Highlands Park 160
Hill, Alan 257
Hill, Jimmy 36
Hillsborough 99, 213
Hilton, Pat 11, 60, 72, 155–7
Hindle, George 189
Hitler, Adolf 88
Hoddle, Glenn 248
Hollins, Dave 22
Hong Kong 279
Hooliganism 188, 222
Horsham 60
Horton, Brian 102, 230–31, 234, 236, 242, 244, 248, 255, 270, 277–8
Houghton, Ray 279
Hove Park 65, 185
Howard, Frankie 7, 8, 13, 156, 232, 255, 278
Howe, Eddie 266
Howell, Graham 160
Howell, Ronnie 12, 16, 69, 95–6, 118, 131–2, 137, 146, 160
Huddersfield Town 60, 131, 215, 218, 277
Hull City 12, 112, 277
Hunter, Norman 180–81, 189
Hurst, Geoff 219, 221

ICI 23
Ipswich 222
Ipswich Town 93, 165, 281
Iran 120, 121–4, 127, 143, 177
Ireland 141, 275
Irvine, Willie 11
Israel 141
Isthmian League 61
Italy 140
ITV 69, 105, 233

Jennings, Nicky 262–3
Jersey 273
Jobbings, Fawcett and Grove 194
Johannesburg 160
Juventus 35, 55, 168

Keane, Roy 26
Kearns, Mick 217
Kelly, Chris 209–10
Kent 270, 277
Kew, Gordon 62
Kinnear, Joe 221, 235

Knight, Dick 270

Labour Party 114–16, 200
Lancashire 284
Land Registry 269
Langfords Hotel 252
Lawrenson, Mark 244–5, 248, 255, 285
League Cup 13
Leandros, Vicky 129
Leather, Alan 88, 262
Leatherhead 209–10, 214
Lee, Gordon 158
Lee, Trevor 235
Leeds 190, 194
Leeds United 27, 35, 37, 41, 54, 56–8, 117, 161, 165–71, 173–8, 179–82, 184, 187–8, 190–96, 199–203, 212, 214, 219, 227, 253, 256, 265–6
Leicester City 280
Lewes 1, 48, 50, 77, 132
Ley, George 51, 72, 77, 81, 160
Lincolnshire 276
Lindley, Maurice 188
Liverpool 35, 54, 80, 92, 161, 165, 171, 189–90, 243, 245, 251, 255–6, 263
Lloyd, Cliff 56, 105, 107
Lobo, Francisco Marques 35
Lofthouse, Nat 21
London 17, 42, 59, 63, 74, 97, 101, 125, 144, 179, 181, 222, 225, 227, 250, 255–6, 269
London Weekend Television 36, 42, 177, 202
Long Eaton 203, 206
'Long Live Love' 130, 139–40
Longson, Sam 34–8, 40, 44, 55, 172, 200, 207
Lord, Bob 80
Luton Town 78, 192, 224, 255
Luxembourg 129, 139
Lyngstad, Anni-Frid 140
Lytham St Annes 80

Macaulay, Archie 89
Macclesfield Town 278
McDonagh, Jim 223
McEwan, Billy 117–19, 127, 131, 137, 146, 206
McFarland, Roy 148, 184
McGovern, John 77, 110, 191–2

299

Machin, Ernie 215, 223
Mackay, Dave 40, 56
McKenzie, Duncan 191
McNeil, Dixie 233
McNeil, Mick 24
Madeley, Paul 175, 193
Madison Square Garden 100
Maidstone United 208, 281
Majorca 77, 133, 144, 152, 155, 157–8, 160–61, 177–8, 179, 185, 192, 221, 237–41, 282
Malmö 243
Manchester City 133, 165, 192, 256, 277
Manchester United 3, 21, 54, 131, 205, 212, 222, 255–6, 258, 264
Marian persecutions 1
Mariner, Paul 93–4
Marlowe, Ricky 176, 183, 215, 218
Martin, Neil 221, 223, 225–6
Marton Grove School 23
Master of the Horse 121
Match of the Day 233, 251
Megson, Don 69
Megson, Gary 104
Mellor, Ian 133, 147–8, 161, 183–4, 188, 215, 226, 230, 244, 248
Mercer, Joe 165
Merrion Centre 189
Metropole Hotel 117, 231
Middlesbrough 23, 115, 174, 202
Middlesbrough FC 21–6, 30, 49
Midland Hotel 44, 121
Midlands Counties League 203
Millwall 230, 234–5, 237, 241, 284
Mitchell, Austin 194
Monaco 140
Moncur, Bobby 67, 79
Moore, Bobby 80, 117, 120
Moore, Brian 69–71
Morecambe, Eric 210, 213, 222
Morgan, Sammy 230, 232–3
Moseley, Graham 247
Motherwell 168
Mourinho, José 51, 76–77
Mullery, Alan 241–2, 244–7, 250, 252, 254–5, 261, 267, 278, 280–81
Murphy, Pat 96

National Union of Mineworkers 113–14
Natural History Museum 63

Newark 206
Newbury 283
Newcastle 48–9, 276
Newcastle United 67, 79, 213, 256
Newman, John 159–60
Newman, Paul 109
Newton-John, Olivia 130, 139–40
New York City 100–102, 117
Nicholson, Bill 252
Nobody Ever Says Thank You 24, 89
Northampton Town 262
Northumberland 49
Norton, Terry 156–7
Norwich City 57, 133, 147, 183, 251, 256
Nottingham 247–8
Nottingham Evening Post 75, 253
Nottingham Forest 26, 40, 77, 79, 89, 98, 104, 117, 161, 173, 183, 191, 212–13, 220, 222, 224–5, 228–9, 237, 239, 242–3, 245, 249–53, 255, 257–8, 262–3, 274–5, 282, 285
Nottinghamshire 276, 282
Notts County 245
Nuneaton 262

O'Connor, Des 18
Old Den, the 235
Oldham Athletic 14, 120, 151, 155
O'Neill, Martin 213
Ord, Ernie 29, 30, 32, 33, 37, 44
O'Sullivan, Peter 3–4, 12, 48, 51, 61, 64, 69, 76–7, 95–6, 99, 111–12, 118, 138, 166, 181, 183, 185, 204–5, 208, 211, 215, 218, 244, 247–9, 251–2, 255, 267, 270, 278–81
Owen, Syd 188, 191
Oxford United 277

Paine, Thomas 1
Palace Pier 16
Parker, Bert 89–90
Patcham Court Farm 268
Peace, David 41
Pennines 257
Perkins, Russell 62, 63
Peterborough 125
Peterborough United 195, 218, 228–9, 274, 281
Peters and Lee 18
Peugeot 87, 276

INDEX

Phillips, Brian 25
Phythian, Ernie 30
Piggott, Lester 252
Piper, Steve 4, 11, 65, 76–7, 90–91, 118–20, 126, 132, 146, 156–8, 161, 163, 208, 214–15, 218, 229–30, 248, 264–6, 279–80
Plymouth Argyle 14, 93–4, 215–16, 222, 262
Poland 164
Poole, Terry 131
Portsmouth 9, 262, 264, 268–9, 281
Port Vale 27, 102, 110, 127–8, 131, 154, 218–19, 221, 231, 234, 277
Powney, Brian 5, 10, 17–18, 44, 62, 69, 71–72, 77–79, 89, 92, 97, 105–6, 110, 125–6, 128, 131, 133, 135–7, 152–3, 155, 181, 213, 263, 265, 280
Preston North End 205, 209, 218–19, 232, 245, 278, 284–5
Preston Park 281
Prince Regent 130
Privy Council 59
Professional Footballers' Association 56, 104–5, 107, 110, 136

Quarndon 194
Queens Park Rangers 191–2, 278

Ramsey, Alf 164–6
Reading 195, 279
Redford, Robert 109
Redknapp, Harry 157
Revie, Don 37, 53, 165–7, 174, 188–9, 194–5, 199, 200
Rhodes, Tony 111
Ringmer 18
River Trent 98, 238
Roberts, Bob 169, 173–4, 192
Robertson, Fyfe 12
Robertson, John 213, 247, 252, 257, 282
Robertson, Lammie 4–5, 11, 17, 51–2, 60, 62, 64, 68, 72, 81, 98–9, 101, 111–12, 138–9, 152–3, 158–9, 161, 280–81
Robson, Bobby 165
Robson, Bryan 248
Rochdale 9, 13, 15, 98, 103, 120, 154, 279, 284
Rogers, Alan 93
Rollings, Andy 147–8, 161–2, 183–4, 208, 210–11, 215, 230, 234, 244, 248–9, 255, 280–81
Rolls-Royce 87, 230, 262, 277
Ross, Bobby 137
Rostron, Phil 193
Rotherham United 223, 232, 234, 284
Rottingdean 208
Rowland, Helen 160
Royal Academy of Arts 87
Royal Albert Hall 144
Royal Salop Infirmary 125
Ryan, Gerry 246–8, 284

Samrah, Paul 269
Sargent, Dave 209
Saudi Arabia 283
Saward, Pat 8, 10–11, 13–18, 39, 78, 89, 92, 282
Scarborough 250
Schulenberg, Gerhard 35
Scotland 164, 174
Scunthorpe United 281
Seaford 181, 280
Seaford Town 280
Seasman, John 235
Seaton Carew 31
Seattle Sounders 263, 285
Secombe, Harry 3
Second World War 32, 129
Shackleton, Len 29, 34
Shanahan, Terry 111
Shankly, Bill 53, 92, 190, 252, 267
Shaw, Don 55
Shaw, Robert 110
Sheen, Michael 41
Sheffield United 274, 284
Sheffield Wednesday 79, 222, 236
Shepherd, John 22
Sheridan, John 64, 97, 104, 142, 219
Shilton, Peter 246, 251
Shoreham 60, 284
Shrewsbury Town 14, 15, 16, 39, 122–3, 125–6, 154, 176, 231
Simon, Sydney 192
Sims, Peter 156
Sizen, Dudley 273
Skeete, Leo 99
Skegness 244, 252
Slovenia 284

Smith, Bobby 21
Smith, Gordon 258
Smith, Tommy 80
Smith, Willie 209
Solti, Dezso 35
South Downs 268
Southend 222
Southend United 141–2, 151, 275, 278
Southport 14, 52, 154
Southwick 181
Spall, Timothy 41
Sparta Rotterdam 249
Spearritt, Eddie 48, 72, 77, 160, 166
Sproson, Roy 231
Stamford 206
Stamford Bridge 187
state of emergency 59–60, 82, 98
Stevens, Gary 248, 251
Stiles, Nobby 284
Sting, The 109
Stock, Alec 241
Stoke City 191, 203
Stoke-on-Trent 254
Storer, Harry 27
Stringer, Len 8, 10, 19
St John, Ian 168
Suddaby, Peter 247
Sunday Express 37, 38, 57, 167
Sunday Mirror 53, 121
Sunday People 25
Sunday Telegraph 247
Sunday Times 55
Sunderland 21, 27, 28, 29, 35, 89, 104, 203
Sussex Express 74
Sussex University 65–6, 185
Swan, Peter 208
Sweden 283
Swindon Town 13, 232, 234, 255, 278, 281, 283
Sykes, Eric 61

Tabor, Arthur 86
Tacoma 285
Tampa Bay Rowdies 285
Tamworth 207–8
Taylor, Lill 190
Taylor, Peter 56
  absences 64–65, 104, 118, 216
  appointed by Brighton 39–47
  at Derby County 34–8
  at Hartlepools United 29–34, 36
  at Nottingham Forest 243, 245–9, 252, 262–3
  becomes Brighton manager 169–77, 182–3
  breakdown in relationship with Clough at Brighton 170–73, 253
  breakdown in relationship with Clough at Nottingham Forest 253–4, 256–8, 282
  bungs 262–3
  coaching style 75–7, 80, 103, 135–6, 148, 159, 267
  death 282
  declines Clough's attempt to take him to Leeds 190–91
  early months as Brighton manager 185–8, 203–212
  fallout with *Evening Argus* 216
  fight to avoid relegation (1974/75) 214–20
  first meeting with Brighton players 1–5, 132
  Iran 122–3
  joins Brian Clough at Nottingham Forest 242
  legacy at Brighton 244, 265–71
  management style 210–12, 223–4, 233, 236–7, 267
  money 30, 171, 262–3
  Nottingham Forest v Brighton (1979/80) 245–8, 251–2
  origins of move to Nottingham Forest 228, 236–9
  playing career 26–7
  politics 115
  push for promotion (1975/76) 226–37
  reaction at Brighton to him leaving for Nottingham Forest 241–2, 244
  resigns as Brighton manager 240–41
Taylor, Tommy 21
Tehran 121
Templeman, John 4, 62, 64, 75, 104, 111–13, 137, 158–9, 161, 176, 182, 262, 280, 283
Thatcher, Margaret 115
This Is Your Life 80
Thomas, Clive 51
Thomson, Ken 25

INDEX

Thorne, Adrian 23
Times, The 45, 54, 165, 252
three-day week 60, 98
Tiler, Ken 206, 211–12, 214–15, 244, 248
Todd, Colin 35
Tomaszewski, Jan 164
Tooting and Mitcham 96, 160
Torquay United 134, 275
Tottenham Hotspur 21, 213, 220, 242
Towner, Tony 11, 53, 66, 77, 99, 112, 162, 208, 215, 217, 223, 227, 244, 248, 280, 284
Tranmere Rovers 79, 145–7, 215
Trump, Donald 88
Turin 35, 62

UEFA 35
Ulvacus, Björn 130, 140
United Counties League 206

Vancouver Whitecaps 285
Vaughan, Frankie 18
Villa Park 125
Vine, David 140
Vinicombe, John 19, 42–3, 55–7, 63, 67, 91, 94, 101, 118, 142, 147, 153–4, 175–6, 218–20, 224, 226, 237

Wainman, Harry 110
Wainwright, Billy 121
Waldorf Hotel 42, 44
Wales 181
Walldorf, Sven-Olof 140
Wallsend 48
Walsall 61, 137–8, 143, 204, 217, 230
Walters, Peter 138
Walton and Hersham 54–5, 61–4, 67–8, 75, 82–3, 93–5, 184, 209
Walton, Ron 119
Warboys, Alan 68–9, 151, 155
Ward, Peter 207–8, 230, 232–5, 237, 244, 247–8, 251, 255, 263–4, 267, 270, 275, 285
Warters, Don 168
Waterhall 268
'Waterloo' 130, 140
Watford 9, 14, 22, 79, 81, 216
Watney 276
We Are The Damned United 193
Weaver, Paul 74
Webb, Stuart 172

Welch, Ronnie 80, 81, 137, 206
Welsh, Alan 93
Wembley Stadium 190, 212, 256–7, 264, 279
West Germany 164
West Indies 101, 122
West Pier 140
Westwood, Danny 235
White Hart Hotel 1–3, 48, 77, 132
Whitehead, Phillip 115–17, 119, 121
Wichita 285
Widmerpool 282
Widmerpool Cricket Club 239
Williams, Gary 247, 251
Williams, Ray 102
Wilson, Glen 3, 5, 64, 91, 136, 162, 185, 255
Wilson, Harold 115
Wilson, Harry 80, 81, 98, 104, 118, 143, 152, 181, 186, 208, 210, 214, 217–18, 236, 244, 247, 284–5
Wilson, Joe 3, 5, 64, 155, 158, 162
Wilson, Jonathan 24, 89
Wilson, Vince 121
Winstanley, Graham 206, 215, 230, 244
Winterbottom, Walter 212
Withdean 270, 277
Witney Town 283
Woffinden, Colin 209
Woking 221
Wolverhampton Wanderers 133, 161, 222, 284
Woodcock, Tony 213
Woodward, Percy 192
World Cup 164, 175
World of Sport 70
Wrexham 118–19, 205, 217
Wycombe 125, 132

Yarwood, Mike 86–7
Yaxley, Mike 86, 281
Yeovil 262
York 29, 222
York City 2, 45–7, 50–54, 60, 82–3, 117, 131, 134–6, 145, 151–2
Yorkshire Evening Post 168, 174
Yorkshire Television 194–5
Yugoslavia 139

ALSO AVAILABLE FROM BITEBACK PUBLISHING

WHEN FOOTBALLERS WERE SKINT
A JOURNEY IN SEARCH OF THE SOUL OF FOOTBALL

JON HENDERSON

336PP HARDBACK, £20

Long before perma-tanned football agents and TV mega-rights ushered in the age of the multimillionaire player, footballers' wages were capped – even the game's biggest names earned barely more than a plumber or electrician.

Footballing legends like Tom Finney and Stanley Matthews shared a bond of borderline penury with the huge crowds they entertained on Saturday afternoons, often on pitches that were a world away from the pristine lawns of the game's modern era. Instead of the gleaming, expensive sports cars driven by today's top players, the stars of yesteryear travelled to matches on public transport and, after the game, returned to homes every bit as modest as those of their supporters. Players and fans would even sometimes be next-door neighbours in a street of working-class terraced houses.

Based on the first-hand accounts of players from a fast-disappearing generation, *When Footballers Were Skint* relates the fascinating story of a truly great sporting era. All of us who call ourselves football fans owe the book's multifarious cast our thanks for bequeathing our national game such a rich and deeply human heritage.

— AVAILABLE FROM ALL GOOD BOOKSHOPS —

WWW.BITEBACKPUBLISHING.COM